Political Traditions in Foreign Policy Series

KENNETH W. THOMPSON, *Editor*

The values, traditions, and assumptions undergirding approaches to foreign policy are often crucial in determining the course of a nation's history. Yet, the interconnections between ideas and policy for landmark periods in our foreign relations remain largely unexamined. The intent of this series is to encourage a marriage between political theory and foreign policy. A secondary objective is to identify theorists with a continuing interest in political thought and international relations, both younger scholars and the small group of established thinkers. Only occasionally have scholarly centers and university presses sought to nurture studies in this area. In the 1950s and 1960s the University of Chicago Center for the Study of American Foreign Policy gave emphasis to such inquiries. Since then the subject has not been the focus of any major intellectual center. The Louisiana State University Press and the series editor, from a base at the Miller Center of Public Affairs at the University of Virginia, have organized this series to meet a need that has remained largely unfulfilled since the mid-1960s.

Antonio Gramsci

Antonio Gramsci

ARCHITECT OF A NEW POLITICS

DANTE GERMINO

Louisiana State University Press
Baton Rouge and London

Copyright © 1990 by Louisiana State University Press
All rights reserved
Manufactured in the United States of America
First printing
99 98 97 96 95 94 93 92 91 90   5 4 3 2 1

Designer: Laura Roubique Gleason
Typeface: Galliard
Typesetter: G&S Typesetters, Inc.
Printer and binder: Thomson-Shore, Inc.

LIBRARY OF CONGRESS CATALOGING-IN-PUBLICATION DATA

Germino, Dante L.
    Antonio Gramsci : architect of a new politics / Dante Germino.
        p.   cm. — (Political traditions in foreign policy series)
    Includes bibliographical references.
    ISBN 0-8071-1553-3 (alk. paper); ISBN 0-8071-1655-6 (alk. paper pbk.)
    1. Gramsci, Antonio, 1891–1937.   2. Communism—Italy—History—20th century.
    3. Communists—Italy—Biography.   I. Title.   II. Series.
    HX289.7.G73G47   1990
    324.245′075′092—dc20
      [B]   89-49081
                                                                       CIP

To Rebecca Eleutheria Lianos,
harbinger of a freer, more musical world

Contents

Series Editor's Preface

With the publication of this important volume on Antonio Gramsci, Professor Dante Germino contributes an important chapter in the Louisiana State University Press's series on political tradition and foreign policy. His work is also somewhat of a departure from the series' emphasis on foreign policy as the main focus of the discourse.

What makes Germino's gripping account of the life and works of Gramsci relevant to us is the powerful impact of Marxism on foreign policy in the period before and after World War II. It is impossible to understand the foreign relations of either the interwar or postwar period without giving attention to the worldwide impact of communism and socialism.

The great virtue of a study of Gramsci is that it puts to rest the illusory notion that Marxism is a monolithic force in the world. Germino shows not only that the interaction of Italian communist and socialist thought with Moscow is complicated and unpredictable, but also that Gramsci's thought, while Marxist in orientation, is infinitely varied and changing over time.

International relations studies have suffered from a paucity of concern with political traditions and political philosophy. Similarly, political theory has often overlooked the interplay of political theories and international politics. Thus, Germino has filled a void to which a too narrow specialization often contributes. His work will have enduring value in breaking new ground for both political theory and international studies.

KENNETH W. THOMPSON

Preface

Some scholars may wonder if yet another book on Antonio Gramsci is justified. Many have been written on the great Sardinian. My answer is that I have found Gramsci so interesting that I have been moved to try to link his political theory with his personal experience in a way that to my knowledge has not been pursued. What interests me—and frankly what I think should interest everyone—is Gramsci *tout ensemble,* the architect of a new politics.

Antonio Gramsci's ideas became familiar to me in the 1960s, when I was writing a book designed to draw out the distinction between political theory and ideology. I began to read Gramsci systematically, however, only in 1971, when Christopher Lasch invited me to present to the American Historical Association a paper on Gramsci and Benedetto Croce. I was able to give some additional time to the reading of Gramsci while on sabbatical in Rome in 1976. From July 1, 1981, to June 30, 1982, I spent full time studying this remarkable man and thinker, thanks to a Senior Research Fellowship from the National Endowment for the Humanities and to a sabbatical from the University of Virginia. In the summer of 1984 I returned to Italy with the support of my university.

A distinguishing feature of the present study is that, instead of concentrating only on the *Prison Notebooks,* it makes extensive use of Gramsci's early journalism and letters as well as the documents relating to his work as the leading figure in the Italian Communist party in the mid-1920s. My rationale for this shift in emphasis from the *Notebooks* to the pre-prison writings is found in Gramsci himself, who in prison repeatedly stressed that he was out of touch with "tactile reality," for him the only source of political knowledge. Seen in context, the *Notebooks* can be understood as a continuation of Gramsci's lifelong effort to sketch in the outlines of a new politics of inclusion.

The present volume is an exercise in *verstehen*. I have sought to present Gramsci from the inside, empathetically, rather than to impose on him some abstract "position." *Tout comprendre c'est ne pas tout pardonner,* but a thinker-practitioner like Antonio Gramsci deserves to be understood before he is judged.

I am grateful to Elsa Fubini of the Istituto Gramsci in Rome and to other personnel of the institute, including especially Vincenzo Di Giovanni, whose gracious assistance is warmly acknowledged. In Turin I had the good fortune to meet and come to know well Sergio Caprioglio, editor of Gramsci's pre-prison writings. I am enormously grateful to him for letting me read the unpublished new attributions by Gramsci that he unearthed and for answering many detailed questions.

Robert H. Evans, chairman of the Woodrow Wilson Department of Government and Foreign Affairs, Kenneth W. Thompson, White Burkett Miller Professor of Government and Foreign Affairs, and Dexter W. Whitehead, dean of the Graduate School of Arts and Sciences at the University of Virginia have assisted me in important ways on this project, and I thank them.

My colleague Richard Arndt, drawing on his rich knowledge of things Italian, read and commented on the first draft in detail. He inspired me to persevere in giving the first draft of my manuscript the thorough revision it needed.

My good friend Bruce Hall has my enduring gratitude for his invaluable assistance in preparing the final manuscript.

This book is dedicated to my granddaughter, whose middle name means "freedom," and who loves the music of the saxophone.

Antonio Gramsci: A Brief Chronology

SARDINIA

1891   One of seven children, is born on January 22 at Ales, a small town north of Cagliari, Sardinia. Spine develops abnormally owing to Pott's disease.

1897–1900   Moves with family to Ghilarza after father is suspended from job for allegedly embezzling electoral funds. Father is imprisoned on August 8, 1898, and is tried and convicted on October 27, 1900.

1903–1905   Interrupts schooling to work ten hours a day six days a week, and Sunday mornings, in local registry office for the equivalent of two kilos of bread per week. Father is released from prison on January 3, 1904.

1905–1911   Resumes schooling, first at the secondary school (*ginnasio*) in Santa Lissurgiu, boarding in peasant's house, then at the high school (*liceo*) Dettori in Cagliari. Lives with older brother Gennaro.

TURIN

1911   Wins meager scholarship of seventy lire per month to University of Turin. Begins studies in November.

1913   Begins to be active in the Italian Socialist party (PSI).

1914   (October) Publishes article in socialist newspaper in ambiguous response to then-socialist Mussolini's call for support of Italy's intervention in World War I. The article is later held against Gramsci by his detractors.

1914   (December) Has scholarship withdrawn for failure to take some examinations even after postponement of them for health reasons. Never completes university degree. Suffers from nervous exhaustion for several months lasting into fall of 1915.

1915   (Fall) Begins active career as journalist for *Il Grido del Popolo,* socialist weekly.

1916   (January or February) Becomes self-avowed professional revolutionary.

1916–1918   Writes regularly for *Avanti!* (Turin edition), edits *Il Grido del Popolo* beginning September, 1917.

1917   (November) Welcomes the Bolshevik Revolution as the "Revolution Against *Das Kapital.*" (December) Founds Club for the Moral Life.

1919   Helps found *L'Ordine Nuovo* (The new order), cultural weekly of the Italian Socialist party (PSI) in Turin.

1920   (September) Actively supports occupation of Fiat factories in Turin and Milan.

1921   (January) Is one of the leading delegates to split from the PSI Congress at Livorno and help found the Communist party of Italy (PCd'I), later renamed PCI. Bordiga emerges as party leader.

1921   Is appointed editor-in-chief of *L'Ordine Nuovo,* now a daily, at a thousand lire per month.

1922   (March) Wins appointment to represent the PCd'I in the Comintern.

MOSCOW

1922   (June) Arrives in Moscow. Suffers from nervous exhaustion. Is patient at Serebranyi Bor (Silver wood) sanatorium outside Moscow. (September) Meets Julia Schucht, his future wife, who is visiting her sister Eugenia at Serebranyi Bor. (October 28) Is still at sanatorium when Fascists gain power in Italy. (December) Fully recovers; resumes full-time duties on the Italian Commission of the Comintern. Meets Trotsky, Zinoviev, and other Soviet leaders. Known to Lenin (now in poor health), does not meet him personally. Learns of Italian Fascist mandate for his arrest.

1923   (November) Leaves Moscow for Vienna to be closer to Italy.

VIENNA

1923   (December) Arrives in Vienna from Moscow to set up liaison office with the PCd'I.

1924   (January to May) Writes letters to allies in Italy urging a new course for the PCd'I and replacement of Bordiga as party leader. (February) Learns Julia Schucht (who remained in Moscow) is pregnant with his child. (April 6) Gains election as Communist deputy in Italian Parliament.

ROME

1924   (May 12) Returns to Italy under parliamentary immunity. (June) Sees murder of Socialist deputy Matteotti provoke crisis in Mussolini's government. (June–December) Is involved in opposition movement to fascism, at first leading party in joining the "Aventine Secession," later leading it back into Parliament. (August) Is elected secretary-general of PCd'I. (August 21) Becomes father, with birth of Delio. The marriage of Antonio and Julia is registered in Moscow.

1925   (January 3) Is still in Italy when Mussolini announces full-fledged Fascist dictatorship. (March) Returns to Moscow for meeting of Comintern Executive, sees Delio for the first time. Returns to Rome after brief visit. (October) Is in Rome when Julia Schucht arrives with Delio and Julia's older sister Eugenia, but lives separately from them. Is now under Fascist police surveillance, but visits them irregularly.

1926   (August) Remains in Italy when Julia, pregnant with their second son, Giuliano, returns to Moscow with her sister. Takes brief Italian holiday with Delio, who then goes to Moscow to join his mother. (October) Sends lengthy letter to Moscow warning the Soviet party against committing excesses against opposition led by Trotsky.

PRISON YEARS

1926   (November 8) Is arrested at his Rome apartment, in violation of parliamentary immunity, and then transported to Ustica, a tiny island off the Sicilian coast, where he is kept in confinement with Bordiga and other Communists.

1927   (January 20 – February 7) Is transported, chained, in cattle car to Milan's San Vittore prison, where he remains for fifteen months.

1928   (May 11) Endures another excruciating journey, this one in a sealed cubicle, to Rome for his trial. (May 28 – June 4) In Il Processone—joint trial of all Communist leaders before the Special Tribunal for the Defense of the State—is sentenced to twenty years, four months, five days. (July 8 – 19) Is transported to prison at Turi (Bari) in southern Italy.

1929   (January) Obtains permission to write in his cell. (February) Begins to write notes in his first *Quaderno* (Notebook). (March) Formulates plan of study for the *Quaderni*.

1930   (November—December) Is left feeling isolated by the debate with comrades at Turi over the new Comintern policy predicting the imminent collapse of fascism.

1931   (August 3) Suffers massive stroke.

1932   (November) Has sentence reduced to twelve years and four months. Refuses to ask for a pardon in return for provisional freedom. (December 30) Is still in prison when his mother dies in Sardinia.

1933   (March 20) Has doctor in attendance who declares his health to require transfer to a hospital. (November 19) Is taken from Turi to a nearby prison infirmary, then to a private clinic at Formia. Bars are put on the windows at Gramsci's expense.

1934   (October 25) Is granted provisional liberty. For the first time, is allowed to take walks outside the clinic. The bars are taken off the windows of his room.

1935   (June) Suffers severe medical crisis. (August 24) Is transferred to clinic in Rome.

1937   (April) Is accorded complete freedom, but is unable to make use of freedom, because of massive cerebral hemorrhage on April 25. Dies on April 27, with ashes deposited in an urn in Rome's English Cemetery, where many famous non-Catholic men of letters are buried.

Source: "Cronologia della vita di Antonio Gramsci," in Sergio Caprioglio and Elsa Fubini (eds.), *Antonio Gramsci, Lettere dal Carcere* (Turin, 1972), xxi–xlvi.

Abbreviations

APC	Archives of the Italian Communist party, Rome, Istituto Gramsci.
Caprioglio MS.	Antonio Gramsci's early journalism, 1920–1921, ed. Sergio Caprioglio.
CPC	Antonio Gramsci, *La costruzione del partito comunista, 1923–1926,* ed. Elsa Fubini (Turin, 1971).
CT	Antonio Gramsci, *Cronache torinese, 1913–1917,* ed. Sergio Caprioglio (Turin, 1980).
Formazione	Palmiro Togliatti (ed.), *La formazione del gruppo dirigente del partito comunista d'Italia nel 1923–1924* (Rome, 1974).
Fubini MS.	Antonio Gramsci's correspondence, 1910–1920, ed. Elsa Fubini.
GAR	Mario Mammucari and Anna Miserocchi (eds.), *Gramsci a Roma, 1924–1926* (Milan, 1979).
INM	Antonio Gramsci, *Il nostro Marx, 1918–1919,* ed. Sergio Caprioglio (Turin, 1984).
LCF	Antonio Gramsci, *La città futura, 1917–1918,* ed. Sergio Caprioglio (Turin, 1982).
LDC	Antonio Gramsci, *Lettere dal carcere,* ed. Elsa Fubini and Sergio Caprioglio (Turin, 1972).
ON	Antonio Gramsci, *L'Ordine Nuovo, 1919–1920* (Turin, 1954).

Quaderni	Antonio Gramsci, *Quaderni del carcere,* ed. Valentino Gerratana (4 vols.; Turin, 1975).
SF	Antonio Gramsci, *Socialismo e fascismo: L'Ordine Nuovo, 1921–1922,* ed. Elsa Fubini (Turin, 1966).
SPN	Antonio Gramsci, *Selections from the Prison Notebooks,* ed. Quintin Hoare and Geoffrey Nowell Smith (New York, 1971).
SPW [1]	Antonio Gramsci, *Selections from Political Writings, 1910–1920,* ed. Quintin Hoare (New York, 1977).
SPW [2]	Antonio Gramsci, *Selections from Political Writings, 1921–1926,* ed. Quintin Hoare (New York, 1978).
2000, II	Giansiro Ferrata and Niccolo Gallo (eds.), *2000 pagine di Gramsci* (2 vols.; Milan, 1964). All quotations are from Volume II.

Antonio Gramsci

I ✦ The World of the Hunchback from Sardinia

You ought to reconstruct my state of mind . . . formed over twenty years of solitude within my family.
             —Antonio Gramsci to Julia Schucht, November 4, 1924

Who was Gramsci? Gramsci was a Sardinian . . .
             —Aldo Garosci, *Il Cittadino*, Rome, April 20, 1949

Seated across from me at a Rome restaurant, my Italian friend suddenly and unexpectedly spoke of how it felt to be a *gobbo*, a hunchback. "*You* can put both elbows on the table," he said, his chin barely resting on the tabletop, "but I can barely see you. For me to climb a set of stairs requires ten times the effort it takes you. Even putting on my clothes is an ordeal. Often I have excruciatingly painful muscle spasms, day and night. Try to imagine what an enormous effort it takes for me to meet someone for the first time, knowing what an 'ugly' first impression I make. So it was with Gramsci as well. I want you to write about the effect of being a *gobbo* on his mind. Most books pass over the subject in silence."[1] I promised my friend that I would and thanked him for his insight, so painfully shared.

Antonio Gramsci never grew to be more than four and three-quarters feet tall. He had two humps, one in front and the other in back, giving him a deformed appearance. His normal-sized head appeared huge and awkward on his short frame. He also walked lamely.

From the perspective of today's medical knowledge, one can say that Gramsci's hunchbacked condition was caused by Pott's disease (a form of tuberculosis, now as uncommon as are hunchbacks themselves in Italy). His family's explanation was that his deformity resulted from an accident (a fall down the stairs from the arms of a maid). None of the "fall" stories is credible. They were attempts on the part of Gramsci's

---

1. These remarks took place in Rome in June, 1984.

family to save face in a culture whose folklore assumed hunchbacks to be possessed by evil spirits.[2]

As a historian of political theory, I have been reluctant to face the possibility that Gramsci's deformity probably affected his teaching about politics more powerfully than did his reading of Croce or Sorel or Marx or Lenin or any number of other thinkers. I recoil from reductionist explanations; beyond that, it would be ironic indeed to say of a thinker who so learnedly attacked the "vulgar" materialist interpretations of history that his ideas had been determined by his physical condition. Most revolutionaries in history have not been hunchbacks, and most hunchbacks have not been revolutionaries. Nonetheless, the fact remains that Antonio Gramsci's deformity very powerfully affected the way he looked at the world.

As a hunchback, Gramsci was visibly and irremediably an outsider. Obviously referring to his physical condition, he wrote in letters to the woman he loved that throughout his childhood he felt like an intruder in his own family. (In fact, his mother and siblings seem to have treated him well, but Gramsci's deformity made it difficult for him to accept affection as genuine.) He hid himself from others "behind a mask of hardness."[3]

None of the above is meant to imply that Gramsci was a pathological case. Most of what we know of his childhood feelings comes from his recollections written in his early thirties to Julia Schucht and from his later letters from prison. That he could write freely about those feelings indicates that he handled his deformity with remarkable maturity. Through the letters to Julia, written soon after they had fallen in love, Antonio tried to let her know what she was in for; in fairness to her he felt an obligation to reveal the bad with the good so that there would be no surprises. He also recounted to her many delightful childhood memories, some of them having to do with nature and wild animals. He deeply loved the spectacularly beautiful countryside around Ghilarza, the small town north of Cagliari and inward from Oristano where he grew up. He came to feel himself very much a Sardinian, in love with its language and food and much of its culture.

2. For variations on the theme of when Gramsci allegedly fell from a servant's arms, see, inter alia, Martin Entwhistle, *Antonio Gramsci: Conservative Schooling for Radical Politics* (London, 1979), 7; John Cammett, *Antonio Gramsci and the Origins of Italian Communism* (Stanford, 1967), 4; and Laurana Lajolo, *Gramsci: Un uomo sconfitto* (Milan, 1980), 19.

3. Antonio Gramsci to his wife, Julia Schucht, March 6, 1924, in *2000*, II, 32–33.

His core experience, however, remained that of someone on the fringes of social life. This basic feeling of exclusion, mixed with other personal qualities, helped him notice and empathize with others who were pushed to society's margins. Perhaps the following account written in prison only a few years before his death most vividly recalls his early empathy for the excluded:

> When I was eight or nine years old, I had an experience that has now returned vividly to memory. . . . I knew a family from a nearby village; the family consisted of a father, a mother, and several children. Energetic people, especially the mother, they were small property owners and ran an inn. I knew (I had heard tell) that in addition to the children mentioned, whom I knew, this woman had another son whom one never saw and of whom she spoke with sighs as if he were a great misfortune—an idiot or a monster or worse. I remember that my mother often referred to this woman as if she were a martyr who made many sacrifices and suffered many sorrows on account of this offspring.
>
> One Sunday morning around ten, I was sent to this woman; I had to leave some crochet work [from my mother] with her and bring back the money for it. When I found her, she had already closed the front door of her house. She was dressed in her Sunday's finest to go to Mass; she had a bag under her arm. Upon seeing me, she hesitated a little and then decided. She told me to accompany her to a certain place and that on returning she would take the crochet work and give me the money. She led me outside the village to a small clearing cluttered with debris and rubble; in one corner there was a hovel resembling a pigsty, four feet high, without windows or openings of any kind and with one heavy door as an entrance. She opened the door, and immediately one heard an animal-like moan; inside was her son, a youth eighteen years old, of very swarthy complexion, who was not able to stand and therefore remained seated and lunged in his seat toward the door as far as the chain around his waist permitted him to go. . . . He was covered with filth and red-eyed like an animal of the night.
>
> His mother emptied the contents of her bag, fodder mixed with leftovers from home, into a stone trough and refilled another container with water. Then she closed the door and we went away.[4]

The young Antonio kept the whole story to himself, convinced that no one would believe him.

4. Gramsci to Tatiana Schucht (Gramsci's sister-in-law), January 30, 1933, in *LDC*, 736–37.

In letters written at different times to different persons, Gramsci later spoke often of his childhood and adolescence in language similar to that evoked by the sight of the retarded boy. In October, 1932, from prison he wrote his sister-in-law Tatiana Schucht (Tania) of his having "almost always known only the most brutal aspects of life," of the "deep scars" that his early life had left on his consciousness, of his character as having been "formed from approximately twenty years of solitude within the family" and of the "lonely life he had been accustomed to lead since infancy." Only a small part of his life had been happy and carefree, he observed.[5]

When Antonio was only seven years old, his father, election registrar in a small town near Nuoro, was fired, tried, and imprisoned for over five years for extortion and embezzlement. It was then that the rest of the family moved to Ghilarza, where a relative of his mother made a small house available to them. He did not learn the reason for his father's long absence until he was ten, and then only by overhearing family gossip—an experience that only deepened his sense of isolation, increased his suspicion toward everyone, and made him almost fanatically insistent on honesty. As the hunchbacked son of a disgraced father, Antonio felt even more excluded than before from the society into which he had been born.[6]

The childhood experience that Gramsci considers the greatest source of his "instinct for rebellion" was that of being forced, out of economic necessity, to interrupt his schooling for two years in order to work. For five and a half years Antonio's mother took in sewing and relied upon the assistance of relatives to make ends meet as she struggled to feed and clothe her seven children. Upon graduation from elementary school, Antonio had to work ten hours a day six days a week, as well as Sunday mornings, carrying large volumes of real estate records around in the local registry office. He wrote of how his body ached so much at night from the effects of this physically demanding work on his small and twisted frame that he often had to cry himself to sleep:

> What saved me [was] my instinct . . . for rebellion against the rich, against the sons of the butcher, the pharmacist, and the clothing store merchant, because I was unable to continue my studies, while they could

5. Gramsci to Tatiana Schucht, October 3, 1932, in *LDC*, 682–83.
6. Lajolo, *Gramsci*, 23.

proceed with theirs—and this despite the fact that I had scored a "10" in all my elementary school subjects.[7]

Out of these early, painful experiences, including his encounter with the grade school principal who refused his request for early promotion because he did not know by heart all eighty-four articles of the 1848 *Statuto* (Savoy constitution),[8] Antonio Gramsci began to develop an empathy for all individuals and groups outside the pale of privilege.

The exceptional emphasis Gramsci placed on the role of will in human affairs can best be understood in relation to his experience as a hunchback. Every action is more difficult for a hunchback than for a person of normal stature, and it requires an enormous act of will to overcome both the physical pain and the psychological feelings of inferiority attendant upon that affliction.[9]

SARDINIA: THE HUNCHBACK OF THE ITALIAN NATIONAL FAMILY

If the physical and psychological suffering endured as a result of a twisted and truncated body was the first formative influence helping to shape Gramsci's early consciousness, growing up in Sardinia was the second. One cannot understand what kind of revolutionary Gramsci became without understanding the effect of his Sardinian upbringing on his consciousness.

Detaching Gramsci's mature revolutionary thought from his Sardinian upbringing is like detaching a coal car from a train engine: the former is needed to fuel the latter. The fact that Gramsci eventually became a revolutionary has everything to do with his early experience of injustices rooted specifically in Sardinian soil. Gramsci's sense of injustice that fueled his quest for a new politics was not abstract but was always colored by the specific injustices he had observed or experienced. In addition to his psychological disposition, conditioned by his physical deformity, the fact that his region was an island at the periphery of Italian national life was crucial to the development of Gramsci's revolutionary sensibility.

Sardinia was a presence that Gramsci always chose to carry with him.

7. Gramsci to Julia Schucht, March 6, 1924, in *2000*, II, 33.
8. Gramsci to Tatiana Schucht, January 2, 1928, in *LDC*, 165.
9. Giuseppe Fiori, *Antonio Gramsci: Life of a Revolutionary* (New York, 1970), 25–26.

His letters, full of descriptions of the island, reveal his passionate interest in Sardinia, its language and its culture. Everywhere he went in later life he sought out his fellow Sardinians and plied them with questions about conditions on the island. It is no exaggeration to say that Gramsci thought of himself as a Sardinian first and an Italian second.

When Palmiro Togliatti said of Gramsci that "from the critique of the structure of Sardinian society he arrived by means of socialism at the critique of the structure of all of Italian society," [10] he was stating the truth, but too abstractly. Gramsci's intellectual "critique" of the Sardinian "social structure" grew out of the specific, concrete feelings and emotions that he experienced in growing up on the island.

Despite his deep affinity with Sardinia, Gramsci never romanticized it. From Sardinia he acquired an attitude of realistic assessment of the enormous practical difficulties impeding radical change. This attitude of realism, not to be confused with the pragmatism of common sense, rendered him always immune to illusions that there is any shortcut to meaningful change. Sardinia taught Gramsci how long the past was and how deeply entrenched were the "habits of the heart" in the way of revolutionary social change. Indeed, it may be that his theories of the "civil society" and "the war of position" grew out of his Sardinian experience of finding behind every near oppressor another who is more distant, and of eventually concluding that the specific Sardinian problem could be resolved only in an international context. Gramsci's tactile way of thinking emerges from his Sardinian existence. [11] He was not a dreamer who sought escape through a magical transfiguring of reality, but a practical visionary who sought to break down the walls that for centuries had kept his compatriots locked into what he called an "anachronistic and fossilized culture." [12]

When in his *Prison Notebooks* Gramsci called himself a "provincial person three or four times over," [13] he can only have been affirming his unbreakable attachment to and empathy with Sardinia. That empathy shows itself repeatedly in his political writings. A most eloquent illustration of it appears in an article he wrote for the Socialist party news-

10. Palmiro Togliatti, *Antonio Gramsci* (Rome, 1965), 51.
11. Ruggero Grieco, "Gramsci," *Il Promoteo*, February 15, 1924, p. 30. The Italian reads, literally, "He experiences things in a tactile way." Courtesy of Sergio Caprioglio.
12. *Quaderni*, 1542.
13. *Ibid.*, 1776.

paper *Avanti!* in 1919. Eight years in Turin had afforded Gramsci ample opportunity to reject and forget his Sardinian past. He could have chosen to write exclusively about the problems of the northern working class. It was the beginning of the so-called Red Biennium when Italian socialism was at its apogee. Listen, however, to Gramsci's voice indignantly protesting the wartime censor's refusal to permit publication of an article on Sardinia:

> Why can't one recall that Sardinian miners are paid starvation wages, while the shareholders in Turin fatten their portfolios with dividends crystallized from the blood of Sardinian miners, who often are reduced to eating roots to avoid dying of hunger? Why should it be prohibited to recall that two-thirds of the inhabitants of Sardinia (especially women and children) go without shoes in the winter and summer, through the thorns and the riverbeds that take the place of roads, because the price of hide has gone sky-high due to the protective tariffs that enrich the Turin industrialists and leather manufacturers?[14]

How did Antonio Gramsci come to perceive what most of his contemporaries overlooked or passed over in silence? Why did the fact that Sardinian shepherds and peasants had to travel in cattle cars and use riverbeds for roads and go without shoes in winter and summer grip him to so great an extent as to inform the kind of life that he would lead? No merely intellectual explanation—that he read a volume by Sorel or Marx or Labriola or Lenin—is sufficient to explain Antonio Gramsci's decision to become a revolutionary and, furthermore, to become a revolutionary of a particular type. Rather, the explanation must begin with Gramsci's concrete experiences of misery in his childhood and youth in Sardinia. To say this in no way implies that his political thought was determined by his childhood experiences. It means, instead, that Gramsci's thought was not something desiccated and unrelated to his life, and that experience was a concrete whole for him.

Thus, the roots of the mature Gramsci's revolutionary critique of society extended deeply into the Sardinian soil of his youth. In the previously cited letter describing his initial anger at the undeserving sons of privileged families in his hometown who could continue their education while he had to work, Gramsci tells how his idea of "the rich . . .

14. Gramsci, "I dolori della Sardegna," *Avanti,* April 16, 1919, in Sergio Caprioglio (ed.), *Antonio Gramsci: Scritti, 1915–1921* (Turin, 1968), 103–104.

became enlarged to include all the rich landowners of Sardinia."[15] The youthful Gramsci did not fall prey to narcissism. His aversion for "the rich" did not remain at the level of petty resentment against individuals more fortunate than he; rather, it broadened into a critique of a social system that made advancement in school dependent on the prestige of a father's occupation. What comes out repeatedly in Gramsci's writings is the vividness with which he recalls a particular injustice. Justice for Gramsci was no intellectual abstraction, but a conception of the world elaborated in reaction to direct experiences of specific, concrete injustices that in time revealed behind them a system of power designed to serve the wants of the prestigious few rather than the needs of the impoverished many.

"RECOLLECT THAT IT IS SARDINIA"—CICERO

Within the Italian national family, the island of Sardinia stood and still stands in the position of a poor relation. Geographically isolated and poor in natural resources, Sardinia had been looked down on by continental politicians ever since Roman times. In one of his letters, Cicero wrote to his brother: "Take care, my brother, of your health; even though it is winter, recollect that it is Sardinia."[16]

Sicily is also an island, it is true, but Sicily has commercial advantages, rich archaeological sites from both Greek and Roman times, and lemon groves (to say nothing of the Mafia). Sicily has been a force to be reckoned with in the national life. By contrast, Sardinia was in Gramsci's time regarded by mainland Italians as nothing more than a breeding ground for malaria and a hideout for bandits. The ancient Greeks had barely penetrated the island, and Rome had planted relatively few colonies—the minimum necessary to achieve control of the sea and supremacy over the indigenous civilization.[17]

Only recently has a literature begun to emerge to do justice to the richness of Sardinia's indigenous culture, the "nuraghic world." Some eight thousand nuraghi (stone fortresses) even today dot the Sardinian

---

15. Gramsci to Julia Schucht, March 6, 1924, in *2000*, II, 33.

16. Quoted in Alan Ross, *The Bandit on the Billiard Table* (London, 1954), 9.

17. The failure of the Greeks to penetrate the island of Sardinia beyond Olbia on the east coast in 55 B.C. was presumably because Sicily was large enough to keep the Greeks fully occupied.

hillsides. They have no equal anywhere. These impressive stone structures, mute reminders of an unjustly neglected past, brood over the Sardinian countryside. Christian Servos, the French archaeologist and author of a major work on the nuraghic world, has written eloquently of the genius of the pre-Roman "Sard" civilization. The richness of Sardinia's indigenous past lies hidden under the mound of prejudices imposed upon it by a series of conquerors.[18]

It is not unreasonable to call Gramsci's Sardinia the hunchback of the Italic world. Throughout his life Gramsci identified himself with Sardinia's plight, and at the end he regarded himself as more Sardinian than Italian. Even though in his prison writings he condemned many aspects of Sardinian culture in the modern period as "fossilized" (*una cultura fossilizzata*), he regarded the brutal aspects of Sardinian life (as illustrated in the treatment of the retarded boy) to have been the result of repression imposed from without. As Gramsci put it:

> The instinct for rebellion, which as a child was directed toward rich people [in Ghilarza] . . . expanded [in adolescence] to include all the rich people who oppressed the peasants of Sardinia, and I thought it was necessary to fight for the national independence of the region. "Into the sea with the Mainlanders!" How many times I repeated these words.[19]

Gramsci's Sardinianism, or "Sardism," was so powerful that Palmiro Togliatti later said of him that even after he became a Socialist he continued to be a champion of Sardinia. For Gramsci "the task of socialism could not be detached from the task of redeeming his own island."[20]

Antonio Gramsci spent the first twenty years of his life in Sardinia. During that time he became exposed to the ideas of the Italian Socialist party primarily through his older brother Gennaro, with whom he lived while attending high school (*liceo*) in Cagliari from 1908 to 1911. Although he did not arrive in Turin ignorant of Italian socialism, he was anything but a party militant. In one of his letters to his mother, in the spring of 1909, Antonio expressed amusement at the idea that the police thought that his brother, who worked as a minor functionary in the local Socialist headquarters, could have been a dangerous anarchist.[21]

18. On the "nuraghic world," see Christian Servos, *La Civilisation de la Sardaigne* (Paris, 1954), and Raimondo Carta Raspi, *Breve storia di Sardegna* (Cagliari, 1950).
19. Gramsci to Julia Schucht, March 6, 1924, in *2000*, II, 33.
20. Togliatti, *Gramsci*, 51.
21. Susanna Carda Marcia, *Il giovane Gramsci* (Cagliari, 1977), 37, 40, 119.

The greatest direct political influence on Gramsci before he went to the University of Turin was not socialism but the movement for Sardinian independence. Although he quickly moved on from this position, becoming a Socialist in 1913 or 1914, Gramsci never ceased to be concerned with Sardinia's powerlessness. Successive Italian national governments, subservient to northern industrialists, agricultural producers, and bankers, mercilessly exploited the island economically while neglecting to provide even the most rudimentary public services. Gramsci wrote often of the region's appalling rate of illiteracy and of the extreme poverty of the vast majority of the population. He was not writing about hunger as just a social problem, for he had often been hungry himself. When he observed that in many areas the island's only roads were riverbeds, he had traveled those same nonroads himself. He also knew of the desperate plight of the miners from observing and talking with them.

Throughout the centuries and in the face of repeated foreign conquests, Sardinia's people managed to retain the quiet dignity that continues today to impress the visitor. This dignity, often confused with reserve, was an important part of Gramsci's Sardism.

Although other Italians—especially the Piedmontese—looked down upon Sardinians, Antonio Gramsci always remained proud of his origins. In one of his last conversations he told a fellow patient in a Rome clinic that his true nationality was not Italian but Sardinian.[22] As Andrea Viglongo, one of Gramsci's closest associates from his Turin days, told the present writer, Gramsci's passionate interest in things Sardinian extended even to the island's religious festivals, in particular Cagliari's annual *corteo* (parade) in honor of St. Efiseo, patron saint of Sardinia. The parade goes on for hours. Each village in Sardinia has its distinctive costume, and inhabitants of many villages ride gaily decorated carts pulled by garlanded oxen. Gramsci's lifelong resistance to the deadening uniformity of much of modern rationalized society owes its original in-

22. Paolo Spriano has recorded the following interview with Lina Corigliano, who reported, among other things, that Gramsci refused to join everyone else in the clinic in listening to Mussolini's famous speech announcing the conquest of Ethiopia. From one conversation he (Gramsci) conveyed the impression that he was a convinced regionalist: "What nationality do you think you are?" he asked me. "I am Italian," I answered, astonished at his question. To which he responded: "Not at all. You are a Calabrese before you are an Italian, just as I am a Sardinian." Quoted in Paolo Spriano, *Gramsci in Carcere* (Rome, 1977), 92.

spiration to Sardinia. Viglongo reports that Antonio Gramsci thought traditional festivals such as that honoring St. Efiseo helped to give a people a sense of identity.[23]

Gramsci had little patience with the folkloric aspects of many accounts of Sardinia, however. He particularly disliked the short stories of Sardinia's most famous nineteenth-century writer, Grazia Deledda, because he thought that they presented the island as quaint.[24] Undoubtedly, he would have had the same reaction to D. H. Lawrence's travelogue *The Sea and Sardinia*. The brutal aspects of everyday life in Sardinia should never be ignored, he insisted. Sardinia, after all, was a very real place, the place where Gramsci had paid out much of his life, where his father, having backed the wrong political faction, had to spend over five years in jail for a petty crime, and where retarded children could be chained in the woods in a pigsty.

Gramsci particularly seethed over descriptions of Sardinians as biologically inferior to Italians on the mainland. He learned early to recognize the intellectually and morally disgraceful tendency of some who belong to social groups temporarily enjoying power, wealth, and prestige to attribute inequalities brought about by their own selfish policies to the genetic "inferiority" of the people who have been oppressed. As Togliatti expressed it, Gramsci "sought for the explanation for the poverty and backwardness of the island in the actual relationships that prevailed between the different social groups."[25] For Antonio Gramsci, Sardinia was the laboratory in which the injustice of the larger world could be measured. As an entity, Sardinia was oppressed by the mainland; as a reflection of the social order prevalent on the Italian peninsula, the island's own social order reflected the pattern, prevalent in Italy, of oppression by the powerful over the weak.

In Sardinia Antonio Gramsci learned early to distinguish the self-serving prejudices and rationalizations of the powerful from historical reality. Sardinians were inferior only because they were caught in the grips of an evil and exploitive social system. Sardinia did not have to be what it had become. Its present economic and cultural backwardness resulted from outside domination (the "outside" in the island's most re-

23. I had the good fortune twice to interview Andrea Viglongo, one of Gramsci's three or four closest associates, in Turin in the spring of 1982.

24. Fiori, *Gramsci*, 56.

25. Togliatti, *Gramsci*, 49.

cent history meaning the ten wealthy industrialists in Turin who used the liberal state erected by the nineteenth-century *risorgimento* for its own illiberal interests).

Gramsci's Sardism could have taken a tribal direction. He could have built on his youthful indignation against outside exploitation to contend for a closed, fossilized society. His rejection of closure in favor of openness and "broadening out" speaks volumes about the astonishing importance that "will" played in his life and thought. As both a *gobbo* and a Sardinian, Gramsci journeyed "beyond the wide waters"[26] with two strikes against him. He suffered severe bouts of depression.[27] His body was often racked by severe muscle spasms, and he was frequently tormented by headaches. Knowing what an unattractive first impression he was sure to make on conventionally minded people, he lived in almost total isolation for months on end. In spite—or perhaps because—of all of his difficulties, however, Gramsci was eventually to convince himself that the world of social relations and attitudes was alterable by human will; that persons, groups, and regions currently ostracized by the prestigious and the powerful could assume their rightful place in the sun because there was more than enough sun to go around for everyone.

"Gramsci's originality begins with the moment when he, having become a Socialist, continued to be a Sardinian," Palmiro Togliatti observed.[28] The progress of Gramsci's quest for a new politics is improperly conceived if one assumes that he tried out one "faith" after another, as if in a clothing store trying to find the right fit. Many interpreters of Gramsci ignore the continuity of his life by attempting artificially to divide it into neat phases, a type of "phase-ism." An account of his life as a series of phases inevitably fails to grasp the fact that Gramsci's twofold experience of exclusion, as a hunchback and as a Sardinian, remains throughout the bedrock of his thought and life.[29]

26. "Di la delle grand' acque." Fiori, *Gramsci*, 70. This was a popular expression in Sardinian, referring to mainland Italy.

27. Gramsci to Julia Schucht, March 29, 1924, in *2000*, II, 39.

28. Togliatti, *Gramsci*, 51.

29. Some examples of "phase-ism" are: Alisdair Davidson, *Antonio Gramsci* (London, 1977), 270; Giuseppe Ferrata, Preface to *2000 pagine di Gramsci*, I, 112; and Fiori, *Gramsci*, 149. The *svolta* (turning point) of Gramsci's life is alleged by the first source to have come in 1919–20, by the second in 1926, and by the third in 1921. I argue that the evidence suggests that there was no *svolta*, or "road to Damascus" experience, at all in Gramsci's life. Rather, Gramsci built on his early experience as a hunchback and as a Sardinian to develop a theory of politics based on including the excluded.

To diminish in any way the importance of Gramsci's commitment first to socialism and then to communism would be a gross inaccuracy, of course; but it is important to note that Gramsci never became a Socialist or even a Communist in the doctrinaire sense of the word. Rather, he saw himself as continuously involved in the process of freeing human beings from specific forms of arbitrary exclusion.

For Antonio Gramsci politics is the process of including people who had been excluded and of merging the periphery with the center. The ultimate objective of the new politics is to include all people in the center.

GRAMSCI IN SARDINIA AND SARDINIA IN GRAMSCI

Sardinia's importance to understanding Antonio Gramsci's mature theory of politics, then, cannot be overestimated. It was in and through his Sardinian experience that Gramsci acquired his dominating and abiding aversion for the politics of prestige. His stormy relationship with those later called the "mandarins" of Italian socialism and communism thus becomes comprehensible. After leaving Sardinia, Gramsci identified first with socialism and then with communism because, of all the available forces on the scene, these two successively seemed to have the best prospects for demolishing the prison of a social order based on prestige.

It should be stressed, however, that Gramsci did not feel that he lacked prestige in all respects. In one of his letters he refers to his advantage over many of the peasant children in elementary school because he had been educated in Italian as well as Sardinian, and they had not. Therefore one of Gramsci's gifts was the ability to transcend immediate, unhealthy narcissistic concern for self and to empathize with the "prestigeless," whoever and wherever they were.

Gramsci's conviction that the distinction between the prestigious few and the prestigeless many is arbitrary and unnecessary led him to the further conviction that all invidious distinctions, being a creation of human will, can be overcome by human will. The differences between individuals, regions, and social groups, while real, are not essentially important. These differences are unnecessarily magnified by the operation of the old politics of prestige. The mistaken idea that Sardinian "inferiority" is an unmodifiable fact of nature is one consequence of the politics of prestige. The notion that a hunchback is not normal is another. Gramsci found out in time that he was able to enjoy sex, and in adulthood he developed physical prowess in his arms and hands.[30] As he broke out of his own shell of inferiority and emerged as a leading figure in the socialist movement in Turin, he found that his deformity mattered less and less to the people who mattered more and more to him.

Palmiro Togliatti has written of Antonio Gramsci:

> From the critique of the structure of Sardinian society he came, by way of socialism, to the critique of the structure of Italian society as a whole, and thus . . . to the discovery of . . . forces for renewal both on the island and in all of Italy and of the means by which one proceeds to achieve this renewal.[31]

While Togliatti has properly noted the crucial importance of Sardinia in Gramsci's life and thought, his characterization is rather too abstract, and it tends to leave out the extent to which Gramsci was always directly and personally involved in the problems he was analyzing. Gramsci was anything but a spectator analyzing structures; he was a participant in an ongoing process. He did not so much discover forces of renewal as enter into and help those forces emerge. Also, *renewal* is a rather tame word for the new politics because it implies that there was something healthy in society's past that should be renewed, while Gramsci committed himself to a kind of qualitative change in political existence—the overcoming and abolition of the distinction between centers of prestige and peripheries of inferiority. Finally, Gramsci's broadening out process was to take him far beyond Italy to include all mankind.

 Gramsci's mature vision of a new politics dedicated to overcoming "marginalization" (*emarginazzione*)[32] can be understood fully and properly, then, only in the context of his youthful formative experiences. As Piero Gobetti suggested, even Gramsci's early contacts with socialism were more the result of his loneliness as a Sardinian émigré in the cold and distant climate of Turin than of a commitment to Italian socialist

---

30. Reference to the adult Gramsci's strength in his arms and hands abound in the literature. He generally won stone-throwing contests with his comrades.

31. Togliatti, *Gramsci*, 51.

32. *Emarginazzione* ("marginalization") may have been coined by Enrico Berlinguer, long-time secretary of the Italian Communist party before his death in June, 1984. Berlinguer, himself a Sardinian, was profoundly influenced by Gramsci. Berlinguer developed the theme of *emarginazzione* in his speeches in 1981. One of Gramsci's last entries in the *Quaderni* concerns *gruppi marginali* (marginal groups). See chapter 9 for a discussion.

doctrine, then permeated with positivism.[33] Christian Riechers has correctly noted that from his most youthful publications to the last page of
the *Prison Notebooks*, Gramsci demonstrates an "uninterrupted coherence of theoretical outlook."[34] My chief purpose is to trace this outlook
by focusing on Gramsci's theory of a new politics. Once more, however,
this outlook cannot be understood apart from the specific experiences—
even sights, sounds, and smells—of Gramsci's personal life, because for
Gramsci a theory of a new politics also implies and is embedded in a
style of life.

I have said that Gramsci's theoretical conception of the world cannot
be understood detached from his tangible experiences of life, and specifically of Sardinian life. This contention is more than borne out by his
letters from prison, which abound with requests for information about
the smallest details of everyday life in his native island. "This news of
the village (Ghilarza) interests me a great deal," he wrote to his mother
from prison. "You shouldn't think that these events are ephemeral or
petty or that news of them bores me. I am always as curious as a mole
(*furetto*), and I value even the smallest tidbits." He had a vivid memory
for particulars. In the same letter he affectionately recalled the memory
of Nina Corrias, an early advocate of feminism, who founded the first
Circolo femminile in Ghilarza. At the same time that he admired her, he
humorously recalled her "pose of mainland superiority."[35]

"You ought always to send me news of Ghilarza," Gramsci wrote his
brother Carlo, "for it is very interesting and significant to me." In the
same letter, Gramsci went on to discuss the role of the outlaw in Sardinian culture. "The classical Sardinian outlaw," Gramsci insisted, "possessed something like a trait of generosity and greatness"; now, instead,
one sees a form of "technically organized, professional criminality developing." Gramsci noted a greater degree of corruption in modern Sardinian banditry in that the thieves were sometimes rich and socially

33. Piero Gobetti, *Opere complete* (3 vols.; Turin, 1960), I, 282. Gramsci appointed
Gobetti, a liberal, to review cultural events for *L'Ordine Nuovo*. Gobetti died in Paris at
age 25 from wounds inflicted by Fascist terrorists.

34. Christian Riechers, *Il marxismo in Italia* (Napoli, 1975), 18. Although at times in-
sightful, Riechers' book presents a distorted picture of Gramsci as a philosophical idealist
and voluntarist at odds with Marx's scientific materialism. Riechers holds that Gramsci's
idea of revolution ends in passivity and contemplation, the very accusation Gramsci
hurled at Bordiga (see chapter 8).

35. Gramsci to his mother, March 5, 1928, in *LDC*, 184.

prestigious; they stole out of "a moral perversion that has nothing in common with [authentic] Sardinian banditry."[36] The spread of suicides among the outlaws was to Gramsci a significant sign of the undesirable transformation that had taken place in recent years. (It is interesting to observe Gramsci's preoccupation with the theme of prestige even when writing about thieves.)

Writing from prison to thank his mother for a loaf of Sardinian bread, Gramsci said that, although it was stale by the time it reached him, "the smell was as strong as ever." A year later he informed his sister-in-law about the peculiar excellences of Sardinian yogurt:

> Don't get it in your head to send me *gioddu* (Sardinian yogurt) . . . because you wouldn't know how to make it. If you think it is easy to prepare *gioddu* . . . you are extremely mistaken. . . . What is called yogurt in Rome is completely repugnant to what Sardinian shepherds make.[37]

Warming to his subject, Gramsci composed a veritable paean to Sardinian yogurt in his next letter to the same person:

> On the question of *gioddu,* it is neither a matter of Sardinian patriotism nor of *campanilismo.* . . . Rather, it is that one can't mail or keep Sardinian yogurt long without it spoiling. And there is also another very important reason: it seems necessary that a certain dose of filth be present . . . in the environment for *gioddu* to be genuine. This element of filth (*sporcizia*) cannot be measured mathematically. . . . To be authentic filth that is natural and spontaneous, it has to stink like a billy goat.[38]

Gramsci's prison letters evoke the sounds, sights, and smells of a world with which he fully identified. Fully aware that Sardinians were outcasts in the Italian body politic, at or near the bottom of the scale of prestige as measured by the Italians on the continent, Gramsci delighted in displaying his appreciation for what he regarded as rough and authentic in Sardinian peasant life.

Gramsci not only acquired from Sardinia a sense of injustice from having been for a time excluded from his own family and from school; he also acquired a love of the island's peasant population and landscape. "How as a boy I loved the valley of the Tirso," he wrote to his mother from prison:

36. Gramsci to his brother Carlo, October 8, 1928, in *LDC,* 232.
37. Gramsci to Tatiana Schucht, March 23, 1931, in *LDC,* 419.
38. Gramsci to Tatiana Schucht, April 7, 1931, in *LDC,* 424.

As a boy I used to remain for hours and hours seated on a rock to marvel at the kind of lake that the river formed right under the church [of San Serafino].

He goes on in the same letter to describe how a snake went into the water to fetch an enormous eel, which it killed and abandoned. "The eel was rigid as a stick and made my hands stink very much."[39]

To his son Delio, then eight years old and far away in Moscow, Gramsci wrote how as a small boy he had watched a family of five porcupines pick up apples from a clearing in the light of a full moon. He caught the animals, kept them as pets, and watched how they killed snakes and then ate them, one piece at a time. He expressed the desire to tell Delio of "other things I have seen and felt as a boy," many of them having to do with animals.[40]

In another letter from prison to his mother, Gramsci recalled the place where he played with paper schooners:

I remember well the courtyard where I played with Luciano and the pond where I maneuvered my great paper floats . . . [and] then destroyed them with shots from toy guns.[41]

Antonio Gramsci's descriptions of the countryside around Ghilarza reveal the depth of his love of nature, specifically of plants and animals. Later in prison, one of his most beautiful letters speaks of his attempt to tame a pair of swallows he had managed to attract into his cell:

One of them was very proud and extremely lively. The other was very timid, with a servile mind and without initiative. The first one immediately became owner of the cell. . . . What pleased me about this swallow is that it did not want to be touched. It rebelled ferociously, with wings unfolded, and pecked at my hand with great energy.[42]

Thus, Antonio Gramsci not only learned dignity from Sardinia; he also learned playfulness. In the testimonials collected about Gramsci and from my own interviews with people who knew him well—for there are even today survivors, because Gramsci died relatively young— almost everyone has stressed the playful side of his personality, a side one never would know from looking at his fierce photographs. One of

39. Gramsci to his mother, October 19, 1931, in *LDC*, 509.
40. Gramsci to his son Delio, n.d., in *LDC*, 893.
41. Gramsci to his mother, September 12, 1932, in *LDC*, 672.
42. Gramsci to Tatiana Schucht, May 19, 1930, in *LDC*, 345.

his most vivid letters concerns his last visit to Sardinia and to his home-town of Ghilarza, when even the local Fascist dignitaries called upon him to pay their respects (he was, after all, a member of the Chamber of Deputies). There, at home for the last time, Gramsci made the house shake with the sounds of his "war" between two imaginary armies of crabs, for his own amusement and that of his four-year-old niece.[43]

Gramsci's appreciation for the playful interludes in his childhood and his delight in the natural world surrounding his native village should not obscure the fact that more than anything else the word *Sardinia* meant a life that for most people, himself included, had been brutal and hard. For Antonio Gramsci, Sardinia meant a place where one was for-tunate to get one good meal a day; where, going to bed hungry, you could hallucinate about an enormous spider waiting to descend and suck your brain out when you fell asleep.

The word *Sardinia* for Gramsci meant attending a wretched second-ary school (*ginnasio*), where the school year began late because of the difficulty of attracting even the three mediocre teachers it had to so re-mote a place as the tiny village of Santa Lissurgiu, and where most of the pupils, of peasant origin, could not speak or write Italian. It meant observing repeated acts of cruelty upon a mildly demented peasant woman by her own daughter.[44] It meant, in order to attend the *liceo* (high school) in Cagliari, he had to live in a tiny room with no plaster on the walls, a room that opened onto "a kind of shaft, more like a latrine than a courtyard."[45] It meant having to stay home from high school on some days for lack of money with which to buy clothes or books despite his pleading letters to his father to send money "for the love of God."[46] Sardinia meant a place where the great majority of the people were peasants who lived in illiteracy, extreme poverty, and su-perstition. This peasant majority was utterly ignored by the "great in-tellectuals" of the liberal state who tended "to conceive of humanity as national groups of intellectuals." To Gramsci, these writers—Benedetto Croce, Guido De Ruggiero, Salvador De Madariaga—liked to think in

43. Gramsci had always delighted in playing with small children. He liked nothing better than to get down on all fours in a comrade's apartment and play games with the children (interview with Andrea Viglongo, Turin, April, 1982).

44. Gramsci to Tatiana Schucht, September 12, 1932, in *LDC*, 674.

45. Gramsci to his brother Carlo, December 9, 1927, in *LDC*, 124–25.

46. Fubini MS. There are five letters here in all, written from Cagliari, where Antonio Gramsci attended *liceo*.

terms of national character, but they failed to see that the true nation consisted of the majority of the population and not the intellectual elite.

> [They] do not see that the peasants, as the majority of the population, really constitute the nation, even if they count for very little in ruling the state. . . .[47]

In Sardinia Antonio Gramsci acquired a zest for the concrete that lasted all his life. Instead of talking about the problem of hunger in the abstract, he constantly inquired about exactly what the people (above all, the peasant majority) ate:

> I would like for Grazietta to let me know what a family of *zorronaderis* and *massaios* (daylaborers and sharecroppers), and of small landowners who work their land themselves, of full-time shepherds, and of artisans eat over a week's time.[48]

Gramsci proceeds through the list of particulars: how much meat (if any), vegetables, pasta, bread, coffee, sugar, or milk for the children. Far from being an impractical or utopian thinker, Gramsci had an emphatic aversion to building "castles in the air." The roots of his practicality grew out of early experiences of family life:

> At my house the members of my family were always making a multitude of plans, hypotheses, and grandiose preparations, and then they would forget something essential, without which seemingly well constructed projects fail.

This "something essential," Gramsci continued, was "the existence of 'others'":

> My father and my brothers believed that they had a great capacity for business. . . . They were always constructing castles in the air and criticizing the absence of a spirit of initiative in other Sardinians. Naturally, none of their ventures ever succeeded, and the fault always belonged to "others" as if these "others" had not also existed beforehand and should not have been taken into consideration before launching . . . [the enterprise].[49]

In the above letter, recalling familial experiences during his adolescence, Gramsci spoke graphically of his aversion to mere ideas. Even

---

47. Gramsci to Tatiana Schucht, October 19, 1931, in *LDC*, 512.
48. Gramsci to his mother, September 13, 1931, in *LDC*, 485.
49. Gramsci to Tatiana Schucht, December 28, 1931, in *LDC*, 548.

the smallest details were discussed at length; everything was analyzed, weighed, discussed, as if one were dealing with affairs of state.

To discuss matters merely abstractly—"in idea"—was always far removed from the adult Gramsci's understanding of the role of theory, and he agreed essentially with Immanuel Kant's essay attacking the popular notion that "it may be true in theory but it won't work in practice."[50] Theory for Gramsci was an intuitive union of disinterested, disciplined speculation and the requirements of a particular, concrete historical situation in which the reactions of "the others" are considered in advance of a project. Gramsci's youthful aversion to building castles in the air, to conceiving proposals in idea only, remained with him to the end and is reflected in his criticism in the *Prison Notebooks* of the utopias of More, Campanella, and others.[51]

GRAMSCI: SARDIST OR SOCIALIST?

Antonio Gramsci's experiences—personal, familial, cultural, and linguistic—in the first twenty years of his life spent in Sardinia were clearly decisive in providing the basis for his revolutionary activism. Before he was a linguist or a Socialist or a Marxist he was and remained a Sardinian. In the *Prison Notebooks* there is a reference to the effect of the elections of 1913 on the Sardinian peasantry, the importance of which has not been noted sufficiently in the literature. Gramsci is talking about the significance of expanding the suffrage for the hopes of the ordinary people—the excluded ones. "The election of 1913," he observes, "is the first [in Italy] with distinct popular characteristics because of the very large participation of the peasants." In Sardinia, he notes, there was a "widespread mystical conviction that everything would be different after the vote," that it was "a real social palingenesis."[52] Very possibly these observations have autobiographical significance.

Everyone now agrees that Gramsci did not join the Italian Socialist party until late 1913 or early 1914. It is very probable that the experience of the 1913 elections and their effect on Sardinia had a decisive role in

50. Immanuel Kant, "Theory and Practice: Concerning the Common Saying 'This May Be True in Theory but Does Not Apply in Practice,'" in C. J. Friedrich (ed.), *The Philosophy of Kant* (New York, 1949), 415–29.

51. *SPN*, 239.

52. *Ibid.*, 243.

Gramsci's move away from a possible career as a professor to that of a direct participant in the political struggle through increasingly revolutionary journalism. Gramsci observed the elections directly while in Sardinia on summer vacation after his first year at Turin University.

According to Susanna Carda Marcia, a major scholarly source for the period from 1910 to 1913 in Gramsci's life, Gramsci's first journalistic activity took place at age 19, when he worked as correspondent for the regionalist paper *Unione Sarda* in the tiny village of Aldo Maggiori, where one of the earliest experiments at a cooperative of shepherds and sheep breeders was organized. Marcia argues that Gramsci came slowly to socialism via his philosophical and linguistic studies. She notes correctly that the Italian Socialist party was at the time under positivist domination. The temper of the young Gramsci's mind was averse to positivism and its logic-chopping, mechanistic, impersonal, and pretentious pseudoscientific schemes.[53] I would revise Marcia's formulation to read that Gramsci came to his own kind of socialism as a development of his primary experiences both as a hunchback and as a Sardinian. As we shall see, Gramsci's attraction to linguistic studies at Turin appears to have been motivated primarily by his appreciation of the Sardinian language (which is more than a dialect) and his conviction that Sardinia was unjustly condemned *tout court* by the powerful groups on the continent who decided what was prestigious and what was contemptible.

It is safe to say that before 1913 or 1914 Gramsci was more a Sardist than a Socialist. Traces of his ferocious opposition to protectionist trade policies imposed on powerless Sardinia from powerful Turin remained in his writings for years after he left the island. As we shall see, one of his reasons for rejecting Italian liberalism was its abandonment of a policy of free trade. In October, 1913, Gramsci, then in Turin, signed an antiprotectionist manifesto in the Sardinian language.[54]

Sardinia's continuing presence in Gramsci's life cannot be disputed. Much of the literature about him is interested only in describing the Marxist motif in his thought. While Marx's writings were to have a major impact upon Gramsci's thought, one cannot understand Gramsci as someone who converted to Marxism, as it were, after a youth preoccupied with Sardinian questions. In time, Gramsci abandoned his sim-

53. Marcia, *Il giovane Gramsci,* 38.

54. *Ibid.,* 46. Marcia discovered Gramsci's signature on the manifesto written in Sardinia in October, 1913.

plistic emphasis on the protective tariff as the major source of all Sardinia's ills, and he quickly left behind the even more simplistic Sardinian nationalism of his youth. The presence that always remained centrally with him, however, was that of Sardinia as the outcast in the Italian national family. From that experience, just as from his own early feelings of being an outcast because his deformity disgraced his family, he learned to identify with marginal groups in general. His dedication to overcoming marginalization (*emarginazzione*) became the core of his theory of politics, of which a nondeterminist kind of Marxism was unquestionably a major part.

As Massino Salvadori observed, Antonio Gramsci arrived at Turin in the fall of 1911 "as a Sardinian with a whole baggage of principles . . . concerning Sardinia and its continental exploiters." Already as well, however, Gramsci sounded a revolutionary theme. To quote Salvadori again, "autonomism [the idea of Sardinian self-government] was not conceived by Gramsci from the perspective of democratizing the bourgeois state."[55] Antonio Gramsci's conviction that meaningful political change could come only by revolution is evident even as early as his senior essay entitled "Oppressed and Oppressors," at the Liceo Giovanni Maria Dettori in Cagliari. Gramsci argues in the essay that humanity has always struggled to free itself from bondage to oppressors, whether they be a single individual, a social class, or an entire people. Sardonically rejecting the rationalization of conquerors that their purpose is to "civilize" the conquered inhabitants, the young Gramsci insists that beneath the skin of the so-called "civilizers" themselves there lies "the hide of the wolf." Although the wolflike instincts present in all human beings have subsided somewhat in modern times, they are still there. However, from the French Revolution of 1789 humanity has learned a new truth—that privileges and social differences, having been produced by society and not by nature, can be surpassed.

"Oppressed and Oppressors" ends with its youthful author's grim prediction that humanity "needs another bloodbath" in order that "the powerful people" (*i dominanti*) should repent for having left mankind in a condition of "ignorance and ferocity."[56]

While one should not attach excessive importance to a high school

55. Massino Salvadori, "Gramsci e la questione sarda," *Studi Storici*, III (1976), 195–222, 207–208.
56. Gramsci, "Oppressi ed oppressori," in Paolo Spriano (ed.), *Scritti politici* (Rome, 1967), 5. There is a translation of the essay in *SPW*[1], 3–5.

essay, perhaps produced in a hurry, it is nonetheless true that "Oppressed and Oppressors" contains the germs of Gramsci's mature political thought. In addition to his obvious identification with the oppressed, one should note Gramsci's extraordinary preoccupation with the savage, or beastly, side of man's nature that lies underneath the veneer of civilization. Beneath the utopian language and the hyperbole of this high school essay there runs a realistic strain that recognized that even after the last revolutionary bloodbath abolishing all man-made privileges had taken place, man would still be a contradiction and a problem to himself. Through his own self-knowledge Gramsci had learned that there are two sides to man's consciousness. For the darker side of his nature Gramsci consistently used animal images. When feeling depressed and self-destructive he compares himself to a "bear in its cave" or a "wolf in its den."[57]

> My imagination has two outlets [he wrote to Julia Schucht in 1924]: when I am at peace it indulges itself by creating bizarre and comical scenes; when I am exhausted and embittered, it fabricates atrocious and unhealthy things.[58]

Above all, however, Gramsci carried with him from his Sardinian upbringing two qualities that were to enable him to stand the physical and psychological sufferings during his long years as a political prisoner in Benito Mussolini's Italy—an iron will and the capacity to recall the simple pleasures of his childhood in his beloved Sardinia. Writing to his mother from prison, he told her that although he recalled many sorrows and sufferings, he also remembered something happy and beautiful about his youth in Sardinia. "I am sure that we shall see each other again," he wrote,

> and we will prepare a huge meal with *kulurzonas* (cheese ravioli), *pardulas* and *zippulas* (Sardinian desserts) . . . and *figu sigada* (a sweet shaped in the form of a doll).[59]

EVERY SARDINIAN IS AN ISLAND WITHIN AN ISLAND

In one of his last letters to his wife, written three and a half months before his death, Antonio Gramsci observed:

57. Gramsci to Julia Schucht, July 7 and August 4, 1924, in *2000,* II, 48, 52.
58. Gramsci to Julia Schucht, March 3, 1924, in Fubini MS.
59. Gramsci to his mother, February 26, 1927, in *LDC,* 53.

> I believe that you have always known that I have a great, even a very great difficulty in exteriorizing my feelings. . . . In Italian literature it is said that if Sardinia is an island, every Sardinian is an island within an island. . . . Perhaps there is a little bit of truth in this, enough at least to give the flavor [of my thought].[60]

Both from what Gramsci wrote about himself and from what those closest to him, such as Alfonso Leonetti, Andrea Viglongo, and Palmiro Togliatti, said about him, it is clear that his Sardinian background provided the "flavor" of his thought. Perhaps Leonetti's distinction between *sardità* (Sardinianness) and *sardismo* (Sardinianism) best captures the manner of Sardinia's presence in Gramsci's mind. Gramsci soon abandoned Sardinianism, but he remained a Sardinian.

This is also true with respect to his deformity: Gramsci would properly have condemned as "Lorianism" [reductionism] any argument that held his political vision to have been a surface reflection of his own torment, physical and spiritual, as a *gobbo*. One need not be a psychoanalyst or even a psycho-historian to make the point that Gramsci's hunchbacked condition should be taken seriously as a formative factor in his thought. In 1921, Gramsci wrote:

> The Communist acknowledges that he is weaker physically, but he does not acknowledge that he is weaker spiritually; his body may be enslaved, but not his soul.[61]

Here he is clearly speaking autobiographically. As a Sardinian hunchback, he had faced long odds before he became engaged in the political struggle as a Communist.

Only by beginning with Gramsci's preintellectual, emotional, and formative experiences can one understand adequately what kind of revolutionary Gramsci became. I do not want to reduce his original and creative theory of a new politics to idiosyncratic experiences; rather, I wish to enhance our understanding of that theory by showing how it is anchored in Gramsci's unusual life experiences. The discovery that Gramsci's theory is anchored in those experiences scarcely invalidates the theory in any way. On the contrary, it could enhance the theory's validity because it underscores the fact that Gramsci did not have to learn about the *emarginati* secondhand: he *was* one of them.

60. Gramsci to Julia Schucht, January 5, 1937, in *LDC,* 880–81.
61. Gramsci, "Chi è communista?" in *ON,* 1.

II 𝔉 From University Student to Revolutionary Journalist, 1911–1918

Awarded a scholarship at the university, Antonio Gramsci arrived in Turin, the great city *al di la delle grand' acque,* unequipped financially, emotionally, or physically to deal with such an enormous change in his life. It is difficult to imagine a sharper contrast than that between Ghilarza, then a town of two thousand inhabitants strung out on a mountain ridge and isolated from any major population centers, and Turin, after Milan the most industrialized city in Italy. Into this utterly unfamiliar environment Antonio Gramsci arrived in October, 1911.

Gramsci recounts at first walking around the city stupefied at its size and fearful of getting hit by a tram. At first he had trouble with the university's bureaucracy over getting his scholarship funds released and had to beg his family for money. He could not afford the room he had rented and was forced to seek another one. The cold of the winter affected him adversely; he shivered in his room at first, lacking even an overcoat. He could not afford to buy enough to eat. He knew absolutely no one and had great difficulty in socializing because of his concern about the effect of his physical appearance on others. Months went by before he established friendships with the two brilliant fellow university students who were to work with him to found *L'Ordine Nuovo:* Palmiro Togliatti and Angelo Tasca.

Having placed ninth among the top ten competitors for a scholarship (set aside for needy Sardinian students) at the Carlo Alberto College of the University of Turin, Gramsci enrolled in the Faculty of Letters for Modern Philology. His first major research project, which was with Professor Matteo Bartoli, dealt with aspects of the Sardinian language. He also attended lectures on Italian literature given by Umberto Cosmo and on the Twelve Tables of the Roman Law given by Giovanni Pachini, where he began to get to know Togliatti, who was also one of the ten special scholars from Sardinia.[1]

Marco Spinella has written that compared with Milan, Florence, and Naples, Turin was a very modest cultural center during Gramsci's years at the university. He compared Gramsci's university environment unfavorably with that of Karl Marx in Germany during the 1840s.[2] Whether or not Spinella's characterization of Turin as a minor cultural center is valid, Matteo Bartoli deepened Gramsci's knowledge of linguistics.

THE IMPORTANCE OF GRAMSCI'S STUDIES OF LINGUISTICS FOR HIS POLITICAL THOUGHT

In a much-discussed book published in 1979, Franco Lo Piparo contends that the first germ of the idea for which Antonio Gramsci has become most famous—that of "hegemony"—lay in the work he did on linguistics with Bartoli at Turin University from 1912 to 1913. Lo Piparo's thesis is worthy of serious consideration, because if it is correct, then Gramsci had already discovered the key concept of his mature political theory before he studied Marx seriously. Lo Piparo bases his thesis primarily upon his reading of Gramsci's *dispensa,* the notes collected and systematized from lectures and reading on linguistics from 1912–1913, forming a document of 213 pages in Gramsci's immaculate handwriting.

Bartoli was Italy's foremost champion of "neolinguistics," a school of thought holding that language is much more than grammar and vocabulary, and that language, politics, and culture are indissolubly related aspects of a worldwide historical process. Bartoli himself had derived inspiration from Graziadio Isaia Ascoli, who in 1873 had written, according to the words of Gramsci's *dispensa,* a "magisterial, and in

1. For an account of Gramsci's desperate unhappiness upon first arriving in Turin, see Giuseppe Fiori, *Antonio Gramsci: Life of a Revolutionary* (New York, 1970), 70–80. In the scholarship competition Gramsci finished ninth, Palmiro Togliatti second.

2. Marco Spinella calls Turin a "very modest cultural center" in his Introduction to *Attualità di Gramsci* (Milan, 1977), xi.

some respects definitive treatise" on the question of an Italian national language. Ascoli had attacked Alessandro Manzoni's project to establish Tuscan (Florentine) Italian as the language of the newly unified Italy. One of the means by which Manzoni had hoped to accomplish this task was by compiling the first "Italian" dictionary. Ascoli had objected that Manzoni had the situation reversed: one could not come up with an Italian dictionary until an Italian language existed. All the people in all the regions of the new nation must participate in creating a national language. It cannot be imposed by "the learned" on "the ignorant," Ascoli had insisted.[3]

Ascoli's reflections influenced Gramsci permanently. Both in his journalism during the Turin years and in the *Prison Notebooks* Gramsci cited Ascoli favorably.

Gramsci saw very early—during his first full year of studies at Turin University—that language and politics cannot be neatly separated, and that in a vital sense language *is* politics, for it affects the way people think about power. Throughout history the powerful have used language to forestall criticism before it starts by establishing themselves as the arbiters of taste.

One of the reasons for Italy's late unification as a nation, Gramsci concluded, was that the masses of the people were excluded from the world of literature by the humanist mandarins of the Renaissance. Knowledge was concentrated in a small minority of intellectuals who formed a caste and who wrote for each other rather than for a wider public of active citizens.

A new culture (including a new language) cannot be forced on a people; this is the burden of Gramsci's opposition to Enlightenment-style rationalistic reformers such as Alessandro Manzoni. Society is not a machine or a mechanism.

THE OLD IN THE NEW

Gramsci learned early in his linguistic studies at Turin University that, although history is a conflict in which there is a winner and a loser, the loser adopts the alien culture only with significant resistance. As Lo

3. Franco Lo Piparo, *Lingua, intellettuali, egemonia in Gramsci* (Bari, 1979), 36, 55, 68–71, 81–85. On Ascoli's importance to Gramsci, see *ibid.*, 103–104, 109–15, 127–29, 205–14, 229–30, 253–57.

Piparo has noted, Gramsci undoubtedly was strongly influenced by Ascoli's conclusion that "the adoption of the conquering language and culture does not lead to a radical substitution and/or destruction of the preceding language and culture." The result is rather that a new "linguistic block" is formed in which elements of the two languages, dominant and dominated, influence one another. What Ascoli calls "new ethnic individuals" arise through the fusion of different national entities.

Gramsci carefully studied Ascoli's distinction between "the language of the substratum" and the "action of the substratum," the former representing the native language of a conquered territory and the latter the "influence of the phonological, morphological, and syntactical structures of the native language on the adopted language."

Only by placing language in a comparative perspective, Ascoli insisted, could one analyze specifically Italian problems. Ascoli held that Tuscan Italian could not be established as the national language by virtue of the government's putting its stamp of approval on Manzoni's proposed dictionary. For a variety of reasons, Florence could not be for Italy what Paris had been for France.

The attack on the fatalism of the positivistically inspired "neogrammarians" was to affect profoundly Gramsci's interpretation of Marxism. Ironclad phonetic laws no more determine a society's language than ironclad economic laws determine a society's political structure, Gramsci concluded. Neogrammarians and deterministic Marxists alike sought to force spontaneous and vital life forms into the procrustean beds of determinism.

In a letter to Leo Galetto written in February, 1918, Gramsci ridiculed the idea of Esperanto as a universal language:

> Down with Esperanto . . .—a linguistic form that is rigidified and mechanized. I am a revolutionary, a "historicist," and I affirm that only those forms of social activity—whether linguistic, economic, or political—that arise spontaneously from the activity of free social energies are "useful and rational." Therefore: down with Esperanto, as well as with all the privileges, all the mechanizations, all the definitive and rigidified forms of life. . . .[4]

4. Gramsci to Leo Galetto, late February, 1918, in *LCF,* 673. Gramsci's article "La lingua unica e l'esperanto," February 16, 1918, in *LCF,* 668–73, had ridiculed the idea of a contrived universal language such as Esperanto.

"Everything moves," wrote Gramsci, quoting Heraclitus in Greek. What was important was "real history." Intellectual schemes are only hypotheses; at best their value is to give a possibly secure direction to practical action.

LINGUISTICS AND "HEGEMONY"?

In a letter from prison, Gramsci contrasted the moment of hegemony or cultural direction with the mechanistic and fatalistic conceptions of economism, claiming that Marx and Lenin could be counted in support of the former, while positivists and reductionists who distorted Marx but claimed to be his disciples supported the latter. Lo Piparo quotes Luciano Gruppi to the effect that the germ of Gramsci's idea of hegemony may be found in the December 24, 1917, article "The Revolution Against *Das Kapital*." In reality, asserts Lo Piparo, the first germ of the idea must be located during the 1912–1913 academic year when Gramsci studied linguistics with Bartoli and became familiar with his battle against the neogrammarians and their rationalistic and fatalistic materialism.

Lo Piparo has done yeoman service in placing Gramsci's notes for the course taught by Bartoli in context. A more biographical approach might have led him to find the germ of Gramsci's opposition to mechanical and fatalistic modes of thinking in Gramsci's early life in Sardinia.

Gramsci was taken with Bartoli's theory that languages spread by virtue of the cultural prestige of the conquering tongue, because he (Gramsci) had earlier become preoccupied with the theme of prestige as a result of his own experience as a marginalized person. To Gramsci, Sardinia was an example of a conquered people, with a language low on the scale of prestige.

Gramsci's new politics of overcoming *emarginazzione* involved both the preservation of what was vital and alive in the indigenous culture—and as we have seen, Gramsci loved the Sardinian language and proudly proclaimed himself a provincial many times over—and the opening out of that culture to the wider world that was Italian, European, and global. The new politics was based on the twin demands that "less prestigious" groups be included in the general culture and that the new culture be truly general. The hegemony of one language or culture over another might be justified at a given point in history because it offers a wider horizon than did the indigenous one, but that hegemony, far from being self-perpetuating, should serve to stir up creative impulses in the people upon whom the hegemonic culture is acting, enabling them to pull themselves up to the height of the "prestigious" culture.

For Gramsci, the difficulty specific to Italy is that the process of self-elevation has been blocked by the confinement of the hegemonic culture to a caste of intellectuals, the "people-nation" having been left to contend with fossilized customs and dialects of restricted communication. Exploitation and oppression were always seen by Gramsci to be cultural as well as economic. The precondition for ending such exploitation had to be the resolve by the subjugated strata and regions of society to rise up and create their own culture instead of waiting for the philanthropic benevolence of the powers that be. To create a counterhegemony was the revolution's first task.

Gramsci's theory of hegemony, then, had its roots in his experiences prior to his intellectual encounter with Marx. Those experiences were unique to him both as a hunchback pushed to the margins of society and as a son of Sardinia, the island-region oppressed economically and culturally by the "mainlanders." His studies in linguistics under Professor Matteo Bartoli only confirmed and gave intellectual depth to his vision of a new politics of liberation of the vast prestigeless majority from an order established by and maintained for the robber barons and intellectual mandarins of the day.

In Turin, when he became active in the Socialist party and came into contact with the workers at the enormous Fiat manufacturing plant, it was natural for Gramsci to marry these formative experiences with Marxism without ever dogmatically becoming a Marxist. There can be no denying the central importance of the Marxist motif to Gramsci's thought, however. Torrents of words have been published about precisely when Gramsci became a Marxist, a question that is wrongly put because it assumes that at sometime or other Gramsci converted, as a result of reading Marx himself, from a vague humanitarian socialism to a scientific doctrine that answered all of life's questions.

Gramsci did indeed begin to read some of Karl Marx's works seriously at Turin. According to Alfonso Leonetti, during the period 1914–1918 when he was between twenty-three and twenty-seven years old, Gramsci "read and studied the following works of Marx: *The Communist Manifesto, Revolution and Counter-Revolution in Germany* [*i.e., Address of the Central Committee to the Communist League*], *The Holy Family, The Poverty of Philosophy,* and the *Introduction to the Critique of Political Economy,* almost always in the French translation edited by Citron."[5]

In the next chapter I will examine Gramsci's use of Marx in the newspaper articles written during the period 1914–1919. Now that a definitive edition of those writings exists, the task of answering the question "What did Marx initially mean to Gramsci?" has been simplified considerably.

GRAMSCI'S EVERYDAY LIFE IN TURIN

Andrea Viglongo, one of Gramsci's closest associates, has published his reminiscences of Gramsci at Turin. There are four noteworthy features of Viglongo's account of Gramsci's daily life in Turin. Viglongo (1) describes in detail the places where Gramsci lived in Turin and explains why he chose them; (2) describes Gramsci's "almost pathological need for company" when he walked around the city, even on the most trivial errand such as buying a pack of Macedonia cigarettes; (3) comments candidly on Gramsci's sexual life; and (4) notes Gramsci's ever-present concern and fascination with Sardinia.

As to choice of residence, Viglongo notes that the terrified youth who arrived in Turin in mid-October, 1911, to compete for his scholarship over several days of exhausting examinations, at first could find only a tiny room for three lire per night, because the fiftieth anniversary celebration of Italian unification had brought a wave of tourists to Italy's first capital city. (The value of his entire scholarship was only seventy lire per month.) With the aid of the college registrar he soon procured a different room for less than half the price, however. Viglongo continues:

> For 25 lire [per month] he found a small room looking on the Dora River, at 57 Corso Firenze, almost at the corner of the Via Periegia, less than five hundred meters from Togliatti's lodging. Perhaps the location was not accidental, because in his two successive choices of rooms he

5. Alfonso Leonetti, *Note su Gramsci* (Urbino, 1970), 70.

showed little initiative in his search. When he returned from Sardinia [after the summer vacation] in the fall of 1912, he chose a room that even though it faced on a funeral home . . . turned out to be two hundred meters from Angelo Tasca's address. [After Togliatti, Tasca was at first Gramsci's closest co-worker in the Socialist party. Eventually Gramsci regarded him as intellectually unreliable.] He did not like either of these rooms, and it was only on returning to Turin for his third year at the university [in November, 1913] that he finally succeeded in finding a room and location he liked. This room turned out to be in the very same building in which Tasca lived.

In the last several years of his eleven-year residence in Turin Antonio Gramsci took his meals regularly with a co-worker and disciple Attilio Carena and his sister Pia. Their home became his true home. Viglongo precisely indicates the locations of Gramsci's residences, eating places, and places of work in order to show how small was the geographical area over which he walked all those years.

Viglongo attributes the narrowness of Gramsci's spatial universe in part to the need to be near people who mattered to him or with whom he had to work; another reason must surely have been Gramsci's physical condition. As a hunchback it took much more effort to traverse long distances on foot, and Gramsci obviously shuddered at the thought of riding long distances on the trams, exposed to stares and possible ridicule.

Viglongo's second, related point concerns Gramsci's almost pathological love of company:

He suffered at the very thought of having to walk three hundred meters up the street by himself to buy cigarettes. He was always with someone; he needed people.

Viglongo recounts always being at Gramsci's side:

All comrades and friends [of Gramsci] of that time remember me as the young man always at his side. I gladly went everywhere with him, and I was grateful for the attention he paid me and the invaluable attention I received from conversing with him. I felt that I was his favorite pupil— not necessarily that I was, but I was pleased to think so and I gloried in it.

With reference to Gramsci's sexual life during these years when he knew him in Turin, Viglongo writes:

Gramsci as a man: . . . Despite his physical deformity, Gramsci was a normal man with all the usual sexual desires. In Sardinia he had not had the opportunity to have sex with women.

However, this was possible in Turin by having recourse to houses of prostitution. Gramsci never spoke with any of us young people about these problems . . . out of the modesty required in that era as a norm of conduct; but I know that once Leo Galetto had to go to rescue him from a brothel because Gramsci did not have enough money to pay for the services he had received.

Viglongo concludes that the relationship between Gramsci and Pia Carena, the woman with whom he worked closely after the founding of *L'Ordine Nuovo,* was platonic in character, in part because of Pia's own wish that they be married before engaging in sexual relations. Whether or not this is true, there can be no doubt that Pia was completely in love with Gramsci. Alfonso Leonetti, whom Pia eventually married after Gramsci left Turin, has said that Gramsci's treatment of her was "an ugly page in his life." After leaving for Moscow, Gramsci never even sent her a postcard.[6]

One reason for introducing these testimonials of the two men who knew Gramsci best during his Turin period is to show that once well established in Turin, Gramsci did not feel excluded from life in the realm of sexuality; despite his deformity he felt himself to be a normal man. His experiences gave him the confidence to declare his love for the beautiful Julia Schucht, whom he later met in Moscow.

Another reason for discussing Gramsci's sexual life is to illumine the meaning of the phrase "the moral life" to Gramsci. When in 1917 he established the Club for the Moral Life, Gramsci scarcely intended to moralize in a Puritan sense. Leading a moral life to him meant caring for and identifying with the oppressed strata of society and developing

6. Andrea Viglongo's reminiscences on Gramsci's life in Turin are found in *Almanacco piemontese* (Turin, 1977) in nine unnumbered pages entitled "Vita torinese di Gramsci." My interviews with Viglongo took place in Turin in May and June, 1982. While the story about Gramsci's being held by the madam of a brothel until he obtained the necessary funds to pay for services rendered might not hold up in court, Viglongo's exceptional reliability in other, weightier matters makes the story credible. (Sergio Caprioglio's own faith in Viglongo's veracity is another important reason to accept the story.) Viglongo talked to me at length about the Club for the Moral Life. Leonetti's remarks are from my interview with him in Rome in May, 1982.

their cultural preparation. Carlo Baccardo, Attilio Carena, and Andrea Viglongo, the three other members of Gramsci's club, were young men forced by their poverty to leave school early. Notwithstanding their lack of formal education, Gramsci was convinced that they could understand and appropriate the cultural legacy of the past. They began by reading Marcus Aurelius' *Meditations*. When in 1918 two of the four members were drafted into the armed forces, the club dissolved. As the only surviving member told me, Gramsci wanted each member to create other clubs or circles. "We were the apostles," Viglongo said humorously.

According to Andrea Viglongo, the club members met and talked informally as they walked in the street. They shared Gramsci's passion for honesty and trust in their personal relations. They passed around a copy of Marcus Aurelius' *Meditations*. Gramsci cared deeply about the club and may have foreseen it as a model for achieving a revolution in culture. That ordinary young working people, with no formal education beyond the fifth grade, could rapidly absorb great ideas of the past can only have impressed Gramsci as a possible model of revolutionary change through the multiplication of such clubs (*circles* is perhaps a better word) among the most intellectually alive of the working class.

THE YEARS AT THE UNIVERSITY: 1911–1915[7]

During his first academic year (1911–1912), Antonio Gramsci lived in a condition of almost complete isolation from other people. Often cold and hungry, he suffered from periodic nervous breakdowns. Nonetheless, his phenomenal willpower pulled him through. When he returned from a summer in Sardinia with his family, he passed three examinations, receiving a perfect score (30) and honors in Linguistics, a 30 in Geography, and a 27 in Greek and Latin Literature.

The academic year 1912–1913 was the most fecund for Gramsci of all his years of study. He attended lectures on many subjects. Palmiro Togliatti, his fellow scholarship holder, reports having seen him everywhere, now listening to Luigi Einaudi's lectures on economics, then attending the classes held by Francesco Ruffini on the church-state relations in Italy.

7. The essential biographical information for this section is found in Caprioglio's chronology of Gramsci's life from 1891 to 1919 in *CT*, xxix–xxxvi.

His hard work notwithstanding, Gramsci kept petitioning to postpone his other examinations, pleading reasons of health. In all probability he rebelled against the academic pedantry and senseless memorization characteristic of examinations at Italian universities of the period. His wide-ranging intellect led him to investigate many subjects at once, and he must have had great difficulty focusing on the rigidly prescribed course of study laid out for him in the Faculty of Letters. In addition, he began to be increasingly distracted by the events around him. In the spring of 1913 the metal workers' union (FIOM) staged a massive strike against the Fiat plant. At this time he had his first direct contact with the workers of a great city. The self-described provincial boy three or four times over began to see what life was like for the masses of working people in the factories of Italy's second most industrialized city. He was also moved to publish two articles in the student newspaper. They subjected the futurist movement to critical scrutiny.

Returning home in the summer of 1913, he supported a Sardinian nationalist movement called the Gruppo di Azione e Propaganda antiprotezionista, sponsored by Attilio Deffenu and Nicole Fancello, in the general elections of October 26 and November 2, the first held under the new law abolishing literacy as a qualification for voting. Gramsci was moved by the sight of Sardinian peasants going to the polls for the first time. More than 172,000 Sardinians voted, over six times the previous number. What was to become Gramsci's repeated emphasis on the potential of impoverished masses who are powerless individually to become powerful collectively has its origins in his observations of what he called the "palingenetic" effect of the Sardinian elections.

Gramsci's return to Turin in November, 1913, marked the last time he was to see Sardinia except for two brief visits. Beginning at this time, late in the year 1913, Antonio Gramsci proceeded to make contact with the Socialist movement in Turin. According to Tasca, Gramsci gradually became active in the youth movement of the Italian Socialist party in Turin and eventually took out his membership card in the party itself. The precise date of his formally joining the party cannot be ascertained.

Pleading serious emotional distress, Gramsci again failed to take his university examinations, scheduled for November, 1913. As a result, he had his scholarship suspended for a brief time. In the spring of 1914 he received the following grades in three examinations: a 25 in Moral Philosophy, a 27 in Modern History, and a 24 in Greek Literature. His scholarship was restored.

Although Gramsci became a Socialist by 1914, he remained fiercely attached to the cause of Sardinian autonomy. He supported anyone who called for reducing or eliminating Piedmont's protective tariff against Sardinia. Gaetano Salvemini's movement for justice for the Italian south, treated like a poor relation ever since Italian unification, greatly interested Gramsci.

During the academic year 1914–1915 Gramsci took a course on Marxism given by Annibale Pastore, from whom he also took private lessons. Pastore later remembered his pupil as having been above all interested in how ideas become practical forces. In April he took his last examination (in Italian Literature). From that moment, Sergio Caprioglio concluded, he in effect left the university. He never bothered to take his degree, which would have required submission of a thesis, although until the end of 1918 he continued to toy with the idea of submitting a thesis on the history of language, in which he would seek to apply the critical methods of historical materialism.

Gramsci as Journalist, 1915–1918

In May, 1915, Antonio Gramsci began to find a vocation as a political journalist, joining the staff of the Turinese Socialist weekly *Il Grido del Popolo,* edited by Giuseppe Bianchi. It was not until December, 1916, when he accepted the Socialist party leader Giacinto Menotti Serrati's invitation to edit the local news page of the Turin edition of the official Socialist party newspaper *Avanti!,* that he had a full-time job sufficient to support himself. Gramsci remained with *Avanti!* until the end of 1920, during which time he wrote numerous reviews of plays, commented on speeches by local figures, and offered wide-ranging reflections on politics in his column *Sotto la Mole.* La Mole, an architecturally distinctive tower erected by Turin's Jewish community in the late nineteenth century, remains today Turin's principal landmark. *Sotto la Mole* means, literally, "under the tower." [8] It could also have meant "under the pile." Gramsci liked to use the double entendre. He also contributed

8. Turin's most prominent architectural monument is the Mole Antoniella, which even today affords the visitor the best view of the city and its environs. *Mole* means "pile" or a massive building.

frequently to *Il Grido*. His articles were almost always unsigned, a conscious effort by Gramsci to avoid achieving journalistic fame as an individual.

To give an idea of both the volume and variety of Gramsci's newspaper writing, one has only to look at his contributions to *Avanti!* for January, 1916, his first full month on the job. He wrote columns on the following subjects: the new year, the controversy over how much Turin had contributed economically to the war effort, the silent screen actor Febo Mari, the exclusion of Socialist representatives from the commission in charge of Turin's Museum for the Risorgimento, the mayor's decision to prohibit the public celebration of Mardi Gras during wartime and the protest of some shop and restaurant owners as a result, what it means to be a true "intellectual," the idiocy of jingoism, the strange utterances of William Jennings Bryan (then American secretary of state), the execution of nurse Edith Louisa Cavell by the Germans in Belgium for having aided many Allied prisoners of war to escape to Holland, an anti-German decree by Turin University's Faculty of Letters restricting chair professorships to Italian citizens, comment on a 1913 speech by Ivanoe Bonomi (who was expelled from the Socialist party in 1912 for having supported Italy's war against Libya), Professor Vittorio Cian's hatred of people of German nationality, a eulogy to a party comrade, a report of speeches by right-wing nationalists on the war, the visit to Turin of Italian Foreign Minister Antonio Salandra (who is described by Gramsci as the spokesman for *Italien über Alles,* and, of most importance, "Socialism and Culture," the latter written for the weekly *Il Grido del Popolo.*[9]

Not bad for a month's writing! During January, 1916, Gramsci also wrote an article entitled "The Syllabus and Hegel," a sarcastic review of a book by the right-wing Catholic publicist Mario Missiroli. According to Gramsci, Missiroli writes in the spirit of Pope Pius IX's *Syllabus of Errors*. Instead, he (Gramsci) extols the spirit of Hegel:

> In the struggle between the *Syllabus* and Hegel, it is Hegel who has won, because Hegel represents the life of thought that does not know limits and posits itself as something transient, something capable of being su-

9. Gramsci, various articles in *CT,* 47–107. Caprioglio concludes that a number of articles previously attributed to Gramsci in this period are doubtful. I have excluded these articles from my list. Caprioglio has also discovered two new attributions for January, which I have included in my discussion.

perseded, something always renewing itself just as history does. The *Syllabus* is an obstacle; it is the death of the inner life; it is a cultural problem and not a historical fact.[10]

The Invisible Army of Books

In "Socialism and Culture" Gramsci continued the debate begun in 1912 in the Socialist Youth Congress at Bologna between Amadeo Bordiga of Naples and Angelo Tasca of Turin about whether a socialist revolution must be preceded by the emergence of a socialist culture. Tasca had answered affirmatively. Bordiga had contended that cultural change would result automatically from economic change. Quoting Novalis and Vico, Gramsci insists that every revolution is preceded by an "intense work of criticism, of cultural penetration." Just as the political thought of the Enlightenment had paved the way for the French Revolution, so socialist political thought must pave the way in Italy for the proletarian revolution. Just as the bayonets of Napoleon's armies found their path "smoothed by an invisible army of books," so the overthrow of capitalism must have its way prepared by a new culture:

> It is through the critique of capitalist civilization that the unitary conscience of the proletariat is formed or is in the process of being formed; critique means culture and not a spontaneous and naturalistic evolution.[11]

Gramsci's interpreters generally judge passages like the above as having been inspired by the philosophical idealism of Benedetto Croce and Giovanni Gentile. If Gramsci had been a merely derivative thinker, these judgments would have merit. If the argument of this book is correct, however, such judgments are superficial and without merit because they do not aid us in understanding Gramsci. On the contrary, they mislead by pasting simplistic labels on this or that phase of his thought. The thesis of this book is that Gramsci's vision of a new politics of including the excluded originated in his formative, preintellectual experiences as a hunchback in Sardinia, and that by the end of his life Antonio Gramsci had used language from a variety of sources—Marx the chief among them—to give amplitude and specificity to that vision.

10. Gramsci, "Il sillabo e Hegel," January 15, 1916, in *CT,* 172.
11. Gramsci, "Socialismo e cultura," January 29, 1916, in *CT,* 99–103. "The invisible army of books" is on p. 102, as is the quotation "It is through the critique. . . ."

Nonetheless, one can definitely say that Gramsci gradually became a Marxist and then remained so to the end. However, to say that Gramsci "became" a Marxist begs the deeper question: What *kind* of Marxist did he "become"? Put simply: Gramsci developed into what in shorthand can be called an "antieconomistic Marxist." [12] Some have argued that he is the greatest antieconomistic Marxist. I am not interested in ranking him as a Marxist; there will always be debates about such rankings, and Rosa Luxemburg and Georg Lukacs have their claim to consideration. Gramsci was more than a Marxist, however; he was a political thinker worthy of study in his own right. The sophisticated, undogmatic, and nuanced character of the best of his thought makes it spill over ideological boundaries and influence non-Marxist movements as well, such as Catholic liberation theology. [13]

In "Socialism and Culture" Gramsci makes clear that by culture he means anything but the encyclopedic mastery of facts. Already here, in January, 1916, Gramsci sounds a theme that resonates through the rest of his gigantic corpus—opposition to a "mandarinate." Nothing would be gained if Socialists were to develop a clique of intellectuals who feel themselves superior to everyone else because they know "a little Latin and a little history." After having just spent four years in a university environment, Gramsci was able on the basis of experience to condemn those professors who "feel themselves to be different from and superior to even the best specialized factory worker." Such prejudice is not culture; it is pedantry: it is not intelligence, but intellectualism.

> Man is above all spirit, that is, historical creation. He is more than [raw] nature. . . . [However], humanity has acquired only gradually a consciousness of its own worth and has conquered *the right to live indepen-dent of the schemes and laws of minorities.* . . . This consciousness has been acquired not under the brutal spur of physiological necessity, but rather through intelligent reflection on the part first of some members and then

12. Economistic Marxism tends to regard ideas as reflections of the material process that make up "the economy." Antieconomistic Marxism stresses that the economy itself is a creation of the human mind and spirit, in interaction with the external material environment.

13. Gramsci's influence on Catholic liberation theology is evident in many ways, but here it is sufficient to note that two leading works of this genre explicitly acknowledge indebtedness to him: Carlos Gutiérrez, *A Theology of Liberation* (New York, 1973) and Leonardo Boff, *Church, Charism, and Power* (New York, 1985). Boff was silenced by the Vatican for a period of time in 1986.

of the entirety of a class. . . . This means that every revolution has been
preceded by an intense work of criticism, of cultural penetration, of the
permeation of human aggregates . . . [with an awareness of their common predicament].[14]

Only slowly do the "aggregates" of human beings, composed of individuals who had each been closed within themselves and preoccupied
with their own economic and political problems, realize their ties of
solidarity with the others in the same exploited condition. From this
realization class consciousness is born; with and through class consciousness a revolution can be made.
Gramsci ends the essay "Socialism and Culture" declaring that the
ultimate end of acquiring a recognition of solidarity with other oppressed people is "better to know ourselves through others and to know
others through ourselves":

If it be true that universal history is a chain of attempts that man has
made to liberate himself from privileges and prejudices and idolatry, . . .
one can understand why the proletariat, which wills to add another link
to this chain, must know how and why and by whom it has been preceded and what benefit it can reap from this knowledge.[15]

The "ultimate end" (*scopo ultimo*) of revolution for Gramsci is "better
to know ourselves."[16] The new politics cannot come about without
a knowledge of the past. History for Gramsci is a treasure-house of
knowledge. From the study of history one learns that man makes history. His conduct is not determined by iron laws. The fundamental
error of the positivists is to confuse nature and history, or better, to
merge history into nature. By studying what a previously subordinate
class like the bourgeoisie was able to achieve in the French Revolution,
one can better understand the possibilities available to the proletariat
today.
One should note the antipalingenetic character of Gramsci's ultimate
vision.[17] The proletariat will not begin from scratch to make its revolu-

14. Gramsci, "Socialismo e cultura," 101. Emphasis added.
15. *Ibid.*, 103.
16. *Ibid.*
17. *Palingenesis* is from the Greek for transformation or new birth. Gramsci almost
always uses it as a derogatory term. To say that Gramsci was antipalingenetic is a fancy
way of saying that he favored sobriety in the rhetoric even of revolutionaries. His whole
style became that of the "sober revolutionary," however paradoxical that may sound.

tion; rather, that revolution will be the latest link in a long chain of attempts for humanity to liberate itself. The revolution will be new, but it will retain its link to the past. It will respect human achievement and creativity wherever it is found in the past. Even the proletarian revolution will only add the latest link to the chain, implying that more links might be added later.

Antonio Gramsci could have chosen to react to the pettiness and charlatanry of academic life by embracing "futurism,"[18] or he could have begun another faddish revolt against contemporary culture. With characteristic taste, however, he emphatically rejected such alternatives and . set out to design a new politics in which the high culture of an elitist past might illumine the lives of ordinary workers in field and factory.

From the beginning of his career as a writer, Gramsci displayed a fierce intransigence on certain points. He knew what he would not compromise; that is, he resisted anything he considered to detract from his ultimate end, a society in which one knew oneself through knowing others, and the reverse. Although he ordinarily abjured crude anticlerical language, Gramsci was adamant about the incompatibility between his vision of a good society and that of a Christianity centered on the fall of man. Such a Christianity insisted that true fulfillment could occur only beyond time and the world. Thus, in an article published in June, 1916, Gramsci reacted sharply against an anonymous statement that inasmuch as socialism was not a philosophical system there was no essential disagreement between it and Catholicism. Intelligent Socialists were now ready to jettison the antireligious orientation adopted twenty years before by the party, the anonymous author had argued.

Gramsci's reply began:

> With such arguments some Catholics wish to show the usefulness of a permanent alliance between the clerical forces and ourselves. . . . It is worth remembering, however, that critical socialism leans heavily on nineteenth-century German idealism, which while not agreeing with the positivistic mode of thinking, has nonetheless guillotined the idea of God. Hegel has always been the black beast of the Catholics because he is not so easily refuted as are Enrico Ferri or Cesare Lombroso.[19]

18. Gramsci emphatically rejected futurism. His first two articles, published in the University of Turin's student newspaper in February and May, 1913, concerned the founder of the Italian futurist movement, Giovanni Papini.

19. Gramsci, "La Consolata e i cattolici," June 21, 1916, in *CT,* 392. Enrico Ferri and Cesare Lombroso were Italian positivists.

After lamenting the rejection of the candidacy of Giovanni Gentile (a professed follower of Hegel who, ironically, later became court philosopher of fascism) from Turin's Faculty of Letters by allegedly "clericalizing" faculty members, Gramsci goes on to describe the strident antithesis between socialism and Catholicism on the question of grace:

> [The Catholics] await redemption through grace—that is, they invoke the good will of the saints when it would be more opportune to appeal to that of men. For them, only authority, revelation, and the word of God matter because they locate the source of human events outside of man, in a supreme will that embraces and judges everything . . . in light of a Semitic conception of good and evil that is more valid for slaves than for men. Instead, [we young Socialists] expect nothing from others except . . . [what we give] ourselves; our conscience as free men imposes a duty, and our organized strength performs it. *Only what is our work, our achievement, has value for us and becomes part of us—not what is granted by a superior power, whether that be the bourgeois state or the Madonna of the Consolation.*[20]

The above formulation, of course, is a caricature of the image of man in both the Hebrew Bible and the New Testament. It reads like a combination of Marx (*The Poverty of Philosophy*) and Nietzsche on their worst days. One can only pause to regret that even a Gramsci could indulge in such a parody of Judaism and Christianity. Nonetheless, one must note that this is not Gramsci's final word on the subject of premodern Judaic and Christian religiousness, and that in practice the Catholicism with which Gramsci had been familiar in his youth was perhaps not too far removed from this sociomorphic degradation of the language of transcendence, at least in certain respects. For centuries the Church had done little or nothing about the illiteracy of the great majority of Sardinian peasants, shepherds, and workers. This is the Catholicism that Gramsci knew.

In any event, even in this article Antonio Gramsci was mainly intent not on attacking Christianity but on affirming a new vision of politics. His opposition to philanthropy is a consistent theme throughout his writing. The lower classes, the excluded ones, cannot become included

20. *Ibid.*, 393. Emphasis added. On the failure of Turin University to offer Giovanni Gentile a Chair, see Caprioglio's note, *ibid.*, 394. Gentile, who broke with Croce in the early 1920s over fascism, wrote much of the famous article by Mussolini on fascist doctrine in the *Enciclopedia Italiana*. He was assassinated in Florence in 1944.

by receiving a gift from the powerful and the privileged. They must win inclusion for themselves and in doing so abolish the distinction between powerful and powerless.

The point is to depend on one's own resources. If one wants to look for influences on Gramsci, here it should be in the direction of Roman stoicism rather than nineteenth-century atheistic humanism. Despite the dramatic—and for Gramsci atypical—imagery about nineteenth-century critical socialism's "guillotining" of God, Gramsci himself was uninterested in whether God was "dead." It was not a question that spoke existentially to him, because from childhood he had felt thrown on his own resources, forced to endure the lot of a hunchback in remote Sardinia. Nonetheless, he was eager to relate to dissident young Catholics who wished to conduct a dialogue with him. He insisted from the beginning, however, that they understand his position that socialism was incompatible with a theocentric vision of reality.

Armenia: Enlarging the Circle of Our Humanity

In March, 1916, Gramsci published an article on the Armenian Massacre of 1915, in which as many as 1,500,000 Armenian people have been estimated to have been killed brutally or left to perish without food and water during the last days of the Ottoman Empire.[21] The article is important for a number of reasons; it shows both how much his sympathies had enlarged since his having left Sardinia less than five years earlier and how on the basis of that expansion his vision of a new politics showed a consequent enlargement. Not only had he established himself in the industrial city of Turin and begun to absorb the way of life of factory workers; he also had acquired a profound capacity for empathy with the suffering of marginal groups everywhere.

Gramsci begins his article on the terrible massacres by observing that ordinarily before a tragedy can move us so deeply that it becomes "part of our inner life" it must happen close by, among people we frequently see and hear, people who are "within our circle of humanity." He quoted Rastignac in Balzac's *Père Goriot* who, when asked whether if he knew that every time he ate an orange a Chinese person would die, he would refrain from eating oranges, replied:

21. Gramsci, "Armenia," March 11, 1916, in *CT,* 184–85. The documentation on the Armenian massacre remains sequestered even today by Turkish authorities.

The oranges and I are near and I am familiar with them, while the Chinese are far away and I am not sure that they even exist.

We, meaning "we good people," would never give Rastignac's cynical answer, Gramsci observes, but

> when we heard that hundreds of thousands of Armenians had been massacred, did we feel that tightening of the stomach muscles that we . . . felt immediately after the Germans invaded Belgium?[22]

The Armenians are as "far away" as Rastignac's Chinese. Thus, the news that the Russians had conquered most of the territory in which the Armenian people had lived under the Ottoman Empire, thereby ending their suffering, had been given less space in French newspapers than a story about the launching of a zeppelin.

In one of his letters, addressed from prison to his son Delio, Gramsci observed that history is concerned with "all the human beings in the world . . . insofar as they unite in society and work and fight to better themselves."[23] The road to that insight was mapped out already in the spring of 1916 when Gramsci wrote of the need to enlarge "the circle of our humanity." The new politics will take all human beings in the world into consideration instead of leaving the individual closed up in his own small, exclusive circle. In a world animated by the new politics the Armenians would not be forgotten.

Typically, Gramsci counsels the Armenian minority in Turin not to wait around for others to recognize the vitality and creativity of their Armenian heritage, but to establish a museum dedicated to Armenian culture and to educate their children to have pride in their past. As a Sardinian accustomed to having his own people viewed as "outside the circle" of Italian (mainland) humanity, Gramsci empathized easily with the Armenian predicament. He was one of a very small number of Italian—and European—journalists to call attention to this monstrous attempt to eliminate an entire minority, an event that helped prepare the way for the Nazi Holocaust.

Gramsci's "circle of humanity" also included Italy's wartime enemies. In one of many newspaper columns deploring Italian anti-German feeling during World War I, Gramsci sympathized with Arturo Toscanini, who upon assuming the podium in Turin's Teatro Reggio to conduct a selection from Richard Wagner's opera *Parsifal*, was greeted with loud

22. *Ibid.*, 184.
23. Gramsci to his son Delio, n.d., in *LDC*, 895.

boos and hisses, thereby illustrating, said foreign minister Salandra the next day, that Turin was "second to none in patriotism." To Gramsci, the spectacle of an Italian audience behaving in such a fashion to Italy's most distinguished conductor showed not only a moral failure; it also showed a collapse of taste. Citing Giosue Carducci's 1872 description of *la borghesia ben pensante che ammira sempre la forza e il successo* (the right-thinking bourgeoisie that always admires force and success), Gramsci heaps ridicule upon the idea that just because a piece of music or a book of philosophy or a poem is part of German culture, it is beyond the circle of Italian humanity.[24]

In his effort to combat cultural jingoism, Gramsci often cited Romain Rolland, a French pacifist and noted author. Rolland was the author to whom Gramsci imputed the maxim "Pessimism of the intellect, optimism of the will." Rolland had a profound appreciation for the genius in much of German culture, and his *Life of Beethoven* achieved a considerable literary success. That Gramsci would reach out repeatedly to a writer such as Rolland, who was fiercely independent of all ideological systems and who was among the few European intellectuals of his time to condemn what Julien Benda called the *traison des clercs* (treason of the intellectuals), is but one of many pieces of evidence that even when he spoke the language of struggle, Gramsci's objective was power of a different order than that of the established elites.[25] Gramsci argued that when those hitherto excluded achieve power under the new politics, they would strive to use it to keep the circle of humanity permanently enlarged rather than to build fences around the privileges they have obtained. As we shall see, one of Gramsci's major disagreements with the Socialists was precisely that they saw no farther than extending privileges "by category," when the real task was to abolish privilege as such. That is to say, the revisionist Socialists sought only gains for the trade unions; caught in their restricted circle of humanity, they did not see the worker or peasant or fisherman or shepherd who had no union, not to mention the dispossessed people in all social classes who have been thrown off their land or out of work or who remain under tyrannical domination.

In his articles for the Turinese edition of the official Socialist party

24. Gramsci, "Omaggio a Toscanini," May 7, 1916, in *CT,* 295–96.
25. Gramsci gave a number of lectures about Romain Rolland's work to Socialist party district meetings in Turin and Milan in the fall of 1916. Caprioglio's indices contain numerous references to Rolland. *CT,* 512, n. 1.

newspaper, Antonio Gramsci frequently drew attention to non-Socialist writers who deserved commendation for the stand they took on a particular issue. For example, he opens his column *Sotto la Mole* for July 20, 1916, with the words "The hunt for the man who thinks for himself, begun May 24, 1915, has claimed its latest victim: Senator Raffael Garofalo."[26] Garofalo, who had opposed the entry of Italy into World War I, asserted:

> This war is not a conflict of civilization against barbarism or . . . of democracy versus autocracy. Rather, this gigantic conflict represents the . . . violent phase of the long preceding economic rivalry between England and Germany that began when the latter, with its industries and new colonies, threatened the former's commercial predominance in the world.[27]

Just as one expects him to continue to pay tribute to Garofalo, the "intelligent and conscientious bourgeois," Gramsci turns tables and attacks the latter's argument that socialism is a superstition that goes against the laws of human nature. Playing with the phrase *a buon diritto* (rightly, justifiably), which includes the word *law* (*diritto*), Gramsci concludes that the bourgeoisie also will have to recognize that the victory of socialism, when it comes, will have been achieved *a buon diritto*. The proletariat's justifiable victory "will be recognized by all . . . , if also with bitterness, by the Garofalos and the Croces of today." Gramsci's argument is characteristically subtle. He opposes the bourgeois idea that there is an abstract, unhistorical standard of justice with the idea that force, or strength (*forza*), decides what is right. However, this strength is not the brute force that has typically sustained bourgeois law and order, but the expansive intellectual and moral force of the proletariat, a force that ultimately will be recognized by all (*tutti*) as legitimate.

ITALIAN SOCIALISTS AS THE GERMANS OF ITALY

In a semi-serious open letter to the prefect of Turin denouncing the arrest of a Socialist young person for distributing leaflets against Italy's participation in the war, Gramsci argued facetiously that Italian Socialists deserved to be treated like "the Germans of Italy."[28] Because of

26. Gramsci, "Il buon diritto," July 20, 1916, in *CT*, 443.
27. *Ibid.*, 444.
28. Gramsci, "Lettera semi-seria all'illustrissimo Signor Prefetto," September 30, 1916, in *CT*, 563–65. This is a new attribution.

their opposition to Italy's holy war for freedom, wrote Gramsci, the Socialist should be reduced to subhuman status:

> The Turinese Socialist is not even human, for philosophy teaches that to be human one must be part of some social aggregate, and the Turinese Socialist rejects the natural aggregate—the country—that destiny has created for him. Therefore he ought not be treated as a human being. . . . Neither the home of a Socialist nor the Socialist party headquarters is inviolable: nothing should be inviolable for the good of the country.[29]

Gramsci's parody of the ultranationalist speeches by Italian politicians, poets, and professors is amusing. His "semi-serious" letter at bottom conveys a deadly serious message, however: the Socialists and others opposed on principle to the war have been transformed from citizens with all rights attendant under the *Statuto* into outsiders by the administrative machinery of the supposedly liberal Italian state. Idolatry of *la patria* (the country) results in the exclusion of those who will not subscribe to the attitude of "my country, right or wrong, but my country."

In "The Territorial Idea," published in his column *Sotto la Mole* in November, 1916, Gramsci again took up the question of how idolatry of the nation as the ultimate form of community is a disease of the human spirit. In the name of realism, observes Gramsci, Italian Socialists have been repeatedly attacked for their refusal to back Italy's entry into the war. The specific attack to which he was responding in "The Territorial Idea" had come from the pen of none other than Italy's most famous and influential cultural figure Benedetto Croce, who in an article entitled "Socialists and the Fatherland" had written on the occasion when the Socialists of Ravenna took down and refused to show the Italian flag:

> Only the saddest boorishness of mind and spirit can take away from citizens of whatever class or party the vision of the Fatherland. . . . However, Socialist ideas have worked for a long time to produce this blindness and spiritual obtuseness. But the people's great struggle, today as in the past, refutes any abstract theory [of internationalism] and shows to everyone that history puts the Fatherland, together with its defense and its glory, in first place and places disputes between parties and classes within the confines of the country in second place.[30]

29. *Ibid.*, 564.

30. Gramsci is referring to Benedetto Croce's speech at Ravenna as reported in the local newspaper *La Libertà*. Caprioglio quotes Croce's article "I socialisti e la patria" as reprinted in *Avanti!* September 9, 1916, in *CT*, 609.

After first drawing out the implications of the above quotation, Gramsci confronts Croce's argument head on:

> From the individual to the family and then to the tribe . . . [and eventually to the modern nation]: nature does not make [further] leaps. Thus, the Socialists [are alleged to be] the idolators of internationalism and of a putrid mythology. The citizen must have a territorial idea if he wants to be completely a man. . . . The proletariat cannot find its home in the territorial idea of the Fatherland because it is without history, *because it has never participated in political life,* because it does not have traditions of a collective life that are confined to the circle of the [national] community. The proletariat became a political being through socialism; in its conscience the territory lacks spiritual concreteness. . . . Its passion, its sufferings, its martyrs are for another idea [than that of the nation]: for the liberation of man from every form of slavery, for the conquest of every possibility of man as such, the man who has no territory, who recognizes no limits except the inhibitions of his conscience. Through socialism man has returned to his generic character; this is why we speak so much of humanity and esteem the International.[31]

As the rise of fascism was to prove all too soon, Gramsci's statement scarcely stood as an accurate description of the mentality of all of Italy's workers; nor was he deluded in this respect. The value of the essay on the territorial idea consists in its eloquent crystallization of Gramsci's theory of a new politics. "The proletariat has never participated in public life." Therefore it is free to create anew and not be bound by the fixations of any merely "territorial" idea, be it that of the city or the empire or the nation-state. The true community of man is more than territorial: it is a work of the human spirit of all ages, and it requires a new politics for a new world in the making. Here in Gramsci's questioning of the territorial idea he comes closer to a breakthrough to a universal theory of mankind as an "open society" than at any other point in his life.[32]

Looking over the more than eight hundred pages of Gramsci's output for the first two years of his journalistic career, one cannot help but be impressed by the conceptual unity of the pieces despite the enor-

---

31. Gramsci, "L'idea territoriale," November 3, 1916, in *CT,* 609. Emphasis added.
32. For a discussion of the distinction, first made by Eric Voegelin, between "universal" and "ecumenic" mankind, see Dante Germino, *Political Philosophy and the Open Society* (Baton Rouge, 1982).

mous variety of their subject matter. The validity of the thesis argued in the first chapter—that Gramsci's bedrock perspective in growing up as a deformed person in an isolated, peripheral culture made him sensitive to the concerns of outsiders in general—is born out repeatedly. His columns comment on the problems of the little people, those without prestige, those who count for little in the existing political and social structure. Sometimes he speaks out for the right of workers' cooperatives to take advantage of the rise in prices for certain products they have stockpiled. One of Gramsci's articles concerns the wartime shortage of foodstuffs for the working population, whereas another supports the demands of workers in the textile mills for better wages and working conditions. One column defends the demand of a father that his child not be required to say the *Pater Noster* at the beginning of the school day, whereas another attacks the so-called Popular University for being "neither popular nor a university." [33] Gramsci asserts that the trouble with this misguided attempt to bring culture to the working masses is that the teachers speak down to their audience and offer courses on subjects like "The Italian Soul in the Literary Art of Recent Generations" and "The European Conflagration Judged from the Perspective of Vico." Instead of aiming to help the workers who take the courses develop their critical faculties so that they can eventually study and understand Vico, the instructors begin with assuming a level of knowledge possessed by a university graduate. [34]

Gramsci comments sardonically in one piece on the abuse of religion on the part of clerics who ask for votive offerings to Turin's Santa Maria Anunziata to implore her to bring victory and peace, as if Mary were on only Italy's side in the war. In another he invokes Rudyard Kipling's poem "If" as an example of a morality that has not been "poisoned" by Christianity, a morality that "can be accepted by all men." [35]

Gramsci's celebration of Kipling's banal poem may be attributed either to an uncharacteristic lapse in taste or to what he perceived to be the poem's resonance of stoicism. (The piece was written at the time of

33. Gramsci, "Le cornacchie e il uacciolo," October 24, 1916; "Socialismo e cooperazione," October 30, 1916; "I ricorsi della storia e le vicende delle cotoniere," December 9, 1916; "Simplicitas," December 15, 1916; and "L'università popolare," December 29, 1916; all in *CT,* 594–96, 600–603, 635–41, 652–54, and 673–76.

34. Gramsci, "L'università popolare," 675–76.

35. Gramsci, "Preoccupazioni," December 31, 1916, and "Breviario per laici," December 17, 1916, in *CT,* 677–78 and 657–58.

the founding of the Club for the Moral Life, whose common reading, as we have seen, was the *Meditations* of Marcus Aurelius.) It should also be remembered that English was the one major European language Gramsci never learned well, so that he quoted the poem in translation. What is noteworthy is Gramsci's total alienation from institutionalized Catholicism and his consequent search for a morality independent of formal Christianity. The irony of invoking the arch-imperialist Rudyard Kipling as a beacon of light for the dispossessed did not escape Gramsci. From prison he later wrote:

> Kipling's morality is imperialist only insofar as it is tied strictly to a specific historical reality. One can still extract from it images of powerful immediacy for any social group fighting for political power.[36]

THE REAL PEOPLE AT THE PERIPHERY

Gramsci's column for January 6, 1917, entitled "Periferici" (Those at the periphery) marked an advance in complexity for his developing theory of a new politics of inclusion. In this column the *periferici* are the representatives of the districts farthest from Turin's urban center. Gramsci declares that after hearing them argue for favors for their districts at every city council meeting, he had come to understand what was wrong with their perspective:

> [Their "peripheralism"] . . . is an abstraction, not a reality. The city exists as a complete whole, not as a center plus a periphery. In this city the two classes of citizens are the proletariat and the bourgeoisie, not the centralists and the peripheralists. There exist unitary interests, whether bourgeois or proletarian. This geographical division of the city is absurd; this wish to make of the city two materially distinctive sections rather than two parts that are intellectually and historically distinct is a grotesque absurdity.[37]

The city council, insists Gramsci, is elected to look after the general interests of the city, of the whole city. The entire city should be concerned if something goes wrong in any particular sector. Similarly, if one sector is privileged over another, the councilors' objective should be to eliminate the privilege in the name of justice, not to create a counter-

---

36. *Quaderni*, 402.
37. Gramsci, "Periferici," January 6, 1917, in *CT*, 687–88.

vailing privilege. The present councilors from Turin's outlying districts want to pit one territorial area against another. The result is "to create two vampires rather than to kill the one vampire now sucking the blood of the majority." The peripheralists are not truly representatives of the suburbs; they are simply traders or "traffickers" in privileges.

Gramsci's imagery here is more than spatial. This article represents his definitive overcoming of his own earlier Sardinian peripheralism in the name of a politics that abolishes the distinction between center and periphery altogether, insofar as it has intellectual and spiritual significance. Among the many ways in which the new politics will differ from the old is that while the latter deals with multiplying privileges for each group involved, the former is dedicated to abolishing privilege altogether. The equation of privilege—meaning special treatment for one district at the expense of the whole community—with the "vampire" is particularly striking. The politics of privilege corrupts everything it touches, Gramsci insists, and he compares the peripheralists to the *irredentisti,* or the ultra-nationalists, who want the boundaries of the Italian nation extended into Yugoslavia or France or Austria or wherever ethnic Italians exist in significant numbers. Although Gramsci is speaking of the local politics of Turin in this column, by analogy what he has to say condemns all tribalistic regionalism, whether Sardinian or otherwise.

THE POLITICS OF *TUTTI* VERSUS THE POLITICS OF *POCHI*

Gramsci's article of December, 1916, deploring sectionalist (and, by implication, interest-group) politics was the precursor of articles written in the ensuing year affirming what for abbreviation I shall call the politics of *tutti.* Applied to social relations, *tutti* is perhaps the ultimately inclusive word in the Italian language. Literally it means "all," or "everyone," as in "All are welcome," regardless of category. The word has a certain ring to it when spoken by Italians. Thus, in his attempt to express the essence of what he understood socialist politics to be, Gramsci wrote in the first number of a new cultural periodical entitled *La Città Futura* (The city of the future):

> Socialists should not substitute one order for another. They should install order itself. The juridical maxim they wish to implement is: *that the possibility of the integral actualization of one's own human personality be granted to all the citizens (tutti i cittadini).* With the enactment of this maxim, all

established privileges will disappear. . . . It will mean that wealth will no longer be the means of keeping many in slavery, but being available to everyone (*tutti*) impersonally, it will give to everyone (*tutti*) the means for the greatest possible well-being.[38]

Of the many examples of Gramsci's invocation of the politics of *tutti* versus the politics of *pochi* (*i pochi* means "the few") is his article entitled "Your Heredity" of May 1, 1918. Contemporary society is analogous to a carnival, Gramsci suggests, in the center of which a merry-go-round rotates at lightning speed. Everyone tries to jump on the back of a horse on the merry-go-round, but only one in ten thousand succeeds in making the right jump. The others fall to the floor, their legs broken.

Competition in capitalist society has the same results as Gramsci's ghastly merry-go-round. Everyone grasps for the brass ring, but most fall to the earth, their "obscene and monkey-like acrobatics" having left them maimed for life.

In place of this bizarre carnival scene, Gramsci sketches in a new architectural design. "The majority must of necessity fail in this atrocious competition." Only the few are in fact free to pursue a human life in the carnival, and they are deluded into thinking that they have achieved it once perched comfortably on the monstrous merry-go-round.

A model of a new society must be built around the knowledge that all men want to share in freedom and to transmit their patrimony to their loved ones. Freedom is above all a spiritual quality, and there is plenty around for everyone to share, provided that the supporting architecture is there. The ugly merry-go-round at the center of the old society must be torn down and replaced with a shelter that protects everyone presently living and provides a cover for future generations as well. True liberty, the patrimony of everyone, will be enjoyed only after the distinction between the *pochi* and the *molti*—the "few" and the "many"—has been overcome. In the present system only the *pochi* are free, in that they have hold of their place on the merry-go-round and after death yield it to their heirs. The transmission of material goods from the few to the few is the essence of the capitalist idea of freedom.

Through association and organization, the many can come into their patrimony and, working disinterestedly for the good of everyone, will also benefit themselves as individuals and those closest to them. The politics of the City of the Future will include everyone in freedom:

38. Gramsci, "Tre principi, tre ordini," February 11, 1917, in *LCF*, 11. Emphasis added.

All men have this aspiration . . . : to become proprietors of freedom, of a freedom that is secure and transmissible [to others]. *If liberty is the highest good*, it is natural to seek to have one's own loved ones share in it, just as it is natural to accept sacrifices for oneself to create this liberty to insure that ones' loved ones will enjoy it, even if one cannot do so oneself.[39]

The real center of the new society, then, will be liberty. Because liberty is everyone's patrimony, however, it is diffused everywhere. The new society of liberty will have no center—or its center will be in everyone.

Philanthropy Versus Organization

In these early articles Gramsci repeatedly attacks the idea that true liberty for the many can develop as a result of concessions by those in power. In an article written in December, 1917, entitled "Philanthropy, Good Will, and Organization" he declares that it is only through solidarity and organization that "the many" will achieve liberty. As we shall see, one of the major reasons for his rejection of reformist socialism is that the latter is willing to accept piecemeal concessions from "the few." The Socialist party must not accept the philanthropy of the powerful few when the latter offers seats on the merry-go-round to those in the working class who will collaborate with them. Accepting philanthropy from the powerful only perpetuates the politics of exclusion, for under the old politics of privilege there are not enough places, nor can there be, for everyone. The only alternative is to tear down the merry-go-round itself and replace it with the architecture of a new politics.[40]

Gramsci's Reaction to the Russian Revolution of 1917

As one would expect, given what we already know about him, the overthrow of the czarist autocracy in Russia in February, 1917 (or March depending on whether the Eastern or Western calendar is used), produced a profound effect on Gramsci. In his first comment (in April) he correctly predicted that the Kerensky regime would be transitory and that eventually a socialist order would be established. Gramsci was fascinated by what he perceived to be the central role of the "soviets," or

39. Gramsci, "La tua eredità," May 1, 1918, in *LCF*, 866–70. Emphasis added.
40. Gramsci, "Filantropia, buona volontà e organizzazione," December 24, 1917, in *LCF*, 518–21.

factory councils, in constructing the new order, and he aligned himself with the so-called intransigent, or revolutionary, faction of the Italian Socialist party (PSI).[41] In August, 1917, he reported on the visit of a delegation from the soviets to Turin, which ended with a massive demonstration by workers in support of Lenin.[42]

In late August numerous strikes and demonstrations (illegal because of the war) erupted all over Turin. Many Socialist leaders were arrested. Gramsci became secretary of the provisional executive of the PSI in Turin and also became editor of the Socialist party weekly, *Il Grido del Popolo,* a position he held until October, 1918. In November he made his first acquaintance with the Neapolitan engineer Amadeo Bordiga, who was in time to be his principal adversary. Initially, however, both men worked together in the intransigent wing of the party.

In December, 1917, Gramsci published his most important single article on the October Revolution. Its striking title was "The Revolution Against *Das Kapital.*"[43]

Between 1917 and 1918, as editor of *Il Grido del Popolo,* Gramsci commissioned translations from the works of Lenin and Trotsky and published interpretations of events as they were happening in Russia.[44] These were the first Italian translations of Russian revolutionary writings.

In October, 1918, Gramsci became one of the principal editors (along with Alfonso Leonetti, Leo Geletto, and later Palmiro Togliatti) of the new Piedmontese edition of *Avanti!.* Pia Carena was his secretary.

Gramsci's general thesis in his various articles on the October Revolution was that these revolutionary events opened a new page in human history. A new order had begun, based on the growing self-awareness

41. Gramsci, "Note sulla rivoluzione russa," April 29, 1917, in *LCF,* 1328–41.

42. Gramsci, "Il comito della rivoluzione russa," August 15, 1917, in *LCF,* 274–77. New attribution.

43. Gramsci, "La rivoluzione contro *Il Capitale,*" December 24, 1917, in *LCF,* 513–17. For some time, Gramsci had foreseen that the revolution in Russia could not stop with Kerensky. See *LCF,* 358–60, 450. Gramsci did not predict Lenin's ascendancy, claiming that he had been kept in ignorance about Lenin's true position and strength by the Italian Socialist party establishment, which promoted V. M. Cernov, a Social Revolutionary. See *ibid.,* 459, n. 2.

44. Gramsci, "Note sulla rivoluzione russa," "I massimalisti russi," and "Kerenski e Lenin," April 29, July 28, and August 25, 1917, in *LCF,* 138–42, 265–67, 285. In the last of the three articles, Gramsci wrote of Kerensky that he "represents historical fatality" while Lenin represents "socialist becoming, and we are with him [Lenin] with all our heart."

by the masses of their power to transform their social relationships, end the reign of privilege, and inaugurate a new politics based on that awareness. Gramsci's emphasis on the capacity of collectively organized outsiders and oppressed people fundamentally to transform social relationships was so great that it brought on him the accusation of "voluntarism" by Socialists inclined toward positivism and a deterministic reading of Marx. In calling the Bolshevik Revolution of October, 1917, "the revolution against *Das Kapital*," Gramsci argued against the idea that Marx had meant to teach that history is governed by "iron laws"; instead, he praised Lenin and his supporters for grasping the real truth of Marx—that in the new order man will make history rather than history making man.

In May, 1918, Gramsci published an important article entitled "Our Marx" in commemoration of the centenary of the German revolutionary's birth. In it he proclaimed that duty of all who followed Marx's influences to abjure hagiography, to appropriate his own critical spirit and independent, intransigent mentality, and to be open to ways in which to assist "the other class"—those who are exploited—to come into their own. Already his fundamental opposition to Bordiga's deterministic Marxism is evident.[45]

45. *LCF,* 518–20, 536–38, 554–58, and *INM,* 3–7.

III ✒ Critical Communism: Gramsci's Vision of a New Politics, 1915–1919

> Then I became familiar with the working class of an industrial city, and I understood what the things really meant that I had read earlier in Marx only out of intellectual curiosity. So a passion for life, for struggle, for the working class gripped me.
>
> —Gramsci to Julia Schucht, March 6, 1924

> The adjective . . . [Marxist] is like money that has been worn out from passing through too many hands.
>
> —Gramsci, "Il Nostro Marx," May 4, 1918

THE MARXIST MOTIF

Gramsci's vision of a new politics cannot be described fully with any simplistic label, including that of "Marxist." However, what I shall call the Marxist motif became a major component of that vision.

As we shall see, Gramsci roundly rejected the idea that Marx's writings comprised a bible. Gramsci's political ideas had their roots in his lived experiences rather than in some bookish lore, whether the books be by Marx, Hegel, Sorel, Lenin, or anyone else. There is no question, however, that, beginning with the October Revolution, Gramsci devoted increasing attention to Marx's writings, and in his important 1918 article "Our Marx" declared Marx to be "a necessary and integral part of our mind and spirit, which would not be the same if he had not lived." [1]

Karl Marx fortified Antonio Gramsci's understanding of politics as the collective overcoming of marginalization by confirming intellectually what Gramsci's instinct for rebellion had told him—that only by struggle and not by philanthropy could such an overcoming be achieved. Marx helped Gramsci recognize that class struggle was essential to human liberation. Marx did not teach him what class struggle meant, however; only direct contact with the working class of Turin could do that.

In Gramsci, "marginalization" and "class struggle" are two complementary and overlapping metaphors. As we have seen, Gramsci's pri-

1. Gramsci, "Il nostro Marx," May 4, 1918, in *INM*, 3–7 at 6.

56

mary experiences in Sardinia were those of the physiologically and psychologically alienated outsider. In Turin he learned to view life from the perspective of an economically subjugated collectivity, the working class of a large city. Whereas before coming to Turin he had read Marx "only out of intellectual curiosity," he now understood what Marx's ideas "really meant." In absorbing Marx's theory of class struggle Gramsci also transformed it. To use spatial images, Gramsci's dominant model remained that of the center and the periphery. While it would be surprising if there were not also traces of this model in Marx himself, Marx's dominant model unquestionably was that of the upper and the lower classes (see figure).

In Marx, the lower class, the proletariat, will rise up(ward) to knock over the bourgeoisie. In Gramsci, the dominant emphasis and the original insight is that of the periphery moving in on the center and dissolving it into itself. Marx and Engels' imagery of the lower class overthrowing the upper class runs the danger of appearing to be prosaic, simplistic, and Manichaean. On the other hand, Gramsci's periphery/center imagery emphasizes the triumph of inclusiveness rather than of resentment against those above one on the social ladder. In making these distinctions, I do not want to suggest that they are mutually exclusive. The two models overlap. Both of them aim to destroy the reign of privilege. Gramsci's model is the philosophically richer and more interesting of the two, however, because it is not so tied to merely economic categories. Because the periphery/center model is not confined to the economic situation, it is possible for Gramsci to make room for the world of culture—of the mind and spirit—in a way that Marx does not. The class struggle idea, or lower–upper model (which I identify as the Marxist motif in Gramsci's thought) was extremely important in giving flavor to Gramsci's center/periphery design for a new politics, however.

One could use the center/periphery model in an unrevolutionary way—to prick the consciences of those at the center and to call for their gradual inclusion of marginalized individuals and groups in the center. One can call this the philanthropic approach, supported by an ethic of charity for the underprivileged and concern for the poor by the rich and powerful. What makes Gramsci's model revolutionary is its marrying of his center/periphery design to Marx's class struggle symbolism. Just as the lower class must rise up and overthrow the upper one, so the mar-

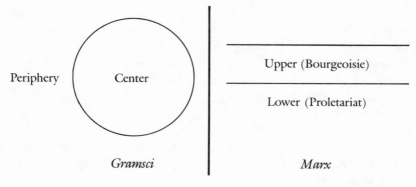

Gramsci   Marx

ginalized sectors of society must move in on the center. By virtue of their having included themselves through their own struggle for recognition, they themselves—the formerly peripheral ones—erase the boundary surrounding the center.

I shall now descend from the heights of the Gramscian paradigm of a new politics to consider specifically and step by step how and when Gramsci made explicit use of Marx's ideas. In doing so, however, I must warn the reader that wherever one finds the class struggle metaphor expressed or implied in Gramsci's writings one finds Marx's footprints. This is another way of saying that one cannot ascertain how Marxist— or un-Marxist—Gramsci is only by discussing his explicit references to Marx. Nonetheless, those explicit references are interesting and revealing up to a point.

Using the indices to Sergio Caprioglio's critical three-volume edition of Gramsci's journalism from 1913 to April, 1919, one finds that for the years February, 1913, to February, 1917, there are only eight explicit references to Marx. From February, 1917, to May 1, 1918, there are thirteen references. From May, 1918 to April 28, 1919, there are eighteen references. Considering that in the third volume there are more references to Lenin, one may be tempted to conclude that Gramsci had relatively little interest in Marx. The problem with that conclusion, however, is that Lenin himself is unintelligible apart from Marx.

Perhaps it is not so surprising that Gramsci infrequently invoked Marx's name, for there were not many readers of the Socialist party newspaper in Turin who would have been all that interested in what a dead German thinker had written about events remote from them in time. His journalism would have been heavy and pedantic if he had "footnoted" each idea from Marx. Gramsci frequently ridiculed the notion that ideas produce other ideas by parthenogenesis. Also, his manner of working was freely to combine ideas from his voluminous reading. He had no awe of intellectual patrimony (a private property notion itself); and because most of his journalism was deliberately left unsigned in order not to encourage a cult following for himself as an individual, he would not have objected in the slightest if others had taken his ideas and used them without giving him credit. Therefore Gramsci did not see the need to give Marx credit every time he used one of his ideas.

Now let us proceed to analyze those articles in which Gramsci either specifically discussed or inferentially drew upon a specific passage in Marx. The first reference concerning Marx is in December, 1915, where Gramsci notes that in his Preface to the third volume of Marx's *Das Kapital,* Friedrich Engels attacked the scientific "charlatanry" of Achille Loria.[2] The second reference is from an article of uncertain attribution merely mentioning Marx's name.[3] The next one (March 11, 1916) occurs in the context of an article ridiculing the disciples of the apostle of Italian republicanism, Giuseppe Mazzini, for having embalmed the words of their master in a sacred text. The article ends: "Who will save you, Oh Christ, Oh Marx, Oh Mazzini, from your superpure and uncontaminated disciples?" Here Gramsci uses the occasion to take a swipe at the positivistic and economistic Marxism of the Socialist party's dominant "maximalist" wing.[4]

On May 26, 1916, Gramsci's column *Sotto la Mole* attacked the nationalist leader Enrico Corradini's idea that the world is divided between capitalist and proletarian nations as at best being only a pale reflection of Marxism. Corradini's division of nations into young and old, proletarian and capitalist, is incoherent and empty of meaning. According to Corradini's logic, Italy should be on the side of the proletarian nations. Although England and France are neither young nor proletarian, Corradini is in favor of Italy's having aligned with them in the war. Corradini's idea that there are old and young nations, just as there are old and young trees or animals, is an example of the absurdity of positivistic

2. Gramsci, "Pietà per la scienza del Prof. Loria," December 16, 1915, in *CT,* 33–34 at 33.
3. [Gramsci (?)], "Sic vos non vobis," February 28, 1916, in *CT,* 163. This is a probable but not certain attribution.
4. Gramsci, "Piccolo mondo antico," March 11, 1916, in *CT,* 189–90 at 190.

reductionism. If a nation were capitalist, it would have a young bourgeoisie, and if it were poor it would have a young proletariat, but the advanced capitalist countries have an old bourgeoisie.[5]

A few months later, in "Class Struggle and War," Gramsci returned to Corradini's attempt to transpose Marxist categories so that they apply to nations rather than to international classes. Corradini, who tries to "plunder" Marx, serves up a mixture of contradictory ideas. The nationalist party leader insists that both the class struggle within the nation and the national struggle on the world scene are historically necessary. The class struggle will redound to the benefit of the nation if it results in greater national productivity. What Corradini does not realize is that Marx's proletariat is *international* and that its aim is to *replace* the bourgeois ruling class of the capitalist order, not to assist it to become more powerful by ensuring that it produces at maximum capacity. Whereas Corradini exalts war between nations and concludes that justice is the dictate of the strongest national power, the international proletariat aims to abolish war. In place of the many (capitalist) nations now at war with each other there will be a single "proletarian nation"— a nation of a qualitatively different kind from that of Corradini:

> This proletarian nation, which is the unification of all the proletariats of the world, will replace the nation. Just as Karl Marx's logic, nourished by historical reality, is superior to that of Enrico Corradini . . . so the class struggle, moral because it is universal, is superior to war, [which is] immoral because it is particularistic and waged . . . for a principle that those engaged in it cannot share with others.[6]

A month later the twenty-five-year-old Gramsci wrote a piece for *Il Grido del Popolo* commenting on a phrase uttered by then Premier Giovanni Giolitti in 1911. In parliamentary debate Giolitti had declared that Italy had changed in recent years and that "Karl Marx has been put in the attic." Gramsci seizes on the phrase to argue that in truth Giolitti and his liberal party had put their founder, Camillo Cavour, in the attic. Cavour, whose diplomatic skills made possible the relatively peaceful unification of Italy in the 1860s, had been opposed to a policy of protectionism by the richer northern areas of Italy toward the poorer southern areas and Sardinia.[7]

5. Gramsci, "Giochi di parole," May 26, 1916, in *CT*, 337–38.
6. Gramsci, "Lotta di classe e guerra," August 19, 1916, in *CT*, 499–500 at 500.
7. Gramsci, "Contro il feudalismo economico," September 16, 1916, in *CT*, 544–45 at 544.

The occasion of this article ("Against Economic Feudalism: Voices from the Attic") was the publication of a selection of Cavour's speeches and writings entitled *Camillo Cavour: Antiprotectionist*. Gramsci's article illustrates again how deeply the poverty of the Italian south and its relationship to the more economically developed north remained at the center of his concerns long after he had left Sardinia. The problems of the "periphery" were always experientially alive to Gramsci.

To turn to the year 1917, Gramsci's references begin with a reference to Marx's Jewish ethnicity (in the context of denouncing a letter espousing "Italic" racism). Gramsci here distinguishes between Italic blood (going back to the Romans) and *Italianità,* a feeling of being Italian. Italian Jews were as Italian as anyone else. By drawing inspiration from Marx, Italian Socialists have transcended questions "of race and blood."[8]

Five months later, in August, 1917, Gramsci quotes a passage[9] from Friedrich Engels' introduction to a 1914 Italian translation of Marx and Engels' *Communist Manifesto* that calls upon Marxists everywhere to reject the "purely philanthropic" proposals of the "bourgeois [or reformist] Socialists" who would distribute economic assistance of one kind or another to the workers within the capitalist order.[10]

Three months later he is writing again about how Corradini defames and "plunders" Marx. Shortly after, Gramsci denounces a jingoistic speech by an Italian war veteran who refused even to admit that Marx, the founder of socialism, had been a German! "Marx learned his socialism in Brussels," the orator had proclaimed.[11]

THE REVOLUTION AGAINST *DAS KAPITAL*

It is not until December 24, 1917, that Gramsci wrote his first full-length treatment of Karl Marx's thought. In "The Revolution Against *Das Kapital*," written to justify the October, 1917, revolution, Gramsci argued against interpreting Marx as a discoverer of iron laws governing history's operation. Lenin's seizure of power in the fall of 1917 was the revolution that flew in the face of a deterministic reading of Marx's analysis of capitalism. According to the determinists (Plekhanov in

8. Gramsci, "Stenterello risponde," March 14, 1917, in *LCF,* 89.
9. Gramsci, "Assicurazione alla vita," August 16, 1917, in *LCF,* 278–80 at 279.
10. Friedrich Engels, as quoted by Gramsci in *LCF,* 279–80.
11. Gramsci, "Grandolini," December 16, 1917, in *LCF,* 493–94 at 494.

Russia represented their view), the revolution had to occur first in the most advanced sectors of the capitalist world—for example, Great Britain or Germany—and not in predominantly agrarian Russia, which with its tiny middle class had not yet even progressed fully from medieval feudalism to modern capitalism. According to an economistic reading of Marx, then, Russia's next stage had to have been capitalism; a society was not free to "skip" a stage and move directly from feudalism to the dictatorship of the proletariat.

The most memorable phrases in Gramsci's article—one of the few signed with his initials—were the following:

Marx's *Das Kapital* was in Russia the book of the bourgeoisie.

The Bolsheviks denied Karl Marx, affirming through action . . . that the canons of historical materialism are not so ironclad as . . . had been thought.

Nevertheless . . . if the Bolsheviks denied some affirmations in *Das Kapital*, they did not deny its immanent, vivifying thought. *They are not "Marxists," that's all. . . . [Instead] they live Marxist thought, [they live that part of it] which will never die, which is a continuation of Italian and German idealism, and which in Marx was contaminated with positivistic and naturalistic incrustations.* And this [Marxist] thought posits always as the greatest factor of history not brute economic facts, but man.[12]

Because of its emphasis on the power of human will to change political and social reality, Gramsci's article has often been attacked as a capitulation to "voluntarism." If the interpretation pursued in this book has any merit, however, there would be no reason for attaching this abstract label to him. His stress on what human will could accomplish grew out of his personal experience and not out of Henri Bergson's metaphysics. Besides, he never anywhere contended that a group or class could will anything it wanted, independent of historical conditions. Marx had not been able to predict the date or physiognomy of World War I. The effect of the war was to bring together in the trenches peasants isolated on the farms. A revolutionary consciousness developed among peasants and workers thrown together by the war, and the centralized czarist state was easily overthrown.

Not long after writing the article "The Revolution Against *Das Ka-*

12. Gramsci, "La rivoluzione contro *Il Capitale*," December 24, 1917, in *LCF*, 513–16 at 513–14. Emphasis added.

pital," Gramsci was back at the hustings, this time contending straight-forwardly that what was at issue was not Marx's writings themselves but a sensible interpretation of those writings. Noting that Claudio Treves, a leader of the reformist wing of the party, had castigated the new generation of party members for its frightful lack of culture, resulting in its accommodation of Marx to whatever it wanted to do, Gramsci replied sardonically:

> Certainly the lack of culture of the "new generation" is great, but it is probably no greater than that of the "old guard." . . . The "new generation," for example, has read, besides the *Manifesto* . . . also the little tract by Marx and Engels on [*The Holy Family*]. . . . It has read and studied also the books [on Marx] written in Europe after the flowering of positivism and has discovered (Oh my! No small discovery!) that the sterilization performed by the positivistic Socialists on Marx's doctrines has not been exactly a great cultural conquest.[13]

Having established the importance of the writings of the so-called young Marx, Gramsci goes on to say that the new generation of Italian Marxists wants to return to the genuine doctrine of Marx. That doctrine sees man and reality "joined to . . . and identified with each other in the historical event." Furthermore, this new generation has discovered that "the canons of historical materialism are valid only *after the fact* [*post factum*] to help us study and understand events of the past." The denial to Marxism of any ability to predict the future becomes with this article one of the abiding themes of Gramsci's Marxism.

Gramsci's article "La critica critica" (taken from the subtitle to *The Holy Family: The Critique of Critical Criticism*) published in January, 1918, is definitive proof that at least by this time he was steadily and seriously reading Marx's works, especially those of the "young Marx." Although Gramsci never got to read the 1844 *Manuscripts on Political Economy,* he imbibed the spirit of that work from some of Marx's other early writings. He knew full well that without Hegel, Marx would not exist, but he also knew that Marx had turned Hegel "on his feet," anchoring ideas in the economic structure of society. Gramsci happily risked being accused of the heresy of voluntarism in order to combat the view of Treves and other older leaders who had reduced Marx's doctrine to an exterior scheme or a natural law. The economistic interpretation of

---

13. Gramsci, "La critica critica," January 12, 1918, in *LCF,* 554–56.

Marx could only cause Socialists passively to wait for events to unfold according to Marx's so-called iron laws.

Gramsci continued to attack positivistic caricatures of Marx. When the editors of *Avanti!* invited Achille Loria to contribute a profile of Marx to the national edition of the party's newspaper, Gramsci exploded with anger. He could scarcely believe that anyone could consider a philistine manipulator of trends such as Loria to be qualified to comment on a genius such as Marx.

"Lorianism" is a consistent theme throughout Gramsci's writing, which drips with contempt whenever discussing Loria's ideas. One initially suspects unfairness on Gramsci's part until one discovers that Loria seriously contended that the invention of the airplane would solve the problem of hunger for the proletariat because hundreds of thousands of airplanes could catch birds on their wings, thereby providing everyone with a culinary delicacy. Gramsci saw Loria as the leading representative of a bankrupt Italian positivism.[14]

Given the corrupting influence of Comtean positivism on Italian socialist thought—the socialist thought that produced the majority, or "maximalist," current in the PSI from its founding in the 1890s—one can affirm with Cesare Luporini that, with the exception of Antonio Labriola, before Gramsci there had been no Marxist tradition at all in Italy. Antonio Gramsci had to create such a tradition singlehandedly; this was no mean achievement.[15]

In February, 1918, according to a recent attribution by Sergio Caprioglio, Gramsci wrote an article praising the "actual idealism" of Giovanni Gentile. Gramsci describes Gentile as "the Italian philosopher who in recent years had produced more in the field of [serious] thought than anyone else." Uncharacteristically, Gramsci extolled the systematic character of Gentile's teaching:

> His [Gentile's] philosophical system is the latest development of that form of German idealism that reached its apex in Georg Hegel, teacher of Karl Marx, and which, being the negation of every transcendentalism, is the identification of philosophy with history, or with the act of thinking,

14. Gramsci, "Achille Loria," January 17, 1918, in *LCF*, 573–74. Gramsci had already ridiculed Loria's reductionist thinking in "Pietà per la scienza del Prof. Loria."

15. From the author's interview with Professor Cesare Luporini, May 6, 1982, in Florence.

in which one unifies truth and fact in a progression that is dialectical, never definitive or perfect.[16]

Gramsci admired the "early" Gentile for having had the courage to write an admiring book on Marx (published in 1899). He had joined with Tasca, Togliatti, and others in lobbying for Gentile to get a chair in philosophy at Turin for which he had applied. In 1916 Gentile had published his *General Theory of the Spirit as Pure Act*. The immediate catalyst for Gramsci's article was the publication of Gentile's interview on the League of Nations condemning the idea of perpetual peace, citing Marx on the inevitability of conflict.

Gramsci was interested in using the resources of philosophical idealism—meaning the current of thought stemming from Hegel and flowing into Marx via the "young Hegelians"—to defeat intellectually the economistic, positivistic Marxists. Philosophical idealism stressed the power of human ideas to organize and shape reality.

GRAMSCI'S MARX, MAY, 1918 – MAY, 1919

On May 4, 1918, the centenary of Marx's birth, Antonio Gramsci published his most important single piece on Karl Marx's politics. A lengthy excerpt is justified:

Our Marx

Are we Marxists? Do Marxists exists? . . . These questions will probably be asked again during these days of the celebration of Marx's centenary. Rivers of ink and stupidity will be spilled. Raving and Byzantinism are the imprescriptible heritage of human beings.

Marx has not composed a neat little doctrine; he is not a messiah who left a string of parables pregnant with categorical imperatives. He has not left a list of indiscussable norms that are absolute and outside the categories of space and time. He has left only a single categorical imperative, only a single norm: "Proletarians of all the world, unite."

The duty to organize . . . and come together should be what distinguishes Marxists from non-Marxists. Too little and too much at once? Who would not be a Marxist?

16. Gramsci, "Il socialismo e la filosofia attuale," February 9, 1918, in *LCF*, 650. New attribution by Sergio Caprioglio.

So be it: all are Marxists, at least to a slight extent, even if unknowingly. Marx was great . . . not because he invented something out of nothing nor because he produced an *original* vision of history, but because what had been fragmentary, incomplete, and undeveloped, achieved maturity, system, consciousness in him. His personal consciousness can become the consciousness of all, just as it already is for many. Because of this fact, he is not only a scholar but also a man of action. He [Marx] is as great and as fruitful in action as he is in thought, because his books have transformed the world while transforming thought.

Gramsci's dramatic opening shows at once both his impatience with the question of who is a "true" Marxist and his awareness of the question's enormous political importance. The sectarians in the Socialist party—those who rave stupidly in the press and at meetings and who exhaust themselves in "Byzantine" debates (recalling the tenth-century controversy over *homoousios* and *homoiousios*) seek to box in Marx's teaching to make it inaccessible to most of mankind. Remaining consistent with his idea of the politics of *tutti,* Gramsci comes down hard for a catholic interpretation of Marx. Marx belongs to everyone, not just to a sect of party bureaucrats and obscurantists: *"Tutti sono marxisti."* Marx's personal discovery can become the discovery of *everyone* (*tutti*). If the intellectual does his work correctly, in writing his books he will engage in the most important kind of political action. Marx has set the example: his books have changed the world.

Gramsci goes on to distinguish Marx both from a merely contemplative mystic and from a metaphysical positivist like Herbert Spencer:

With Marx history continues to be the dominion of ideas, . . . but these ideas attain substance and lose the arbitrariness they formerly had; they are no longer fictitious—religious or sociological abstractions. Their substance is in economics, in practical activity, in the systems and relationships of production and exchange. . . . An idea realizes itself not so much as it is logically coherent in pure truth . . . but insofar as it finds in economic reality its justification and the means for affirming itself. In order to know precisely what are the historical ends of a country, of a society, of a social group, one must above all know what are the systems of production and exchange of that country or society.

Who knows himself? Not man in general but he who submits to the yoke of necessity. Research into the substance of history, anchoring it . . . in the relations of production and exchange, *allows one to discover how the society of men is divided into two classes.* The class that disposes of the instruments of production already of necessity knows itself, already has an awareness, even fragmentary and confused, of its power and its mission. (Emphasis added)

Gramsci proceeds to extol Marx's objectivity and disinterestedness. It is not Karl Marx who is "partisan" (read "sectarian"), but the historians of past regimes:

> Here is the intrinsic defect of previous works of history—to take into account only a part of the record. This part is chosen not on the basis of historical will but on partisan prejudice, even if it is unconscious and in good faith. Research has not had as its end truth, precision, the integral recreation of the life of the past, but the portrayal of a particular activity considered according to a thesis adopted *a priori*. Man was considered only as spirit and as pure consciousness.

Toward the end of this highly significant essay Gramsci introduces an important term inspired by reading Marx: "*l'altra classe,*" or "the other class." The other class consists of those who have been forgotten, neglected, mistreated, and oppressed. Here again one senses Gramsci marrying his view from the periphery with Marx's class struggle insight in such a way as to add sensitivity and depth to Marx's teaching.

The other class comprises the great majority of the people in most societies throughout history, people whom one rarely sees within the pages of history books. To the other class Marx's insights into historical causality come as a revelation. This immense, previously formless multitude begins to affirm itself, to acquire a consciousness of itself.

On the centenary of his birth, the other class owes Karl Marx thanks for having revealed to it the need to organize and to struggle against the oppression of the ruling class. Marx has shown that the great mass of mankind can come into its full humanity only through being conscious of its exploited condition and of the need to organize in order to acquire and express its collective will to overcome that condition. To do that, the other class, or the class of the *emarginati,* of those who have been outside history, must develop its own ideas and programs of action in response to the contemporary struggle. Memorizing Marx's words will not do the trick. Instead, in every situation the oppressed as a class must use Marx's insights to acquire the will to change the specific features of their subjugation:

Understood in a Marxist way, "will" signifies the consciousness of the end, which at the same time signifies a precise notion of one's own power and of the means necessary for expressing it in action. It [will] signifies above all . . . individuation of class, an independent political life for the "other class." . . . It signifies a direct impulse to achieve the chief end . . . [without being distracted by] morbid declarations of esteem and of love.

Gramsci's warning to the *emarginati* against being distracted by mere "declarations of esteem and love" is framed in the context of his already familiar attack on philanthropy. The other class will remain in a state of dependency, will remain as sheep unless they rouse themselves to bring down the entire hierarchical system that has prevailed in various forms from the beginning of civilization.

Marx should not be pictured "as a shepherd armed with a crook," Gramsci insists. Instead, he should be viewed as a catalyst combating intellectual laziness and awakening energies "for the good fight." Karl Marx's legacy is activism in service of the oppressed.

"Marxists" and "in the Marxist fashion" (*marxisticamente*) are worn-out phrases. The spirit of Marx's teaching has been deformed into the dogma of the Marxism of the First and Second Communist Internationals.

Gramsci concludes with these ringing words:

Glorifying Karl Marx on the centenary of his birth, the international proletariat glorifies itself, its conscious force, the dynamism of its conquering aggressiveness that is exposing (*va scalzando*) the dominion of privilege and preparing for the final struggle that will crown all its efforts and sacrifices.[17]

MARX'S "TWO FACES"?

Writing a week later, Gramsci, demonstrating what was to become one of his most notable characteristics, furiously attacked an essay in the "bourgeois press" written by none other than his old teacher and friend Umberto Cosmo. The venerable maxim that truth is no respecter of persons never had a better champion than Antonio Gramsci.

Cosmo, writing anonymously as a Socialist "sympathizer," claimed that the ideological schism in the Italian Socialist party originated

17. Gramsci, "Il nostro Marx," 3–7.

in the split personality of Karl Marx himself, who was part "mystic-revolutionary" and part "concrete historian." The "intransigent factions of the Italian Socialist party," Cosmo had argued, "drew their inspiration from Marx's mystic-revolutionary side," while the "collaborationist" group drew it from the concrete historical side. Gramsci rejected Cosmo's dichotomy both on philosophical and biographical grounds. Intellectually, he said, the division itself is artificial, because facts do not exist independent of "specific men, who have a specific culture, and who propose a specific end." Deceived by the "hallucination of empiricism" one forgets that "the facts . . . are above all consciousness, judgment, valuation, and that these beautiful things are possible only if men, grouped together, propose a general aim to their action." Ideas, "even if they do not result immediately in victory," are the most concrete entities, the most brutal facts there are.

Cosmo's alleged two faces of Marx—mysticism and historicism—are rhetorical exaggerations, Gramsci insists. Marx the sober analyst of records and Marx the passionate (but scarcely mystical) champion of revolution are one and the same, the two moments being dialectically united. In attempting to detach Marx the revolutionary from Marx the historian, Cosmo missed the whole point of Marx's research in the first place, which was to illustrate that ideas are the catalysts capable of turning weakness into strength. So long as they remain atomized, the individuals of the oppressed class will always remain disunited and weak.

Cosmo, the alleged sympathizer, had actually done socialism a great disservice by praising collaboration and condemning those Socialists who favor those who opt for intransigence. In truth, Gramsci insists, collaboration is the death of the spirit, while intransigence is the quality indispensable for the proletariat to possess if it is to play its part in the dialectic of history.

The master of collaboration, Giovanni Giolitti, who had been recalled to the premiership after a decade of prewar service, shows what Socialists can expect if they work with him:

> The vacuous . . . "democratism" of Giovanni Giolitti concretely has always meant protectionism in trade, centralization of the state, bureaucratic tyranny, the corruption of Parliament, favors to the privileged castes, gunfire in the streets against striking workers, and elections won with nightsticks.

Gramsci's essay "Abstractism Versus Intransigence" argued that Italian Socialists should abide by their duty to follow a policy of intransigence—or noncollaboration—with Giolitti's government, because its small pieces of social legislation would not reduce or erase privileges but only create new categories of them, creating invidious distinctions within the working class itself by establishing privileges by category. The new politics of inclusion, politics "in the classist sense," has no alternative in the Italy of 1918 but to follow the line of intransigence. Far from being doctrinaire or abstract, the duty of intransigence was empirical and concrete. It is the collaborationists who are abstract, even if they are called "realists." [18]

UTOPIA

By now, the principal themes of Gramsci's Marxism are evident. Avoiding both economistic determinism and revisionist collaboration, Gramsci sought to portray authentic Marxism as a form of materialistic idealism, or idealistic materialism. Fusing his knowledge of Marx with his personal experience as someone on the fringes of society, Gramsci created his own version of antieconomistic Marxism.

Gramsci's July, 1918, article "Utopia" weaves together most of the strands of Gramsci's Marxism and applies them to the situation in the USSR. As Gramsci understood it, Marxism holds that although political constitutions are necessarily dependent upon the economic structure, the relationship between the two is anything but simple and direct, and the history of a people is not documented solely from economic facts. Marxism is not a predictive science. It is only long after the historical events have taken place that the historian can trace the precise relationship of these events to economic "facts." The general proposition that a given political constitution can survive only if anchored in a compatible economic structure cannot explain why revolutions occur at one time rather than another, because history is not a mathematical calculation. The economic structure has to be understood and interpreted by human beings, and it has weight on the scale of history only when it affects their lives in a specific way. Human beings may be mistaken

18. Gramsci, "Astrattismo e intrasigenza," May 11, 1918, in *INM*, 15–19 at 15–16 and 19, n. 2.

about the economic structure, and their intellectual error can retard the process of change. Economic laws are not to be confused with natural laws, because the latter operate mechanically, while the former are laws only in a metaphorical sense, as the product of human will. As always, Gramsci relates intellectual discussions to the concrete historical context. In the name of his antieconomistic theory he again defends the October Revolution. The economistic Marxists mistakenly concluded that Russia was not ready for revolution in 1917; they failed to understand that through organization "weakness can become strength." By taking advantage of the chaos of wartime conditions, Lenin was able to lead the proletariat from weakness to strength. Unlike the economistic Marxists, whose judgments were imprisoned in their abstract schemes, Lenin understood that historical development is "governed by the rhythm of liberty."

The Great War had equalized conditions everywhere. Economically backward Russia had to fight under the same conditions as the advanced capitalist countries:

> In the Russian events [of 1917] there undoubtedly existed a relationship of capitalist necessity. The war was the economic condition, the system of practical life that determined the new state, that substantiated the necessity of the dictatorship of the proletariat—the war *that backward Russia had to fight in the same way as the most progressive capitalist states*. (Emphasis in the original)

Whereas under the Russia of the czars the proletariat was atomized and prevented from coming together in sufficient numbers to constitute a revolutionary force, in World War I proletarians were able to get to know one another, organize themselves, and acquire consciousness of their power as a class to bring a universal human end to fruition.

World War I, the capitalist war par excellence, proved the ideal setting for the rapid maturation of the class struggle in Russia, for it had produced the greatest concentration of economic power in the hands of the few and the greatest concentration of individuals in the fortresses and trenches.

In a few short years, World War I brought about in Russia the equivalent of what decades of peace had nurtured in the West—the necessary conditions for revolution, including the "development of new sentiments," making possible a new politics:

The great masses of . . . solitary individuals . . . [now] confined within a small geographical space, developed new sentiments and an unheard of human solidarity.

The more they had felt weak and submissive before, the greater now was the force of the revelation of their collective strength along with their desire to conserve it and construct a new society on its foundations.

For Gramsci both the economistic and the revisionist Marxists are the "true utopians," who attempt to govern by procrustean formulas and lack sensitivity to the rhythms of history. Whereas history is the story of freedom, economistic Marxists seek to imprison it in their philistine schemes. He who alleges that Lenin was a utopian because he established the dictatorship of the proletariat before its time has failed to understand the meaning of historical materialism. Such an individual is the true utopian, not Lenin.

In the aftermath of czarist and bourgeois misgovernment, the proletariat needed to centralize power in its own hands. Those who accuse the Bolshevik Revolution in Russia of having established a despotism equivalent to the one it overthrew could not be more mistaken:

> The dictatorship [of the proletariat] is the fundamental institution for guaranteeing liberty because it impedes factious minorities from staging *coups d'état*. It guarantees liberty because it does not aim to perpetuate itself but rather to solidify the permanent organisms into which the dictatorship will dissolve after completing its mission.

After deposing the czar, Russia still was unfree because the Kerensky government did not understand the need to develop a new style of leadership eliminating privileges of caste and class. If a new order really were to begin, institutions in immediate touch with the people had to exist:

> The live nuclei of this [open] hierarchy were the soviets and the parties of the people. The soviets were the primordial organizations to develop, and the Bolsheviks became the governing party because they agreed that the powers of the state ought to depend on and be controlled by the soviets.
>
> The Russian chaos coagulated around these elements of order; the new order began. A hierarchy constitutes itself: from the disorganized and suffering mass one proceeds to the organized workers and peasants, then to the soviets, next to the Bolshevik party, and finally to the one person—

Lenin. It is a gradual hierarchy of prestige and trust, spontaneously formed and maintained by free choice.

For Gramsci, a genuinely Marxist revolution must develop out of the spontaneous activity of the proletariat and not be forced. Spontaneity to Gramsci means overcoming the spirit of caste and careerism. It means constant contact with ordinary, unprivileged people, people who lack prestige. It means including those who have always been excluded. Reversing conventional word usage, Gramsci insists that utopia is authority, not spontaneity, and utopia insofar as it becomes careerism becomes caste and presumes itself to be eternal. Liberty, on the other hand, the kind of liberty expressed through the soviets, is not something utopian. Rather, liberty is the primordial aspiration of people who throughout history have fought to liberate themselves from oppression.

Both the soviets and the Bolshevik party are the guarantors of liberty. They are not castes; they are open to the variations of history. All Russian workers can participate in the soviets and express their will and desires through them. An illiterate, uneducated worker can acquire the skills necessary to become a member of the soviets:

> He acquires a sense of social responsibility and becomes an active citizen in deciding the destinies of his own country. His power and consciousness (*consapevolezza*), along with that of many others, flow through the channel of the leadership structure, and a society the likes of which has never been seen appears in history.

The Bolshevik Revolution then is not utopian; it does not run according to some preestablished plan. It is moving toward freedom, and it is based upon consent rather than violence. Gramsci concludes the article on the Russian utopia with a sarcastic reply to those Marxists who argue that Lenin and the Bolsheviks have failed to create socialism:

> But then, [the Bolshevik Revolution] . . . is not socialism? *No, it is not socialism in the simple-minded sense of the philistine constructors of mastodonic projects;* it is human society as it develops under the control of the proletariat. . . . Socialism does not install itself at a fixed date but is a continuous becoming, an infinite development in a regime of liberty organized and controlled by the majority of the citizens, the proletariat.[19]

19. Gramsci, "Utopia," July 25, 1918, in *INM*, 204–11 at 207–208 and 210–11. Emphasis added.

THE NEW POLITICS IN GRAMSCI'S MARXISM OF 1918

The chief basis of Antonio Gramsci's opposition to a positivistic and deterministic interpretation of Karl Marx's teaching is his unrelenting opposition to a politics based on privilege and prestige. One might almost say that Gramsci forced Marx to conform to the new politics rather than accommodating the new politics to Marx, were it not for the fact that Gramsci recognized that there were positivistic incrustations in Marx that needed to be scraped away. Gramsci deliberately did not claim to have interpreted Marx "correctly," that is, literally, because he held the creative core of Marxism to be a quality of openness to the flux and change of history rather than a set of doctrines extracted from Marx's texts. Marx was not to be treated as a messiah; he was not to be thought of as the author of a procrustean system to be imposed on history. If he were so conceived, then a new caste of privileged experts would arise to give orders to the untutored masses. The October Revolution created an open hierarchy that could not crystallize into an order of caste and class. Both the Bolshevik party and the soviets were the opposite of castes; they were organisms in continuous development, representing the progression of consciousness, of organizability in Russian society.

Gramsci especially valued Marx for having provided better tools for identifying the sources of dominion in the bourgeois political order. Through his emphasis upon the class struggle and his analysis of the evolution of capitalism, Marx showed how the political power of parliaments was a facade for the economic power of the various social formations within the bourgeoisie. Gramsci did not simply copy Marx, however. What was needed was an analysis of present conditions, an analysis based on a creative application of Marx's approach.

GRAMSCI'S ANALYSIS OF ITALY'S POLITICAL ECONOMY

Gramsci used nontechnical language to examine the Italian capitalist political order from a fresh perspective. Not surprisingly, he concluded that Italy did not fit neatly into an abstract scheme of a liberal political economy. There were too many residues from the feudal past, too many ties of the secular, liberal state to the power of the Church, and above all far too much incompetence in a regime that supposedly selected its elites on the basis of merit.

Italy, wrote Gramsci in May, 1918, was in truth "a democracy that wants to become an aristocracy."[20] Whereas liberty should oblige one to improve one's technology to produce more efficiently, the so-called liberal-democratic regime in Italy protected economic parasites and rewarded incompetence.

Through his grim portrait of Italian economic and political life in the wake of the war, Gramsci sought to convince the working class that Italy's incompetent elites did not deserve prestige and power. Through study and intellectual discipline the working class itself could manage affairs more competently than the present elites. This faith in the potential competence of workers (who were branded as "ordinary" by the caste-ridden Italian social order) to manage the instruments of production more capably than their bosses was to make Gramsci immediately appreciative of the possibilities in the factory occupations in Turin and Milan in 1920.

Gramsci harshly characterized the Italian state as the "product of international mimicry." Instead of having evolved organically as an instrument of work, Italy is the artificial creation of nineteenth-century lawyers. It is a semifeudal, caste-ridden, precapitalist society. Its government is despotic in every respect, and its "foreign policy is arch-secret."

Under such conditions, Gramsci concludes, Italy may not be a class society in the Marxist sense. Free competition, the cardinal principle of a capitalist economy, has only superficially influenced the major activities of the national life. The more fully Italian capitalism develops, the sharper will be the class conflict, because the proletariat will finally rid itself of habits of deference inherited from the feudal past. At present, however, the parliamentary system is a democratic facade concealing a semifeudal society, and the deputies resemble messengers of the Third Estate who in eighteenth-century France went to the capital to ask for special privileges on behalf of local groups of peasants.

Gramsci attacked Socialists favoring a policy of collaboration with Giolitti for having embraced "a Marxist Hegelianism"! By Hegelianism, Gramsci means, with considerable injustice to Hegel, acceptance of whatever is as right. Against such "collaborationist realism" or "empiricism" of brute facts, Gramsci argues that the proletariat should prepare itself to govern when capitalism's defects are apparent to everyone but the small minority benefiting from it.

20. Gramsci, "Bolscevismo intellettuale," May 16, 1918, in *INM*, 22–26 at 24 and 25.

Intransigence is not the same thing as passivity or inertia, Gramsci insists. Intransigence is a method of action and a politics of principle:

> It is the politics of a proletariat conscious of its revolutionary mission as accelerator of the capitalist evolution of society, as the reagent that clarifies the chaos of production and of bourgeois politics, that constrains the modern states to continue their natural mission as the forces that break apart the feudal institutions still . . . hindering [the progress of] history.

"We intransigents are liberals (*liberisti*)," insists Gramsci. "We do not want barons in government any more than in sugar and iron."

The removal of feudal controls will allow the law of liberty to operate so that it continually breaks up settled arrangements and requires everyone to improve and perfect himself. Silently dissenting from Marx's prediction of the increasing misery of the proletariat in *Das Kapital*, Gramsci insists that the proletariat will eventually gain from an intransigent policy, for free competition (*libera concorrenza*) brings "bread at a good price" and a vastly increased productive capacity for the nation. It will also bring to the helm new liberal elites who insist on more effective guarantees for the right of association, a right that has been only a chimera in Italy.[21]

If in championing free competition Gramsci sounds like an admirer of capitalism, it is only because he abhorred feudalism even more. Feudalism was in principle a regime based on castes and privileges. Giovanni Giolitti, the past master of Italy's political semifeudalism, had championed a policy of protectionism in trade that in Gramsci's opinion had brought his native Sardinia to its knees. At least Giolitti would be defeated if relatively left-wing liberals took control of the government. Socialists should not put themselves in Giolitti's pocket by playing the game of *trasformismo*. Unadulterated capitalism was preferable to the feudal politics of deference because it sharpened class conflict and prepared the conditions for a socialist revolution.

Capitalism represents the rule of quantity and the destruction of quality. "Bourgeois civilization," Gramsci writes, "has not enriched humanity with originating experience." While it has changed numerical relationships, it has not changed relationships of a qualitative kind. Its

21. Gramsci, "L'intransigenza di classe e la storia italiana," May 18, 1918, in *INM*, 27–37 at 36.

progress has been merely mechanical. In particular, its architecture is ugly: capitalism has not created beautiful buildings (an achievement of quality) but has only "increased the number of nonhovels." The growth of capitalism is parallel to the increased use of tobacco; it is "the civilization of smoke and snuff."

Repeatedly, Gramsci emphasizes the theme that existing politics, whether feudalistic or capitalist, is repetitive and mechanical, concerned merely with quantitative measurements and distinctions. For Gramsci, "our Marx" was anything but a leveler.[22]

THE IMPORTANCE OF STYLE FOR THE NEW POLITICS

Increasingly, Gramsci emphasized the need for Italian Marxism to build a culture, a whole way of life and feeling, to distinguish it from the prevailing capitalist mentality. The Socialist party's policy of intransigence in the face of offers to become part of the "pseudodemocratic" coalition should not be mistaken for inertia. For Socialists to wait passively for the revolution would amount to surrendering to philistine, or vulgar, ideas of Marxism. Instead, Socialists should use the period prior to the eventual collapse of the Italian political economy to create, in effect, a state within a state, to build a new culture ready to take the place of the old one. Even in the present situation of capitalist domination, those among the *emarginati* who choose to do so can begin immediately to live a socialist "style of life." Indeed, the conversion of the working masses to an authentic socialist culture is indispensable to the revolution. Thus, in June of 1918 he wrote:

> Socialists (and here we speak of those who have made socialism all of one piece with their interior life, of those in whom the socialist idea has enlivened all their actions, whether intellectual, moral, or aesthetic) in all seriousness propose as their aim the inauguration of communist civilization. To this end they subordinate all their actions, for this end they educate themselves, for this end they weave all their relationships with the world. They subordinate continuously their affections, their sentiments, the unconscious echoes of their instincts, to this end. . . . They do not want to be . . . dilettantes either in their socialist faith, or in their studies, in art, or in the trade that they follow.[23]

22. *Ibid.*, 31, 33, 36, 37.
23. Gramsci, "Vita nuova!" July 18, 1918, in *INM*, 167–68.

The Revolutionary Party

For Antonio Gramsci, the term *revolution* meant the replacement of capitalism with a new political economy based on a new style of life. Although force might be required in the final stage to overthrow the present oppressive system, a revolution based on force alone would be a revolution in name only. In rejecting the conventional image of a revolution as the seizure of power with guns and tanks, Gramsci also rejected the conventional view of a revolutionary party as a bureaucracy run like an army. The role of the party was rather to exemplify, promote, and sustain a new style of life:

> The Socialist party is the organ for achieving this end; it is the elaborator of those forms and modes through which the class will achieve victory. Because the party . . . transforms and organizes the social forces, it is necessary that it be entirely one with the . . . [working] class.

Over and over again Gramsci emphasizes the importance of the party's maintaining close contact with the working class as its only source of strength. The party "becomes an element of order in the chaos that still exists, since economic evolution has not arrived at its apex, and humanity is not [yet] neatly divided into two classes," insists Gramsci. Thus the party can play a role not only in voicing the concerns of the exploited class, *but in helping to form that class itself.* If it is to assist in bringing isolated oppressed individuals together into a social force and turning that force into a self-conscious class, then the party must retain its distinctive physiognomy and not confuse the workers by supporting or participating in liberal governments in Parliament. Above all, the party must maintain contact and unity with the economic class that it represents (the workers), rather than collaborating with a government headed by the representatives of the rich.

Gramsci labels the view that one can obtain a great success with little strength (*forza*) "parliamentary utopianism," concluding that the only real conquest is that which depends on strength and which can be defended and preserved by strength. In order to possess this strength, much more than a victory, however substantial, in parliamentary elections will be necessary. It will be necessary "better to organize the [working] class spiritually, better to educate it about our goal, without grotesque presumption but also without cowardly abdication."[24]

24. Gramsci, "Fiorisce l'illusione," June 15, 1918, in *INM,* 110–12 at 110–11 and 112.

GRAMSCI'S COMMUNISM

The ultimate goal to which Gramsci refers is communism. By July, 1918, or two and one-half years before the schism at Livorno, Gramsci had become a committed Communist. His communism, however, was based upon his previously developed politics of the liberation of the oppressed class, the substitution of "the other class" for the bourgeoisie, and the eventual elimination of all barriers of privilege and distinctions of prestige.

The revolution had to begin immediately through the spread of a new culture. "The problem is moral more than it is [a question of] mechanical organization: it is a problem of responsibility, of culture, of the deepening of the socialist consciousness."[25] To that end the party needed to support a new kind of newspaper. On June 15, 1918, Gramsci proclaimed the need for what was to become *L'Ordine Nuovo,* a publication devoted to conceptualizing and disseminating the idea of the new politics.

CRITICAL COMMUNISM

Antonio Labriola, the first important thinker to attempt to introduce Marx's ideas into Italy, described Marxist doctrine as a form of "critical communism." In an essay published in 1895, Labriola wrote:

> Critical communism—this is its true name, and there is no more accurate one for such a doctrine [*i.e.,* Marxism].[26]

Gramsci probably unknowingly borrowed the phrase from Labriola. In any event, it seems to be an appropriate label for Gramsci's brand of Marxism. According to Gramsci's article of October 19, 1918:

> Critical communism has nothing in common with philosophical positivism. . . . Marxism is based upon philosophical idealism, which, however, has little in common with what is ordinarily meant by the word *idealism.* . . . Philosophical idealism is a doctrine of [the identity of] being and of consciousness. . . . That Marx had introduced positivistic elements into his works is not surprising and may be explained by the fact

25. Gramsci, "La conferenza di Londra," June 15, 1918, in *INM,* 118–19.
26. Sergio Caprioglio in *INM,* 351, n. 4.

that Marx was not a professional philosopher, and [like Homer] at times even he nods.

Gramsci's admission that there are positivistic elements in Marx no doubt refers to passages where Marx carelessly implies that the material base determines the legal and political superstructure. What is certain, Gramsci insists, is that in its essentials Marxism depends upon philosophic idealism rather than positivism:

> One has only to think of the prominent use that Socialists make of the terms 'consciousness', 'class consciousness', and 'socialist and proletarian consciousness'; implicit in this language is the philosophical conception that one "is" only when one "knows," or "has consciousness of," his own being. A worker "is" proletarian when he "knows" this truth and works and thinks according to this "knowing."

All of the above means that so-called natural categories are purely verbal expressions.

> [For critical communism,] history is the production of a humanity that divides itself into classes and sects, of which from time to time one is predominant and directs (*dirige*) society according to its ends, opposed by the other part [of society] that tends to affirm itself and *substitute* itself in this direction; history is thus not an evolution, but a *substitution,* for which conscious and disciplined strength is the necessary means.[27]

As the above passage illustrates, Gramsci related even his most refined philosophical speculation to the practical exigencies of the day. He did not just talk about Marxist praxis (or the unification of theory and practice); he illustrated it through his own life. The attack on positivistic interpretations of Marx's thought was not grounded on merely textual questions. Gramsci admitted that vulgar or economistic Marxism could support itself on some passages from Marx himself. Marx's greatness, however, lay elsewhere. In an earlier article Gramsci had characterized Marxist praxis as follows:

> What one may call external reality is not something fixed, rigid, completely separated from and independent of the idea; economic and political institutions are not outside of our will and influence. Positivism, it is true, teaches one to abstract the subject from the object, the idea from the

27. Gramsci, "Misteri della cultura e della poesia," October 19, 1918, in *INM*, 346–50 at 348, 349.

action, the form from the matter. But all contemporary philosophical schools learned to correct the error: [they] no longer [speak of] abstraction and separation, but [of] reciprocal action and unity. The form is not empty, but efficient; the object is in the subject and the reverse; to act is to understand, to understand is to act.[28]

Marxist doctrine for Gramsci was self-conscious action to advance the victory of society's "other part"—the excluded and oppressed. Marxism's intellectual dependence on philosophical idealism in no way implies neglect of the importance of the experimental and positive method, however. What is crucial to grasp is that critical communism *makes use of* the experimental method. In the economistic variety of Marxism, on the other hand, it is the experimental method that is allowed to define Marxism:

> The experimental and positivist method, as a dispassionate and disinterested method of scientific research, is also [a part] of historical materialism but is not dependent on it. It is the method proper to the sciences, and Galilei was the first to systematize it. *Historical materialism has demonstrated that historical research must revolve . . . around economic phenomena,* without whose knowledge history is purely externality without substance. . . . Historical materialism thus has integrated the experimental and positive method applied to the . . . study of . . . social phenomena, and should not be confused either with it or with philosophical positivism.[29]

Gramsci's insistence that historical research "must revolve around economic phenomena" is one of the many passages proving that Gramsci was neither a solipsist nor a subjectivist. That history is not objective in the sense of being "out there," divorced from human consciousness, hardly meant to Gramsci that there was no reality except consciousness.

UNCRITICAL LIBERALISM

Gramsci's fierce opposition to collaboration with what we may loosely call Italian liberalism—the center of the Italian parliamentary system— was based on something other than an abstract idea of what true Marxism dictated. His theory of the need for a radically new politics grew

28. Gramsci, "La vera crisi," September 21, 1918, in *INM,* 300–302 at 301. New attribution by Sergio Caprioglio.
29. Gramsci, "Misteri della cultura e della poesia," 349. Emphasis added.

out of his own keenly felt experiences of what he took to be the injustice of the Italian state. He thought Italian liberal democracy of 1918 was based upon unexamined premises about freedom. Thus, in one of his June, 1918, articles he wrote about the distinction between "free thought" (*libero pensiero*) and "thought that is free" (*pensiero libero*):

> Free thought is not the same thing as thought that is free. Free thought is a bourgeois, philistine expression dependent on Jacobin individualism; this is why we find Masons, radicals, and libertarians grouped around it.
>
> The free thinker is a utopian. . . . He conceives liberty in a narrow and limited framework, as liberty only for certain opinions, for certain constellations of opinions. One can say that at bottom he thinks of liberty only for himself. . . .
>
> Socialists, on the other hand, want "thought that is free" (*pensiero libero*). They want to escape from all conventions, all limitations, all prejudices. For them thought . . . is not something mushy. . . . Thought, then, being free, is conditioned, and it is conditioned precisely by history.[30]

Unlike the liberal, who thinks ahistorically and dogmatically, the Socialist has a feel for context and shows great tolerance in discussions and debate. For Gramsci, liberals proclaim themselves free but demonstrate the slavishness of their thought. Liberal thinkers are conformists, because they cannot imagine anyone's disagreeing with them except those governed by ill will and base motives.

Liberal individualism for Gramsci is one of the major sources of economic and social injustice. The doctrine of individualism spawns a vicious competitiveness. The greed for consumer goods must be abolished, along with the entire competitive system, for such a system leads individuals to war and in itself is only a thinly veiled substitute for war.

Liberalism's poverty of thought about freedom is confirmed in practice, insists Gramsci, typically tying theory and practice together. In Italy liberalism has produced a regime of privilege that serves the interests of only a small percentage of the people. Its most prominent representative, Giovanni Giolitti, "chained Italian life to a whirl of artificial interests, of which he had always been the prisoner." Every institution of the state, including Parliament itself, has been corrupted.[31]

Under liberalism "Italian political life had been reduced to a nul-

30. Gramsci, "Libero pensiero e pensiero libero," June 15, 1918, in *INM*, 113–16 at 113, 114.
31. Gramsci, "Giolitti, guerra, e la pace," August 14, 1918, in *INM*, 241–60 at 247.

lity . . . without parties, associations, discussions, control, 'public opinion,' 'country.'" It possesses a ruling class in name only, a class that
instead of governing effectively parasitically enjoys the fruits of its un-
earned prestige.[32]

Italian liberalism violates its own individualistic principles. Italian
life is not like a soccer game played in public according to fixed rules,
but is like *scopone,* a card game played with the blinds drawn in a casino-
like atmosphere, where the result is always to the advantage of the
management:

> *Scopone* is the form of sport for a . . . backward society, [typified by] . . .
> the cult of incompetence, the anonymous letter, and careerism. . . .
>
> Sport gives rise also in politics to the concept of the "loyal opposition."
>
> *Scopone* produces "gentlemen" who kick the workman who in free discus-
> sion dared to dispute their thought right out the front door.[33]

The last reference is to a workman who was fired for daring to contra-
dict baseless anti-Socialist statements by the owner of the home where
he was working. The owner had initiated the conversation, profess-
ing delight in talking with an "authentic" member of the "proletariat."[34]

Although Gramsci deplores Italy's failure to reach the economic and
political level of the United States and Great Britain, he does not sanc-
tion the liberal competitive system as such. If "Italian liberals are a bad
joke" because they are not true liberals but perpetuators of the caste system, true (or consistent) liberals deserve commendation when they
hasten communism's victory by stirring up the contradictions necessary
for the class struggle. It is in this sense that Gramsci's otherwise in-
comprehensible statement that Woodrow Wilson "is the living symbol
of Marxist doctrine in the United States" needs to be interpreted.[35]

Gramsci asserts that Wilson's proposal for a League of Nations should
not mislead Socialists. Instead of representing true humanitarianism,
Wilson's words "are the measure of civilization that for us Socialists
constitutes the presupposition of our triumph. In Wilson, the capitalist
world has attained the awareness of its function and the will to organize
internationally." Indeed, the ideology implicit in Wilson's project for a

32. Gramsci, "L'irresponsabilità sociale," August 23, 1918, in *INM,* 261–62 at 261.
33. Gramsci, "Il 'Foot-Ball' e lo scopone," August 26, 1918, in *INM,* 265–66.
34. Gramsci, "Infortuno sul lavoro," August 24, 1918, in *INM,* 263–64.
35. Gramsci, "Wilson e i socialisti," October 12, 1918, in *INM,* 313–17 at 315.

League of Nations represents the most perfect scheme for international cooperation that one might possibly reach under capitalism. As Karl Marx had foreseen, the effective growth of a Communist International would necessarily accompany the internationalization of capitalism.

Writing at the height of Woodrow Wilson's prestige during his tour of Europe, where everywhere he was received by tumultuous crowds, Gramsci insisted that Socialists not be taken in by the pseudohumanitarianism of Wilson's appeal. Far from being the "idyllic paradise of the peoples," the League of Nations would be the scene of "ferocious antagonisms and colossal struggles between the forces of capitalism, organized to perfection, wherein the proletariat will meet only suffering and humiliation."

The prestige of the American president ought not influence Socialist tactics. "He does not . . . express our will and our faith," Gramsci concluded.

Gramsci's distrust of philanthropy, of the haves giving to the have-nots out of the apparent goodness of their hearts, surfaces repeatedly in his denunciations of Wilson's internationalism, which he labels a pseudo-humanitarian ideology. The good intentions of individual statesmen and philanthropists notwithstanding, the expansion of capitalism only exacerbates the class struggle. The state under capitalism is the "executive organ of capitalist interests" and "individual good will is powerless to change its essence." The capitalist state can never serve as the "impartial regulator of class conflict."[36]

In an important article published on November 19, 1918, Gramsci further clarified his idea of a new politics by contrasting it to Wilson's program for a world made safe for democracy and free trade:

> President Wilson is not even close to being a Socialist. Free trade is not a socialist doctrine but is intrinsically dependent on the capitalist regime. *Socialists are neither protectionists nor free traders (liberisti),* for *in the society they are constructing there cannot be any competition, just as there will be neither classes, social strata, nor states.*[37]

After the world's productive forces have been socialized and internationalized, competition will give way to civic emulation, and moral

---

36. Gramsci, "Disillusioni e speranze," October 15, 1918, in *INM,* 330–33 at 332.

37. Gramsci, "Semplici riflessioni," November 19, 1918, in *INM,* 409–11 at 410. Emphasis added.

duty rather than private property will be the stimulus for greater productivity between individuals, communes, and nations. Socialists are not terrorists; they are revolutionaries in the sense that they expect the progressive development of capitalism through free trade to produce changes of so revolutionary a nature that only socialism will be able to cope with them. In the meantime socialism must proceed with the task of organizing the proletariat to achieve victory over the collection of rootless bourgeois individualists making up Wilson's "people." Wilsonianism, a form of "Calvinist puritanism," will play a progressive role in Italy insofar as it helps to create a true bourgeoisie devoted to modernizing Italy's semifeudal economy. Socialism—Marxist socialism, which is critical communism—needs the bourgeoisie as its counterforce. Italian socialism "as doctrine, as disciplined method of struggle and not only as instinctive rebellion, has little success in *Italy because it has lacked the concrete object* [a mature bourgeoisie] *to criticize and dialectically transcend.*"[38]

Lest his readers mistake him for a "philistine," or vulgar (positivist), Marxist claiming to predict the future on the basis of economic laws and conceiving one's duty to be simply to wait for the inevitable coming of the revolution, Gramsci concludes his "Simple Reflections" with this exhortation:

> We ought to be prepared for everything: *to conquer political power if liberalism does not succeed in resolving the conflicts that shortly will come to pass,* but also to continue with tenacity and clear-sighted perseverance our systematic activity of organizing and educating the masses disoriented from being tossed about in the chaos of ideas and historical situations experienced for the first time.[39]

THE REALISM OF REVOLUTION: GRAMSCI'S ANTIMESSIANISM

Demonstrating his remarkable combination of theoretical vision of a new politics without "classes, social strata, or states" and tactile understanding of concrete situations, Gramsci reiterates in the preceding article the conviction he felt in his bones about the realism of revolution. Luciano Pellicani could not be more incorrect when he accuses Gramsci

38. *Ibid.,* 411. Emphasis added.
39. *Ibid.* Emphasis added.

of having embraced "social palingenesis," or the idea that political reality could be overturned through the revolution, here conceived of as an apocalyptic event. Distorting and misusing Eric Voegelin's insights into gnosticism, Pellicani describes Gramsci's plan to revolutionize society as a "secularized version of the Judeo-Christian ideal of the overturning of reality."[40]

Pellicani's thesis is all the more unsustainable because Gramsci, already in his writings of 1918, specifically and repeatedly attacked apocalyptic and palingenetic notions of revolution.[41] Gramsci's hard-headed realism led him to conclude that Western capitalism

> is physiologically incapable of giving what is asked. Good will founders against the nexus of laws that will lead to new suffering, to more monstrous forms of exploitation, and to the exclusion of power through ever more violent means of the multitudes who instead want power, all power, without intermediaries, without complicated representative mechanisms based on blind and unlimited trust.[42]

Far from expecting the apocalyptic victory of the excluded ones, of "the multitudes without power," Gramsci foresaw with chilling accuracy the rise of fascism, the force that would "through ever more violent means" exclude those same multitudes from power.[43]

Antonio Gramsci thought that only the victory of the Communist revolution could end the economic and social chaos prevailing in postwar Europe. However, that victory would not be achieved artificially through terror.

Gramsci's aversion to violence such as the terror of the French Revolution often appears in his writings, and it is ironic that he who would suffer from Fascist violence should be accused by Pellicani of fostering the very climate he abhorred. Gramsci was not a pacifist, but the whole tenor of his thought reveals his temperamental aversion to violence. Indeed, the violence committed by the capitalist system, whether intended or not, against the faceless, innumerable mass of human beings

40. Luciano Pellicani, *Gramsci: An Alternative Communism?* (Stanford, 1981), 36.

41. See Gramsci's articles "La politica del sè," June 29, 1918, in *INM,* 147–53 at 148–49, where he condemns "Jacobin Messianism"; "Vita nuova!" July 6, 1918, in *INM,* 167–68 at 167, where he ridicules the idea that revolution will bring about a "universal palingenesis"; and "Il popolo e Wilson," January 7, 1919, in *INM,* 484–87 at 485, where he attacks the notion that Woodrow Wilson as "mythical hero" can bring about peace through some "palingenetic miracle."

42. Gramsci, "Il popolo e Wilson," January 7, 1919, in *INM,* 486.

43. *Ibid.*

who made up "the other class" impelled Gramsci to become a Communist. Writing in February, 1919, Gramsci observed:

> The concrete problem of today . . . is to assist the working class in assum-
> ing political power [and] to study . . . the means by which the transfer of
> power of the state [to the working class] can be carried out with the
> smallest possible shedding of blood, so that the new communist state will
> be put into effect . . . *after a brief period of revolutionary terror.*[44]

Gramsci had discussed the terror in the French Revolution in an article concerning requisition of farm animals by the Committee of Public
Safety. Sympathizing with the peasants' resistance, Gramsci proclaimed
that the violence of the French Revolution could be avoided in the coming Communist revolution, because the way will have been prepared
intellectually and morally through the development of a new consciousness in the working masses.[45]

Civil life should be "civilized": this theme resounds through everything that Antonio Gramsci wrote. He writes contemptuously about
those who want to run history like a military barracks. If he seemed to
see the October Revolution through rose-colored glasses, it was because he preferred to give the Bolsheviks the benefit of the doubt rather
than to credit wild stories from Russian expatriates or foreign travelers
about the extent of Bolshevik terror. In that theory, violence and coercion had a minimal place, for he believed that the new politics was for
the benefit of everyone, and that when the time was ripe the overwhelming majority of the people would welcome it.

In the meantime, reality of bourgeois violence in Italy confronted
everyone, Gramsci concluded. The bourgeois order makes an offer you
can't afford to refuse: "Your purse or your life." Here Gramsci referred
to the conditions attached by the Argentine government in December,
1918, when it informed the government of newly independent Austria
that it would receive aid in the form of agricultural products only if
order were preserved, which meant specifically:

> At the slightest beginning of a Bolshevik . . . or Socialist–Commu-
> nist uprising, the transportation and consignment of foodstuffs will be
> suspended.[46]

44. Gramsci, "Stato e sovranità," February 28, 1919, in *INM,* 518–22 at 522. Emphasis
added.
45. Gramsci, "I contadini e lo stato," June 6, 1918, in *INM,* 81–86.
46. Gramsci, "O la borsa o la vita," December 16, 1918, in *INM,* 443–44.

GRAMSCI ATTACKS VIOLENCE

While fascism did not exist as an organized political movement under Benito Mussolini's leadership before March, 1919 (the date of its then little-noticed founding congress in Milan's Piazza San Sepolcro), its real beginnings date from 1914, when Mussolini broke dramatically with the Socialist party over the issue of Italy's intervention in World War I. At war's end, when demobilization gradually took place, some of the ex-soldiers, especially those from the ranks of the *arditi,* or special shock troops, took to the streets intimidating those who had opposed or had been lukewarm to Italy's participation in the war. *Arditismo* became a kind of fad with a minority of Italian youth, some of whom were caught up in the spirit of the Futurist movement led by Filippo Tomassi Marinetti. Gabriele D'Annunzio's occupation of Fiume provided the rallying point for the cult of adventurism and jingoism that can conveniently be called *arditismo.* Mussolini's newspaper *Il Popolo d'Italia* defended and promulgated *arditismo.* Out of the *arditi* and D'Annunzio's ill-fated Fiume expedition (designed to keep the city in Italian hands rather than let it pass to the newly created state of Yugoslavia, as the Versailles treaty required) were to come the Fascist "action squads" that terrorized much of the area centered around Bologna and the Po valley. We shall return to this theme in chapter 8 in the discussion of Gramsci's article "The Monkey People."

Gramsci fought Italian chauvinism tooth and nail, distinguishing himself from the cult of *arditismo* at every opportunity. Although there has been speculation that he may have sympathized with D'Annunzio, in fact Gramsci denounced with contempt the poet-adventurer's invidious terms (*caporettista, sventurati, e sciagurati*) directed at Italian neutralists and even at prisoners of war. A *caporettista* was a defeatist—after the battle of Caporetto, Italy's worst defeat in World War I—and the *sventurati* and *sciagurati* were the unfortunate and ill-starred (adjectives D'Annunzio applied to all prisoners of war, who presumably should have died fighting rather than been taken captive).[47]

Antonio Gramsci was the enemy of any "gladiatorial politics,"[48] and

47. Gramsci, "Il trattamento dei prigionieri," January 3, 1919, in *INM,* 479–80. New attribution.
48. Gramsci, "Demagogia," November 14, 1918, in *INM,* 397–99.

he attacked *arditismo* as the embodiment of philistinism, banality, anti-intellectualism, and puerile activism.[49]

His synonym for *arditismo* is *lazzaronismo,* or "vagabondism." All of the rhetoric about Italy's great Roman past, including the evocation of the memory of Balilla, the child-hero of ancient Rome, was in truth only a mask for indiscipline, self-indulgence, and mindless activism. Gramsci concludes:

> The [so-called] heroic soul of the younger generations refuses to confine itself to the old schemes of discipline and order, just as the classic vaga-bond refuses to sacrifice his beautiful liberty, contemptible but absolute, to constrain himself to follow the discipline required for ongoing and systematic work.[50]

If Gramsci sounds here like a traditionalist on education, it is because he cannot imagine a true revolution without culture, a culture that makes all the learning of the past available to everyone. His contempt for brainless *arditismo* is a logical extension of his critique of positivistic Marxism. For Gramsci, culture was a matter of taste, of preintellectual disposition, and one best acquires such taste by coming into contact with the classics, the best that has been thought and said.

In a withering attack on the futurists and their celebration of the more boorish instincts, Gramsci concluded that the school had to be a serious institution. As Martin Entwhistle has written, Gramsci advocated "conservative schooling for radical politics."[51]

Arditismo represented the antithesis of everything in which Gramsci believed. In the last analysis the militaristic superpatriots who paved the way for Mussolini's fascism sought "to govern with rifles and machine guns" and "to win [imperialistic] wars with terrorism," as Gramsci put it.[52] On April 15, 1919, at the end of a Socialist rally in Milan, a group of Fascists, nationalists, and *arditi* broke into and set fire to the headquarters of *Avanti!* Gramsci reacted fiercely in two columns, one comparing history to "a very fruitful and astute woman, who would not be intimidated by daggers, or incendiary bombs, or machine guns." History is

49. Gramsci, "Lazzaronismo," December 18, 1918, in *INM,* 446–47.

50. *Ibid.,* 447.

51. Martin Entwhistle, *Antonio Gramsci: Conservative Schooling for Radical Politics* (London, 1979).

52. Gramsci, "I trionfi della democrazia wilsoniana," January 13, 1919, in *INM,* 492.

liberty, and always favors the physically weaker side. The resort to violence by the Fascists shows the spiritual weakness of their cause.[53]

In the second column Gramsci linked *arditismo* and Benito Mussolini's Fascist movement to the destruction of the Milan headquarters of *Avanti!* and correctly predicted that, far from being an isolated incident, the attack was a harbinger of things to come. Although a grotesque phenomenon, wrote Gramsci, Fascist *arditismo* served the interests of Italy's great centers of business and banking. Already in the fall of 1918 and the spring of 1919, Antonio Gramsci had diagnosed the emerging Italian Fascist movement as a culture centered on violence as a way of life. Seen in this perspective, far from typifying or exalting violence, socialism was the chief adversary of the culture of violence. Because it understood the link between the economic base and the psychological experience of the culture of violence, socialism was that culture's principal target and victim, Gramsci argued.[54]

By the spring of 1919, Gramsci had concluded that Italian "liberal democracy" was complicit in the rise of the Fascist violence. As he put it:

> Ah, if the Socialists had attacked the building of the Corriere della Sera, then those famous machine guns . . . that the government so willingly exhibits to the workers as a warning [against attempting a *coup d'état*] would have appeared in five minutes. But *Avanti!* can be devastated and destroyed without any concern whatsoever [by the government]. . . .[55]

THE SUFFERINGS OF SARDINIA

As was emphasized in chapter 1, Gramsci never shed his "Sardinianism." The youth who arrived in Turin, "provincialized four, five, six times over," had renewed occasion to write of his native island with the arrival of the Sassari Brigade of soldiers in April, 1919. Already in March he had published a column deploring the city of Turin's decision to boycott the importation of Sardinian lambs and goats so that Piedmontese peasants could earn more for their rabbits. A delegation of four thousand Sardinian shepherds and peasants had descended upon the city to protest the decision.

53. Gramsci, "Le astuzie della storia," April 18, 1919, in *INM*, 602. Hegel had written of the *List der Vernunft*, or "cunning of reason."

54. Gramsci, "La sfida," April 18, 1919, in *INM*, 604–607.

55. *Ibid.*, 606.

Although Gramsci remained self-consciously Sardinian all his life, now that in his late twenties his political thought and experience had fully matured he was able to place economic discrimination against his native island in a larger theoretical perspective. The root of the problem lay in the general politics of privilege practiced by representatives of the Italian state who played the game of enriching their friends at the expense of other citizens. Protectionism, or erecting trade barriers between one region of Italy and another, was a means of "enriching a particular group or stratum (*ceto*) of citizens, in whose ranks are enrolled one's best friends . . . ," even if the result is forcing the majority to eat rabbit, wrote Gramsci in an article sarcastically entitled "Lambs and Rabbits."[56]

On their arrival in Turin, the Sassari Brigade of Sardinian soldiers was feted by the city administration. Many of the community's leading citizens turned out for the parade and festival. The column Gramsci wrote about the occasion was scheduled for publication in *Avanti!* for April 14, 1919, but it was censored entirely and has only recently been published by Sergio Caprioglio. In this important piece, Gramsci commented on the hypocrisy of the Turin establishment in commemorating anything Sardinian after having relentlessly pursued policies that "have reduced Sardinia to squalor." In this article on his native habitat, Gramsci demonstrated his passion for concreteness, his "tactile sensibility," to the utmost. Rattling off a chain of abuses, including exploitation of the natural environment and the semistarvation of the island's peasant majority, Gramsci asked rhetorically how the stockholders, large industrialists, and bankers of Turin could in good faith dare to bestow the Sassari Brigade with flowers, cigars, and ribbons. The Piedmontese ruling class, which made enormous profits from Sardinian agricultural products and raw materials, had given the island nothing in return.

Reading this essay, one is again struck with Gramsci's exceptional capacity for communicating the feeling of pain and deprivation suffered by those at the periphery. He denounced

> the leather manufacturers, who choke the peasants, shepherds, and artisans of Sardinia with enormous prices, that make the price of shoes rise, [and] that force a third of the peasants . . . to go shoeless among the thorns and rocks that cut their feet, that oblige the mothers, daughters,

56. Gramsci, "Agnelli e conigli," March 4, 1919, in *INM*, 552–55 at 554.

and wives of the . . . shepherds always to go without shoes, winter and summer. . . .[57]

In chapter 1 I maintained that the roots of Gramsci's theory of a new politics of inclusion lay in the soil of Sardinia rather than in the books of Marx and the actions of Lenin. However much the latter influenced the growth of the leaves and branches, the trunk remained rooted in Antonio Gramsci's concrete experiences of exclusion in his childhood and youth as a hunchback in Sardinia.

The above thesis appears to be born out with specific reference to his theory of "critical communism," for in the same article one encounters the following passage:

> The word "commune" is one of the most widespread terms in the Sardinian dialect; *there exists among Sardinian peasants and shepherds a religious longing for the 'commune'*, for fraternal collaboration with all men who work and suffer, for eliminating parasites—the super-rich (*riccone*), who steal the bread of the poor, and *who make the little poor boy work and then reward him with a tiny morsel of bread.*[58]

Through his journalism—a unique combination of partisan polemics and theoretical sophistication—Antonio Gramsci had already by the spring of 1919 formulated the vision that would inspire and the themes that would inform the political thought of the great *Prison Notebooks*. Requiring further development were his ideas about the need for a new style of leadership—explained fully only when Gramsci himself assumed the role of secretary-general of the newly formed Italian Communist party—and the theory of revolution through building a counterculture strong enough to resist and even replace the prevailing liberal-capitalist hegemony. In general, however, the principles essential to both of these developments may also be found in the 1918–1919 writings. Especially in his reviews of plays performed on the Turin stage, Gramsci stresses the opposition between the deadness of mechanical repetitiveness and the life of spiritual creativity. Gramsci is as unafraid as was Marx in his youth to use spiritual metaphors. Thus, he declares that

57. Gramsci, "La brigata Sassari," April 14, 1919, in *INM*, 590–92. In "I dolori della Sardegna," April 16, 1919, in *INM*, 599, Gramsci estimated that two-thirds of the Sardinian people were without shoes.

58. Gramsci, "La brigata Sassari," 592. Emphasis added.

"humanity as poetry, spirit, and intelligence" includes and transcends "physical being."[59]

In another column Gramsci expresses the conviction that culture and art will end by also finding their place in proletarian activity, not as the gift of the already existing society, but as vital energy of the proletariat itself, as its specific activity. A new form of civilization will emerge, with its art and culture perhaps rough and confused at the beginning, but which through experience will clarify and refine itself.[60]

In December, 1918, Gramsci wrote a column in *Avanti!* entitled "*Lo Spettro*" ("The Specter"). He opened by quoting the famous lines by Marx and Engels in the *Communist Manifesto* of 1848: "A specter is haunting Europe—the specter of communism. All the powers of old Europe have joined in a holy alliance to hunt out this specter." Gramsci goes on to note that for the Europe of 1918 that specter had become flesh and blood in the new Soviet state. From having been a mere exercise in negative criticism, the *Manifesto* had become an inheritance of positive experiences and a method of practical action that makes theory come alive in a new practice.[61]

This chapter has sought to illustrate how unbookish Gramsci's Marxism was and how Gramsci always concentrated upon the concrete forms of the struggle for the liberation of those masses of human beings who had been excluded from civilization's vital center. What excited him about the October Revolution was the spectacle of tens of millions of history's masses mobilizing themselves to overthrow the czarist regime and substitute a "new order" led by Lenin and by the Bolshevik party. Gramsci had become a committed Communist, but he also remained a "critical Communist." He saw no contradiction between these two terms, because for him the Communist movement as an organized entity was scarcely an end in itself but a means for implementing a new politics. He never ceased to think in a tactile way and always related his communism to the concrete, specific tasks at hand to advance the cause of a new order in which groups hitherto declared marginal by the privileged and the powerful would enjoy full and equal participation in political and social life.

59. Gramsci, "Ridi, Pagliaccio," March 21, 1919, in *INM*, 676.
60. Gramsci, "Arsenaleide," June 11, 1918, in *INM*, 633.
61. Gramsci, "Lo spettro," December 13, 1918, in *INM*, 440.

IV ✒ *L'Ordine Nuovo* and the Occupation of the Factories, 1919—1920

The years 1919 and 1920 came to be known as the *biennio rosso,* or "red biennium." To many supporters of the established order, Italy seemed to be on the verge of revolution. Strikes in the factories occurred with unprecedented magnitude, frequency, and duration. Especially in the fertile Po valley, sharecroppers and day laborers organized themselves for the first time and demanded land reform.[1]

For Gramsci, the *biennio rosso* was a period of strenuous, dedicated work during which he helped to found a new socialist newspaper devoted chiefly to inspiring a movement for workers' democracy in the factories in Turin and Milan. Toward the end of the period Gramsci participated personally in the dramatic attempt by the workers to run the factories by themselves without the help of middle-class professional managers. He also agonized with the workers' defeat. Ever the sober revolutionary, Gramsci knew well how many obstacles lay in the path of the working class before real enduring power could be attained, and so he could endure the failure of the factory occupations better than his comrades who had been led to confuse revolutionary rhetoric with reality.

L'ORDINE NUOVO

In April, 1919, Gramsci, Angelo Tasca, Umberto Terracini, and Palmiro Togliatti founded a weekly newspaper in Turin named, significantly,

1. James Joll, *Antonio Gramsci* (New York, 1977), 52–53.

L'Ordine Nuovo (The new order). Tasca supplied the capital for the venture. Within a year the paper had enough subscribers to be financially self-sufficient. The first issue appeared on May 1, the traditional socialist holiday. The paper's subtitle on the masthead was "A Weekly Review of Socialist Culture." Gramsci was chosen secretary by the editorial group, and he appointed his close companion Pia Carena administrative secretary.

THE FACTORY COUNCIL MOVEMENT

In June of the same year, Gramsci published the first of his many articles, some signed and others not, devoted to the subject of the factory councils. A substantial secondary literature exists on Gramsci's so-called conciliar period.[2]

If one reads some of his articles, draft constitutions, and programs literally and in isolation from the rest of his life and thought, Gramsci would appear to have endorsed the very kind of utopianism he had earlier denounced. Gramsci knew, however, that a mere change of institutions can never magically change men. He never believed in the factory councils as ends in themselves. Rather, they were important because they demonstrated that the proletariat had as much capacity as the bourgeoisie to run a modern state. The council movement, having risen spontaneously, deserved the support of the Socialist party. The party should not allow the cautious trade union bureaucrats in its midst to isolate and defeat the councils out of fear that the latter would trespass on the unions' turf. On the contrary, the party should encourage the council movement and suggest various possibilities for its further development. He also thought that workers' councils should be seen as potential mechanisms for overcoming *emarginazzione,* for bringing in the hitherto passive people at the periphery to the active, directing center of society's life.

Gramsci did not conceive of the Turin factory councils as replicas of the soviets developed during the Bolshevik Revolution. Rather, he thought that in a number of countries at roughly the same time workers had begun to develop comparable institutions for self-government in

2. Joseph Femia cites some of the literature in English in "The Gramsci Phenomenon: Some Reflections," *Political Studies,* XXVII (September, 1979), 472–83.

factories. For example, the "shop stewards" movement in Great Britain greatly interested him, and he acquired information about it principally through his friend Piero Sraffa.[3] A native of Turin, Sraffa, who went on to become a distinguished economist in the circle around John Maynard Keynes at Cambridge University, met Gramsci in 1919 and translated English texts for *L'Ordine Nuovo*. Apart from Tatiana Schucht, Sraffa was to do more than anyone else to assist Gramsci during his long prison ordeal beginning in 1926.

The emerging factory council movement in the gigantic automobile factories at Turin and Milan helped Gramsci perceive the profound inadequacy of the national bureaucracy of the PSI and its trade union organization, the General Confederation of Labor (CGL), as instruments for a new politics. Gramsci thought the bureaucrats of both groups were more interested in their careers than in making a revolution in Italy.

The factory council, consisting of all the workshop inspectors (*commissari di reparto*) elected by all the workers regardless of party or union affiliation, comprised around 250 members at Turin's huge Fiat plant. In turn, this assembly elected a five-member executive committee. The factory council and its executive committee were concerned with ways to improve safety and health conditions at the workplace. It was also charged with enforcing discipline.[4] Beginning in June, 1919, through his articles in *L'Ordine Nuovo* and through direct conversations with the factory workers, Gramsci encouraged the council movement to strengthen and broaden itself to become a vehicle for improving the education, literacy, and revolutionary consciousness of the workers, with the eventual objective of replacing the bourgeois management. Gramsci saw the factory council movement as a means of breaking down the walls separating the workers in one category from those in another, so that each worker, regardless of whether he was an engineer, a designer, an electrician, or an assembly-line operator, would develop a primary sense of loyalty to the work force as a whole, thereby making it impossible for management to bribe one sector of the work force with higher wages and other benefits while keeping down the rest.

One can immediately see why the factory council movement was unpopular with management and also why it aroused strenuous opposition from the trade unions, organized as they were by category and be-

3. See "The Unknown Sraffa," *New Left Review,* CXII (November-December, 1978), 62–83.

4. Martin Clark, *Antonio Gramsci and the Revolution That Failed* (New Haven, 1977), xi.

holden to increasing wages and benefits for their members exclusively. The reason that the factory council movement would immediately pick up Gramsci's enthusiastic support should also be obvious, for it seemed to be eminently compatible with his vision of a new politics of inclusion. Thus, in his first article on the factory councils, "Workers' Democracy," written in June, 1919, Gramsci wrote:

> The socialist state already exists potentially in the institutions of social life characteristic of the exploited laboring class. To bind together these institutions, to coordinate them and subordinate them to a hierarchy of competencies and powers, *strongly centralizing them while still respecting their necessary autonomy and articulations,* means to create already, beginning now, a true and proper workers' democracy in opposition . . . to the bourgeois state. This hierarchy is even now prepared to replace the bourgeois state in all its essential functions of managing and leading the national patrimony.[5]

Having posed the question of how to create a "workers' democracy" in Italy, Gramsci goes on to observe that, while the Socialist party and its companion trade union organization together lead the Italian workers' movement, their influence is exercised only indirectly on the great mass of workers. The party and the union exercise their power by virtue of their prestige as well as through authoritarian pressure.

Gramsci explains to the party and trade union bureaucracy that although eventually the party and the trade unions will presumably absorb the whole of the working class, if they want to see the revolution occur in the first place, they had better welcome developments taking place in the factories to further the cause of workers' democracy. He goes on to hail the internal commissions as organs of workers' democracy which, once developed and enriched, can become the organs of proletarian power, replacing all the functions of management and administration now carried out by the capitalist elite. All over Italy the workers, he declares, should proceed at once to elect workshop commissars and then have them elect internal commissions under the rallying cries of "All Power in the Factory Committees" and "All State Power to the Workers' and Peasants' Councils."[6]

Gramsci proceeds to describe how the entire country could be organized around such councils, the aim being to elect one delegate for

5. Gramsci, "Workers' Democracy," June 21, 1919, in *SPW*[1], 65. Emphasis added.
6. *Ibid.,* 66–67.

every fifteen workers, thereby, through a series of elections, ending up with a committee of factory delegates representing every aspect of labor (manual workers, clerical workers, technicians). Workers such as waiters, cabdrivers, tram conductors, railroad employees, street sweepers, and clerks who labor neither in the factory nor on the farm could be organized in committees at the neighborhood level.

Far from considering "Workers' Democracy" a proposal written in granite, however, Gramsci stresses that "these rapid notes" should stimulate thought and action. He emphasizes that only communist practice can provide an integral and concrete solution to the problems of socialist life. Only through a general discussion that transforms and unifies the consciences of each participant can the ground be laid for a new type of state. Unless discussion, organization, and discipline precede action, "dictatorship of the proletariat" will remain only an empty phrase.[7] Gramsci's use of this famous phrase from the *Communist Manifesto* illustrates the influence both of Marx's writings and Lenin's advent to power. As the last chapter demonstrated, Gramsci had no bookish interest in Marx's writings *per se,* but he became deeply stirred by them when they seemed to have born fruit, as in the October Revolution and subsequent developments in Russia.

Gramsci's September, 1919, article addressed to the workshop delegates at the Fiat factories in Turin and Milan claimed no small role for *L'Ordine Nuovo* in bringing about the new form for administering the two plants. However, Gramsci was under no illusion that his newspaper had *caused* the new movement to happen; rather, *L'Ordine Nuovo* had helped to give concrete shape to an aspiration latent in the consciousness of the working masses.[8]

To Gramsci, the action taken by the workers to create their own organs of self-government in the factories of northern Italy, in the fields of Russia, and in the mines of England sounded capitalism's death knell. The working class "now conceives the possibility of *doing things on its own (fare da sè)* and of doing them well." Far from continuing to need the paternalistic rule of the bourgeoisie, the working class was daily acquiring an awareness, even a certain conviction, that it alone could save the entire world from ruin and desolation.[9]

7. *Ibid.,* 67.
8. Gramsci, "To the Workshop Delegates," September 13, 1919, in *SPW*[1], 94.
9. *Ibid.,* 95.

The newly elected workshop representatives would be responsible for keeping discipline in the workplace in order to maintain and increase productivity just as the previous inspectors had done. The discipline enforced by the new representatives would be qualitatively different from that of the old order, however, in that it would be based on labor's rights rather than on property rights. Whereas the managers appointed by the owners looked down on the workers from a position of privilege, the new workshop representatives would look up to their fellow workers who freely elected them.[10]

Gramsci ends this message to the newly elected workshop commissars in the great plants of Turin and Milan by sketching a pyramid of assemblies and committees to be set up in the future. "For every group of workplaces, for every group of factories, for every city, for every region," appropriate representative councils will be organized, culminating in a "supreme national workers' council," to the end that the entire working class will be prepared to conquer and to govern.[11]

GRAMSCI'S "PROGRAM OF THE WORKSHOP REPRESENTATIVES"

In November, 1919, *L'Ordine Nuovo* published the program of the first quasi-general assembly of the workshop representatives in the Turin factories. Although Gramsci subsequently credited the program to a study group of the inspectors themselves, he himself was the author. The program's preamble states in part that "this assembly does not arrogate to itself the right to formulate a definitive program." On the contrary, any "program of revolutionary work" should be open to "continuous and even radical innovation," its whole purpose being to move Italy to undertake "the practical experiment of realizing a communist society." Gramsci shows his aversion to fixed schemes in this passage and in the subsequent declaration that "the program, we repeat, should not and will not be definitive. Future regional and then national assemblies should revise it continuously, developing the concepts contained in it."[12]

The most important of the program's six "declarations of principle"

---

10. *Ibid.*, 97.
11. *Ibid.*
12. Gramsci, "The Program of the Workshop Delegates," November 8, 1919, in *SPW*[1], 114–15.

is that the factory council members are the sole social (economic and political) representatives of the proletarian class because they have been elected by the universal suffrage of all the workers at their workplaces. The council system is applicable to every organism of production, even in agriculture. The program envisages a system of workers' councils extending from the smallest work unit through assemblies at the city, regional, and national levels, culminating in a worldwide assembly.[13]

Other provisions call for the continuation of trade and craft unions as presently organized so long as the order of capitalist production reigns. The council system is organized on a factory or plant basis; the trade unions are organized on a category basis, meaning, for example, that all textile workers in the nation would be in the same union. The CGL will continue to negotiate for better hours, wages, and working conditions for given categories of workers. Above all, the bitter experience of the Hungarian Revolution, wherein the councils and the unions fought each other, must not be repeated.[14]

One of the program's more notable passages declares that the Turin workers organized into unions reject as artificial, parliamentary-like, and false any other system than that of the councils for finding out the will of the organized masses. "Workers' democracy does not base itself on [mere] numbers and on the bourgeois concept of the citizen, but on the functions performed by the laborer, *i.e.*, on the order that the working class naturally assumes in the process of production."[15] Here Gramsci and his study group are intent on combating the claims of the trade unions to represent the will of their members simply through having their bureaucrats vote *en bloc* for resolutions at conferences, while they may never have asked the opinion of their rank and file members. The declaration also states that the vote of the passive, ill-informed, and indifferent worker should not have the same weight as that of the active, informed, and involved one. One of Gramsci's earliest articles, entitled "The Indifferent Ones," constituted a withering attack upon individuals who stood aside, refusing to become fully involved in the controversies around them.[16]

Other provisions of this elaborate program established the equal

13. *Ibid.*, 116.
14. *Ibid.*, 115–17.
15. *Ibid.*, 117.
16. Gramsci, "Indifferenti," February 11, 1917, in *LCF*, 13–15.

right to vote for all workers, whether manual or intellectual, and specified that administrative and directive personnel be divided into engineers, technical supervisers, draftsmen, and clerical personnel of various types. Some middle-management and white-collar employees were clearly included under Gramsci's definition of the proletariat. The general regulations for the new factory council system called for election of the factory's executive commission (the old five-member internal commission) every six months and also provided that a majority of workers could vote to recall instantly any workshop inspector or executive committee member. Only those union members committed to the class struggle were eligible to run for membership on the factory councils and, as a result, to serve on the new factory executive commission. This new workers' executive commission would have a permanent office. Its members, given leave from work, would collect and act upon the complaints received from the members of the factory council. The entire work force would unite around the instructions of the executive commission.[17]

Throughout the program various sops were thrown to the PSI and the CGL. *Avanti!,* the Socialist party newspaper, was recognized as the sole political daily of the region. Also, the program required all unions to affiliate with the CGL. This can only have disturbed trade union officials, for the factory councils would be the organs of the revolution, and the unions' role would be substantially curtailed after the revolution.[18]

GRAMSCI'S EFFORTS TO RENEW THE SOCIALIST PARTY

In January, 1920, Gramsci authored another program, this one concerned with the failure of the Socialist party actively to support the factory council movement. This document, entitled "Program of Action for Turin's Socialist Section,"[19] castigated the national organization of the Socialist party for failing to grasp the revolutionary significance of Turin's factory council movement, for allowing the term *workers' councils* to be adopted indiscriminantly, and for cooperating with the liberal-capitalist regime. Gramsci asserted that commitment to the class

17. Gramsci, "The Program of the Workshop Delegates," 118–23.
18. *Ibid.,* 124, 117.
19. Gramsci, "Program of Action for Turin's Socialist Section," January 24–31, 1920, in *SPW*[1], 158–61.

struggle must take precedence over temporary gains in wages, hours, and working conditions for only a small percentage of the total work force. Turin's Socialist party organization must press the national PSI "to promote the creation of workers' and peasants' councils in the whole of Italy on the initial basis of promoting trade union action no longer directed toward winning improvements in wages and hours, but toward imposing . . . proletarian oversight (*controllo*) over the instruments of labor and of industrial and agricultural production."[20]

Far from discounting or eliminating the party's role in the revolution in favor of the councils, Gramsci argued in 1919–1920 that the party should be the main initiator of a truly revolutionary councils' movement. Achievement of oversight (the Italian word *controllo* has a less heavy-handed meaning than the English word *control*) of the instruments of production by the proletariat through the kind of council system outlined in the previously discussed "Program of the Workshop Representatives" would, if anything, increase the party's influence on the working class, Gramsci argued. That will be the result, provided that the Turin party organization promotes in every league and union the formation of what might be called "permanent groups of Communists." In other words, the flabby PSI bureaucracy would have to transform itself into a revolutionary force.

The party could collaborate closely with these groups to defeat those individuals and groups, the reformist Socialists among them, who have no interest in bringing about a new order but who are eager only to gain a better place for themselves in the old one. New and better mechanisms of workers' control and communist management of production can be created, so that a new phase in the history of the class struggle in Italy can commence. Instead of leaving the party's relationship with the workers in the factory to unstable and *ad hoc* alliances that may change with the circumstances, that relationship henceforth would be based on an intimate fusion and identity of programs.[21]

Gramsci's January, 1920, program of action for Turin's Socialist party organization recognized the very real danger that fascism or an equivalent movement might ascend to power:

> We hold that the bourgeoisie cannot evade the destiny that awaits it except through . . . a reactionary and military dictatorship, and that sooner

20. *Ibid.*, 159.
21. *Ibid.*, 160.

or later it will have recourse to just such a policy. . . . If it is to protect the proletariat and its conquests . . . [the party] must prepare itself materially.[22]

"Material" preparation was a Gramscian euphemism for "arming the proletariat" and creating a strong movement of poor peasants and small land owners to work in solidarity with the industrial movement.

In May, 1920, in his article "Toward a Renewal of the Socialist Party," Gramsci, writing on behalf of Turin's city and provincial representatives to the national council meeting of the PSI, urged that the Italian Socialist party leadership wake up and recognize that accommodation to the bourgeois agenda and muddling through will not work, because "the present order or production and distribution no longer satisfies the elementary exigencies of human life." Only "the armed force of the bourgeois state" sustains the old order, and "the present phase of the class struggle in Italy is the phase that precedes either the conquest of power by the revolutionary proletariat . . . or a ferocious reaction by the propertied class or the governing caste."[23]

The task of the Socialist party is to coordinate the national resistance to the old order. Now in its twilight, that order will use every violent means in a misguided attempt to forestall the inevitable. However, the party has failed miserably to provide such needed coordination. The leading organs of the Socialist party have revealed their total incomprehension of the present crisis. Instead of assisting in the old order's demise, the party has been merely a spectator of events:

> [The Socialist party] never has its own opinion to express in accordance with the revolutionary theses of Marxism and the Communist International; it never issues rallying cries to give a general direction to and to unify and concentrate the revolutionary action of the masses.[24]

Even after the Congress of Bologna of October, 1919, wherein the party accepted the Comintern's "21 points" imposed on all Socialist or Communist parties as a condition for membership, the PSI "has remained a merely parliamentary party, transfixed between the narrow limits of bourgeois democracy and exclusively preoccupied with the governing caste's superficial political affirmations,"[25] Gramsci insisted.

22. *Ibid.*, 161.
23. Gramsci, "Toward a Renewal of the Socialist Party," May 8, 1920, in *SPW*[1], 191.
24. *Ibid.*
25. *Ibid.*, 192.

Gramsci's May, 1920, proposal for renewing the Italian Socialist party repeatedly stresses his view that for a revolution to be successful it must be led by a *revolutionary* party. Gramsci was a party man first and a conciliarist second. However, Gramsci extolled the worker's councils against what was then his party's national leadership, because the latter had turned the PSI into just another parliamentary party passively awaiting the bourgeois governing caste to set the agenda. Far from elevating the faculty councils above the party, Gramsci thought that a truly revolutionary party should be forming nuclei in the factories, on the farm, in the offices, in the mines, and in the military barracks. Through the high quality and timeliness of their proposals, these nuclei would gain the acceptance of the masses of the working class, organized in councils.[26]

The end, or aim, of the revolution, Gramsci explained in his July, 1920, article "Two Revolutions" was

> the construction of a new order of relations of production and distribution, a new order wherein class divisions become impossible and whose systematic development tends to coincide with . . . the exhaustion of state power and with the . . . dissolution of the political organization set up to defend the proletarian class which itself will dissolve, becoming coextensive with humanity.[27]

Viewed in terms of the end of the revolutionary process, both the councils and the party are means. Neither one is ultimate, but both are instruments for overthrowing the bourgeois system of economic and social relationships. The construction of a new politics of inclusion eventually embracing all of humanity was Gramsci's goal in 1920, just as it had been in his graduation essay "Oppressed and Oppressors" at Cagliari in 1911.

Although Gramsci had predicted in July, 1919, that the factory councils movement would spread throughout Italy, a year later he wrote a report to the Comintern acknowledging the movement's failure. He blamed this result squarely on the national leadership of the Italian Socialist party:

> At the head of the movement to form factory councils were the Communists belonging to the Socialist party and trade unions. . . . However, the movement encountered fierce opposition from union bureaucrats, from

26. *Ibid.*, 196.
27. Gramsci, "Two Revolutions," July 3, 1920, in *SPW*[1], 305.

the Socialist party leadership, and from *Avanti!* These people based their polemic on the difference between the concept of the factory council and that of the *soviet*. Their conclusions had a purely theoretical, abstract, and bureaucratic aspect. *Behind their high-sounding phrases lay the desire to keep the masses from participating directly in the revolutionary struggle.* . . .

Therefore the Turin movement did not succeed in expanding beyond its local environment, because the unions' entire bureaucratic mechanism was set in motion to prevent the working class in other parts of Italy from following its example. The Turin movement was derided, sneered at, slandered, and criticized in every way. The bitter criticisms by the union bureaucrats and Socialist party leaders encouraged the capitalists to struggle all the more vigorously against the proletariat of Turin and its factory councils.[28]

Gramsci's repeated inveighing against the Socialist party leadership and the union bureaucracy on the grounds that they sought to keep the masses from participating directly in the revolutionary struggle is in line with his vision of a new politics of inclusion. The major reason for his advocacy of a separate Communist party undoubtedly was his conviction that the dominant Socialist party faction—the so-called maximalists, then headed by Giacinto Serrati—was incapable of overcoming a paternalistic and elitist attitude toward the working masses.

In late August, 1920, on the eve of the occupations by the workers of the Fiat factories in Turin and Milan, Antonio Gramsci discussed the evolution of what he called the "program" of *L'Ordine Nuovo* regarding the workers' council movement. In this context he attacked the idea his coeditor, Angelo Tasca, had of culture as bookish. While the factory council movement was developing under their noses, Tasca was arguing that the proletariat should study Louis Blanc, Eugene Fournier, and other "worn-out" pieces of intellectual "junk." Tasca's idea of socialist culture, then, was to recall for today's workers the third-rate ideas of past "socialist" thinkers. Such a program smacked of condescension. The workers did not need a course on eccentric and utopian political ideas of the past. Rather, the proletariat needed assistance in drawing out the creative possibilities in the factory council movement *of the present*. Proletarian culture consisted in creative action here and now directed at drawing out the proletariat's potential for self-liberation.[29]

28. Gramsci, "The Turin Factory Councils Movement," March 14, 1921, in *SPW*[1], 318–19. Emphasis added. This report was written by Gramsci much earlier (July, 1920).

29. Gramsci, "Program for *L'Ordine Nuovo*," August 14, 1920, in *SPW*[1], 291–98.

Throughout Gramsci's involvement in the factory council movement, one is repeatedly impressed with how he related his stands to concrete, specific events. To him, the factory council movement was no mere
idea; it was an *event* that had occurred independent of any would-be intellectual's devising.

Using an architectural metaphor, Gramsci describes how

> *L'Ordine Nuovo* became for us and for the many who followed us "the
> journal of the factory councils." The workers loved *L'Ordine Nuovo* . . .
> because they recognized in its articles a part, the better part, of them-
> selves . . . and *because the articles were not like architecture that is cold and
> intellectual. . . .*[30]

Antonio Gramsci would have nothing to do with an architecture for
a new politics that gives a mechanical, lifeless, cold, or merely intellectual impression. Rather, that architecture must reflect the aspirations
and passions of those living human beings who have been excluded
from wealth and power, confined within ugly, standardized housing, or
"nonhovels," and chained to boring, routinized jobs that dull their
mind and spirit.

If the workers' councils and the party were alike essential to the creation of a revolutionary new order, what precisely was the difference between them? For Gramsci that difference consists in the party's volun-
tary character. Both the party and the unions have a contractual basis,
with individual workers deciding whether or not to adhere to them.
The councils, on the other hand, arise morphologically out of the structure of the workplace. Those who are poor are forced to work in order
to live. Up to now the poor have had to work under conditions set for
them by others (the employer and the union). Through the councils, on
the other hand, the ordinary worker can participate directly in continuously supervising, modifying, and improving the conditions under
which he works. For the first time he experiences himself as an active,
autonomous force in history.

Ignazio Silone, who knew Gramsci at the time of the factory occupations in September, 1920, has written that "his idea of the 'soviets' was
very beautiful but completely imaginary. While he spoke of the [Rus-
sian] soviets as if they were still the same as they had been in 1917, in

30. *Ibid.,* 293. Emphasis added.

truth they had preserved only the name." [31] Judging from what Gramsci actually wrote about the workers' councils, Silone failed to understand Gramsci's views. Gramsci did not advocate the factory council system for Italy out of a desire to copy the soviets, whether of 1917 or later, in the USSR. Rather, he thought the workers' council movement was indigenous to Italian conditions and that, given the proper support from the whole socialist movement, it could have spread to the rest of the country, including the countryside. Here one needs to recall Gramsci's first article on "Workers' Democracy," wherein he wrote that no one could lay out a detailed, procrustean blueprint of what such a democracy should be. If after 1920 Gramsci ceased emphasizing the councils, it was not because he ever abandoned the idea that they were in principle worthy of support and possible of realization. Ever the political architect, he moved on from one set of designs to another as the landscape and materials changed. [32]

GRAMSCI ON THE FACTORY OCCUPATIONS OF SEPTEMBER, 1920

The 1920 factory occupations in Turin and Milan were preceded on August 20 by an act of defiance by skilled workers against the Fiat Company's refusal even to consider a wage increase. Fearing a lockout, the workers reported every day but did no work. On August 31 management declared a lockout. On September 1 the workers occupied the factories around the clock, declared them under the direction of the factory councils, and began to produce automobiles at about three-fifths the normal rate. Most white-collar workers did not participate in the occupation.

The first factory council had been elected in early September, 1919, at Turins' Brevetti plant. Now a year later, the workers in major automobile factories in Turin and Milan had for months staged a spectacular demonstration of their capacity for self-management. When, as a result of a referendum supported by the PSI national leadership, the vote was

31. Remembrance by Ignazio Silone, in Mimma Paulesu Quercioli (ed.), *Gramsci vivo* (Milan, 1977), 187.

32. Joseph Femia has improperly maintained on p. 479 of his article "The Gramsci Phenomenon," cited in note 2, that Gramsci later abandoned the workers' council concept altogether. Only if he abandoned his commitment to building a new politics from below or outside the currently powerful structures of the state would such an assertion be true. This entire book should be sufficient rebuttal to Femia's contention.

taken to return control of the factories to the owners in exchange for vague promises of national legislation supporting "workers' control," the Italian factory council movement no longer held out any hope of being the catalyst for a new participation by those at the periphery.

Although Gramsci had called the factory seizures an event of major historical importance, he had also emphasized that the proletariat lacked the military means to defend the conquest, and he had urged workers not to confuse the occupations with the revolution itself. The main value of the occupations was to prove to their bourgeois op-pressors what they, the workers, had already learned from their experi-ence with the councils—that the working class was capable of running something as complicated as a modern factory without the benefit of higher bourgeois management.[33]

TOWARD A SEPARATE COMMUNIST PARTY

In an article entitled "The Communist Party," published near the begin-ning of the factory occupations in early September, Gramsci came close to advocating explicitly and publicly secession from the PSI and the creation of a separate Communist party.[34] Far from representing a shift in Gramsci's attitudes about the importance of the councils, however, this article explicitly linked the party to the council system. To Gramsci, the party was an expression of the proletarian vanguard, the same van-guard of the working class that created the soviets in Russia and the councils in Italy to begin with.[35]

> In Russia, the fusion of the unions with the factory councils took place about six months after the October Revolution. Today, after three years of the workers' state, there is now discussion on whether the time has come to pay great attention once more to the councils in order to prevent new forms of syndicalism and to combat the new bureaucratic sedimenta-tions that have been forming for three years.[36]

In summary, Gramsci thought the factory councils were the first stir-rings of a new consciousness in the workers. He believed that through

33. Gramsci, in Sergio Caprioglio (ed.), *Antonio Gramsci: Scritti, 1915–1921* (Milan, 1968), 130–32.

34. Gramsci, "The Communist Party," September 4 and 9, 1920, in *SPW*[1], 330–39.

35. *Ibid.,* 336.

36. Gramsci, "Unions and Councils," March 5, 1921, in *SPW*[2], 19–22.

the councils the workers could gain further confidence in their capability to create new modes of production. They would be tools of the capitalist system no longer. Furthermore, by bringing together highly skilled and unskilled workers, the workers' councils could serve as a place for training the unskilled and for including them as full-fledged members of the workers' movement. Gramsci also saw the factory councils as an international phenomenon, the embryo of the eventual worldwide communist revolution. Finally, he viewed the councils as a fruitful field in which the party might pursue a policy of alliances with other social forces, because the councils were open to workers regardless of ideological or party orientation. Specifically, this meant that he defended the presence of anarchist, reformist Socialist, and *popolari* (Catholic) workers in the councils.[37]

From the beginning, Gramsci viewed the councils from the perspective of his overall theory of the new politics of inclusion. As we saw in the previous chapters, Gramsci had acquired this perspective of a new politics long before the councils became a central issue. It is crucial to recognize that for Gramsci the workers' councils were not part of his own abstract, rationalistic scheme for a utopian society. The revolution could not be secured simply by establishing any particular institution, conciliar or otherwise, for it involved first and foremost the diffusion of a new idea of politics—not an idea in the merely abstract sense of the term, but a new style of life emerging out of the concrete, immediate sufferings and struggles of the oppressed.

The relative importance of the councils and their relationship to the party and the union did become a major point of contention between Gramsci and the Neapolitan engineer Amadeo Bordiga, however. Bordiga's position can be summed up in his article sarcastically entitled "Seize Power or Seize the Factory?" of February 22, 1920, in his publication named (ironically) *Il Soviet:*

> It is rumored that factory councils . . . [took] over the management of the workshops [in Liguria, where the workers seized a factory and kept it running]. . . . We would not like the working masses to get the idea that all they need to do to take over the factories and get rid of the capitalists is to set up councils. The factory will be conquered by the working class—and not only by the work force employed in it, which would be

37. Gramsci, "The Problem of Power," November 29, 1919, *SPW*[1], 134.

too weak and noncommunist—*only after the working class as a whole has seized political power.*[38]

To Antonio Gramsci, Bordiga's words perfectly exemplified philistine, or vulgar, Marxism, which lacked the flexibility to respond to real historical developments. According to Gramsci, Bordiga's ideological blinkers rendered him incapable of attending to opportunities for expanding revolutionary consciousness right under his nose.

Gramsci's involvement in the Turin factory council movement was a logical extension of his idea of a new politics. The councils encouraged hitherto marginal groups to participate actively in the mainstream of society. The councils appealed to Gramsci as enclaves wherein relations of equality could be established between assembly-line workers and technicians, and where jobs could be redesigned so that no one would have to perform a task as monotonous as "the clicking of a set of rosary beads."[39] To the extent that institutions like the councils took hold, capitalist competition would gradually become redundant, along with the accompanying invidious comparisons between winners and losers. Everyone would be indispensable, from the most "civil" of engineers to the most ignorant worker.

As the architect of a new politics, Gramsci made various sketches for the new construction. The building could be designed in a variety of ways; if it contributed physically and spiritually to eradicating claims of prestige and assumptions of deference, the details did not matter. Gramsci was no Jeremy Bentham devising the panopticon model prison. On the contrary, the Sardinian revolutionary sought to liberate everyone from the prison of the politics of exclusion. The councils were not ends but means for acquiring a communist consciousness.

Gramsci's writings about the councils convey the further lesson that he did not simply respond to events; he developed a method for interpreting them and communicated the results of using that method to the workers themselves. When the movement for greater worker participation began in the great Turin factories, Gramsci placed it in broader perspective by comparing it with the shop steward movement in Great Britain and with developments in other countries as well as in the

38. Amadeo Bordiga, "Seize Power or Seize the Factory?" February 22, 1920, in *SPW*[1], 236. Emphasis added.
39. Gramsci, "The Communist Party," 333.

USSR. He did more than describe the movement, however; he drew out its revolutionary implications. As we have seen, he was the chief drafter of the September, 1919, communique to the workshop representatives of the Fiat Centro and Brevetti plants. The communique is remarkable in seeking to draw the Fiat workers' attention to the implications of their actions for workers and peasants and the excluded and powerless everywhere in the world. Gramsci found implicit in the workers' councils the vision of a new politics of inclusion, and it was this latent universality—so different from the particularism of the trade union seeking special advantages for its members—that excited and drew him to the councils.

On March 27, 1924, Gramsci wrote to Togliatti from Vienna about refounding *L'Ordine Nuovo*. Noting that the paper could no longer be the organ for a specific movement—*i.e.,* that of the workers' councils— he still contended that "the *specific* program of the journal should continue to be the factory and the organization of the factory."[40] The Gramsci who in 1924 proposed the government of workers and peasants as the rallying cry for Italian communism was still the same Gramsci who had designed a new architecture for the factory in 1919–1920. Only now he would focus his attention on situating the radical restructuring of industrial work in the larger landscape of the national and international political and economic life.

In *Antonio Gramsci and the Revolution That Failed,* Martin Clark declares that Gramsci "was opposed in principle to factory seizure as a method of class struggle."[41] To speak of Antonio Gramsci as having been opposed in principle to any form of class struggle originating with the workers amounts to mistaking his whole manner of thinking.

The takeover of major factories by workers below the white-collar level in northern Italy appears to have begun as a protest to the seizure of Milan's Romeo works by the police on August 30 and the proclamation of a general lockout by the factory owners on September 1, 1920.[42] The occupations—chiefly in Milan, Turin, and Genoa—gave the workers the opportunity to keep the plants running without the aid of top management. One month later, on October 4, the workers left the factories. They had gained only a promise from Premier Giovanni Giolitti

40. Palmiro Togliatti, *Gramsci* (Rome, 1965), 256.
41. Clark, *Antonio Gramsci and the Revolution That Failed,* 162.
42. Hoare, Notes to *SPW*[1], 386–87. The entirety of n. 129 is relevant.

that he would introduce a bill guaranteeing workers' control over the industry.

As we have seen, Gramsci's reaction to the occupations was complicated. He thought it crucial for the workers to be aware of the enormous risks involved, but he despised the Socialist party trade unions for giving in so easily. According to Teresa Noce, Gramsci harshly criticized his allies, including Togliatti, who participated in the General Confederation of Labor meeting where the decision was made to abandon the factories, for "not having fought *hard enough*, even if they were in a small minority" against the decision.[43]

Clark's contention that Gramsci was "opposed in principle to factory seizure as a method of class struggle"[44] flies in the face of Gramsci's article hailing the factory occupations as "a historical development of greatest significance" and as "*a necessary movement in the revolutionary process and the class struggle.*"[45]

For all his praise of the occupations, Gramsci went out of his way to call on the workers in the seized factories to use "the greatest possible cold-bloodedness" (*il massimo sangue freddo*) in choosing their course of action.[46] They were to have no illusions that by this one act they had achieved a communist society. The occupations were portents of the revolution but not the revolution itself.

Ignazio Silone was a party comrade during the September factory occupations. He has given this description of one of many speeches by Gramsci to the workers during this period:

> We went together to the Bianchi factory [in Milan]. Gramsci was warmly introduced, and the workers listened to him with great respect. I knew that Gramsci . . . was hesitant to speak in public, especially before large crowds. Later he would not even speak at [the Congress of] Livorno. . . . But this time, in response to the interest and anxiety evident in the faces of the workers, he spoke.
>
> He spoke in a very curious and unusual way. He said that at that time there were many people in Italy who fantasized about revolution and who spoke as if it were something easy to achieve. He, however, did not know how things were going to come out in the end. In Milan and Turin

43. Teresa Noce, in Quercioli (ed.), *Gramsci Vivo*, 84.
44. Clark, *Antonio Gramsci and the Revolution That Failed*, 162.
45. Gramsci, "The Occupation," September 2, 1920, in *SPW*[1], 328. Emphasis added.
46. *Ibid.*, 326.

there was a great deal of enthusiasm among the workers and a great deal of fear among the bourgeoisie. Therefore it was not surprising that talk of revolution was in the air; but it was important to keep in mind that there were also dangers and risks involved. The important thing was to remain united no matter what happened. "If the reaction gains the upper hand," he said, "it will be easier to resist if we are united; if we are divided, everything will be more difficult."[47]

Gramsci's was a historicism of eventual, not ephemeral, success. His was a pragmatism of long strides. Despite the fact that the occupation of the factories may have aided the rise of fascism, Gramsci's faith in the capacity of the ordinary worker to create a new order never flagged. His vision of a new politics centered on those excluded from prestige, wealth, and power. What was called by Hegel and Marx "alienation" was for Gramsci not a general property of the modern spirit. It was the result of a twisting of that spirit in a way that left the majority in exile, strangers in their own land. He believed that through active participation from below in shaping their own conditions of work and life, the exiles for the first time in history could come home.

47. Ignazio Silone, in Quercioli (ed.), *Grasmci vivo,* 244–45.

V ✔ From Livorno to Moscow: Gramsci Helps Found the Party, 1921–1922

Antonio Gramsci is today known as the founder of the Italian Communist party (PCd'I), a correct designation if important qualifications are added. At the party's founding Congress of Livorno in January, 1921, Gramsci was by no means the principal actor; that role fell to Amadeo Bordiga. Gramsci deserves to be called *the* founder only in relation to the process of establishing the party as a viable, independent political force. As we shall see, this process took several years to complete itself.

How did Antonio Gramsci conceive of the new party? What place did it occupy in the architecture of a new politics? In the next four chapters we will follow Gramsci's trail as we try to answer these questions. We must take care not to become preoccupied with issues of a mainly doctrinal and sectarian character, however, for we are concerned not with the history of the Italian Communist party, but with Gramsci's vision of a new politics and the place of "the party" therein.

THE PLACE OF THE PARTY IN GRAMSCI'S ARCHITECTURE OF A NEW POLITICS

In his famous 1937 address commemorating Antonio Gramsci's death, Palmiro Togliatti observed, "Above all, Gramsci was and remains a party man."[1] Togliatti's phrase "party man" (*uomo di partito*) should not be interpreted as implying an uncritical or slavish devotion to "the

---

1. Palmiro Togliatti, *Antonio Gramsci* (Rome, 1965), 11.

party." Rather, the phrase means first that Gramsci never conceived of himself as a bookish intellectual, but rather as an active partisan functioning in behalf of the revolution of the masses at society's periphery. Second, the phrase "party man" means that Gramsci saw himself as a man of the Communist party, as he understood and helped to shape that institution.

Ever since the overthrow of the czarist autocracy in February, 1917, Gramsci had been a man of the *Communist* party. Furthermore, he had consistently supported the Bolsheviks and had defended them after their seizure of power in October, 1917, against those Marxist economic determinists who maintained that such a seizure was premature because Russia had just emerged from feudalism and needed to go through the capitalist phase. Although he tended to be a loner in the factional struggles in the PSI, he had been closer to the "revolutionary and intransigent faction," later renamed the "Communist faction," than with either the maximalists or the reformists, the other two main groupings of the PSI. Amadeo Bordiga, with whom Gramsci was later locked in a bitter struggle, had founded his Communist faction immediately after the October Revolution, and Gramsci had attended its first conference. Italian police reports listed him in April to June, 1918, as a Communist "subversive."[2] In July, 1919, Gramsci gave prominent attention in *L'Ordine Nuovo* to the program of the Communist faction.

Through all the intricacies of Socialist party life, Gramsci held fast to two qualities: First, he never surrendered his mind to any party bureaucracy, national or international. He remained a "critical Communist" to the last. Second, he conceived of the Communist party as above all *international* in scope. This second aspect is well captured by Guido Zamis, Gramsci's comrade during his stay in Vienna, who wrote:

> When Togliatti described Gramsci above all as a "party man," he meant by such a designation to specify precisely that Gramsci was a man of the Communist International. He regarded the Italian party as a section of a much greater party, a world party.[3]

From 1917 until the spring of 1920 Gramsci had been strongly opposed to the creation of an Italian Communist party in opposition to the PSI. He and his *L'Ordine Nuovo* group thought instead that the

2. Sergio Caprioglio, "Cronologia," in *LDC,* xxiv.
3. Guido Zamis, *Gramsci zur Politik, Geschichte, Kultur* (Frankfurt, 1980), 121.

PSI's Communist faction should fight for increased influence in the PSI itself. He opposed purist ideas about the party and rejected demands by Bordiga and others that the PSI abstain from elections on the grounds that Parliament was a bourgeois institution.

By September, 1920, however, Gramsci had changed his mind. He called for the Communist faction to become "in word and deed the Italian Communist party, a section of the Third Communist International." The break should come at the next PSI congress, he argued. He was fed up with the passivity of the PSI bureaucracy in the face of spontaneous actions of the masses. The party had become "nothing but a notary public" dutifully recording what the masses were doing.[4]

In a remarkable article entitled "The Communist Party," Gramsci declared:

> In the present period, the Communist party is the only institution that can seriously be compared with the religious communities of primitive Christianity. To the degree that the party already exists on an international scale, one can attempt a comparison . . . between the militants for the City of God and those for the City of Man. The Communist is certainly not inferior to the Christian of the catacombs.[5]

Continuing, he insists that "the fighters for the working class are greater than the fighters for God . . ." because Communists must draw on their "reserves of character and determination . . . without looking for any reward." Thus, Rosa Luxemburg and Karl Liebknecht are "greater than the greatest saints of Christ."[6]

Christianity and communism, of course, had fundamentally different goals and ways of relating to the world. Communism's cause, asserted Gramsci, is "concrete, human, and restricted" by comparison with Christianity. Communists have a definite goal, while the early Christian's goal was allegedly mystical and ephemeral.[7]

Christianity proclaims its miracles, but communism knows the true

---

4. Gramsci, "Il partito comunista," September 4 and 9, 1920, in *ON*, 154–63, and *SPW*[1], 330–39. Where two sets of page numbers are given in the footnotes of this chapter, the first set refers to the Italian original in *ON* and the second to the English translation in *SPW*[1] and *SPW*[2]. The author sometimes prefers his own translation, however.

5. *Ibid.*, 156 and 332.

6. *Ibid.*, 156–57 and 332. Rosa Luxemburg and Karl Liebknecht, leaders of the Spartacist League in Germany, had been assassinated in 1919.

7. *Ibid.*, 156 and 332.

miracle to be that of "the worker who takes charge each day of his own intellectual autonomy . . . by struggling against fatigue, against boredom, and against the monotony of a job that tends to mechanize and thus to kill his inner life."[8] The Communist party helps the exhausted and degraded worker to pick himself up off the floor and look at conditions as they really are, instead of how the capitalist tells him they are:

> The Communist party is the instrument . . . of inner liberation through which the worker is transformed from *executor* to *initiator,* from mass to leader and guide, from arm to brain and will.[9]

Early Christianity helped the slave

> to attain his own liberation by participating in a Christian community, where he concretely experienced himself as an equal, a brother, because he was the son of the same father. Similarly, *the worker* who participates in the Communist party "discovers" and "invents" original ways of life. . . . [He] becomes an organizer rather than someone who is organized, and *feels that he forms a vanguard* that runs ahead and draws all the mass of the people after it.[10]

Gramsci's choice of words in the above passage is interesting. It is not the party bureaucracy that becomes "*the* vanguard," but the worker who by participating in the party experiences himself as part of "*a* vanguard" (*un avanguardia*) of the revolution. In this article Gramsci once more denounces the idea that the party is a bureaucracy independent of the workers; instead the party is the workers' natural habitat. Far from thinking the councils antithetical to the party—the Communist party in the making, that is, as distinguished from the sterile Socialist party bureaucracy—Gramsci perceives the party as the councils' logical extension and completion.[11] The vanguard is a force *composed of* rather than *forced on* the workers. The most energetic and self-conscious workers make up the Communist party and pull the masses along with them.

By comparing early Christianity and modern communism, Gramsci aimed to accomplish several objectives. First, he wanted to inspire the

8. *Ibid.,* 157 and 333.
9. *Ibid.* Emphasis added.
10. *Ibid.,* 157–58 and 333. Emphasis added.
11. *Ibid.,* 160–61 and 336. Here Gramsci writes of the Communist party as an expression of the proletarian vanguard, a very different idea from Lenin's notion of the party as *the* vanguard of the proletariat.

supporters of the Communist faction by drawing a parallel between the two movements. Just as Christianity had begun as a tiny, persecuted sect at the fringes of ancient society and had proceeded to conquer the mighty Roman Empire, so communism had begun as a small, persecuted movement on the fringes of modern society and had gone on to conquer the imposing Russian czarist autocracy. Although no hard and fast predictions could be made about when communism would be victorious in Italy and other European countries, and although the means used would vary according to the circumstances, there was no doubt that a revolution of comparable magnitude to that made by Christianity would be carried out by communism.

After stressing certain parallels, however, Gramsci turned to highlighting differences between the two revolutions. Whereas Christianity had promised an eventual end to all the problems, tensions, and suffering of this worldly existence, communism envisaged a down-to-earth practical change in social relations. Christianity had left the slaves in their outward slavery; communism would combine inner and outward liberation. All forms of slavery and marginalization would be ended. Such a transformation as the Communists envisaged would not bring the Kingdom of God on earth. The heavenly City of God and the earthly City of Man were fundamentally different.

After the Communist revolution men would still be men, not angels. There was nothing sacred about the Communist revolution. It had no church. The party, the councils, and all other new institutions were mere practical tools for reversing the centuries-long domination of the few at the center over the many at the periphery.

Gramsci did not envisage the Communist party as a cadre of bureaucrats in an office building, but as a collection of human beings who are in most respects imperfect and ordinary. He spoke of himself as an "average man." For Gramsci, the party was simply the most active and energetic segment of the working class capable of rallying consent among them. Unless the basic understanding of the Communist party and its role in the revolution, as expressed above all in the article "The Communist Party," be kept always in mind, Gramsci's occasional use of military analogies will be misunderstood.

As his September 24 article, "Political Capacity," illustrates, Gramsci sometimes compares the proletarian revolution to an army with the party as its general staff. However, he never intends these metaphors to be taken literally. In "Political Capacity" Gramsci uses the military metaphor not to propose a model of how to conceive the Communist party, but as a tool with which to attack the PSI's passivity and incompetence in agreeing to hold a national referendum on whether to end the Turin factory occupations in exchange for a vague promise by Premier Giovanni Giolitti to introduce legislation on workers' control in Parliament. Gramsci was enraged at the PSI for having called for a referendum instead of having urged workers in the rest of Italy to stand behind their Turin comrades through protests, strikes, and so forth. It is in this context that the following passage, directed against the national leadership of the socialist trade union, should be interpreted:

> Revolution is like war; it must be minutely prepared by a working-class general staff, just as war is by the army's general staff. Assemblies can only ratify what has already happened, praise successes, and implacably punish failures.[12]

Placed in context, then, Gramsci's September 24 article was a bitter protest against the inability of the Italian Socialist party leadership to lead. Four years later, looking back on these events, Gramsci wrote that the Italian Socialist party had lacked "an organic activity of agitation and propaganda." The party should have responded actively to every event in the month-long factory occupation, staging mass demonstrations, calling meetings, and circulating manifestos. Above all, the party should have formed cells in the factories to encourage the workers who wanted to use the occupation as a base for expanding proletarian power. Instead, the PSI's leaders feared the mass of the workers. They insisted that nothing should be done *"without a formal order from the center,"* that is, from themselves.[13]

The above passage is from one of Gramsci's Vienna letters, which will be analyzed more fully in chapter 7. These letters are all the more significant in light of the fact that Gramsci had just returned from eighteen months in Moscow where he had served on an influential body of the Comintern. In Moscow Gramsci had every opportunity to absorb the Leninist language of "democratic centralism." Instead, the Vienna letters—which were to inform Gramsci's praxis as secretary-general of

---

12. Gramsci, "Capacità politica," September 24, 1920, in *ON*, 171, and *SPW*[1], 347–49.
13. Gramsci to Palmiro Togliatti and Umberto Terracini, February 9, 1924, in *Formazione*, 195. Emphasis added.

the Italian Communist party from August, 1924, to November, 1926—reveal continuing preoccupation with keeping the party organization flexible and responsive to initiatives from below.

Ever the opponent of a Communist party composed of purists, Gramsci's support of the workers' councils as potential instruments for making the revolution never flagged. The councils, of course, contained many workers, perhaps even a majority, who were not Communists. The role of Communist party members in the councils was to serve as a catalyst for unleashing the reserves of creative revolutionary energy in the working class as a whole. The Communists were to take the lead in mobilizing the consent of the workers but not to dictate to them.

Having said the above, it must not be assumed that Gramsci held a liberal-democratic view of party governance. Because they had been kept isolated and ignorant at society's margins, the workers as an unorganized assembly could not act authentically. Voting in the mass on referenda prepared to be ratified, the workers were as ripe for manipulation and mind control as the crowd analyzed by Gustav Le Bon in his famous study of mass psychology.

Inevitably any political theory calling for rebuilding society's foundations is going to be called elitist by those who maintain that the passive majority is satisfied with things as they are. Gramsci's recurrent refrain in numerous articles comparing the Communist and Socialist parties was that a revolutionary party needed to represent and be responsive to newly emerging social forces. Those social forces were clearly in evidence in Turin and Milan and elsewhere in Italy during the *biennio rosso*.

Gramsci remained throughout his life a vigorous opponent of the idea that a revolutionary party can guide the working class on the basis of doctrinaire formulae derived from books, whether written by Marx or Lenin or (to come down several steps) Bordiga. Unless it continuously receives fresh stimuli from the workers, the party either will perish or turn into a "police organ," he insisted.[14]

Throughout his life, Gramsci held up the Turin movement for factory councils (*consigli di fabbrica*) as an example to the nation of how the proletariat already possessed as much capacity as the bourgeoisie to run a modern economy. He later had only one regret—that he and his fel-

14. Gramsci, in *Quaderni,* 1692.

low *Ordinovisti* had not attacked the PSI leadership much more sharply than they had done, "even at the risk of being expelled." [15] Clearly, Antonio Gramsci did not believe in being a party man at any price.

In a letter from Vienna in 1924, Gramsci deplored the fact that the Italian Communist party had been formed at Livorno in January, 1921, only on a concrete and immediate issue, namely, that of whether the PSI should have expelled the reformist wing led by Filipo Turati. [16] What had been missing at Livorno was any serious discussion of what a revolutionary party should be and do.

ISOLATED IN THE PARTY

In the first two chapters we saw how Gramsci had endured a life of painful isolation during much of his early life. At first he was similarly isolated in the newly formed Italian Communist party. He was almost left off the Central Committee. [17] Under Bordiga's leadership Gramsci at first was assigned only minor party duties. The Italian Communist party's memoranda for the spring of 1921 refer infrequently to Gramsci; in the campaign for the May 15 parliamentary elections he was listed as a speaker only at rallies in the smaller, less important cities and towns. [18]

Although he should have been the top vote-getter among the candidates presented on the Communist party's Turin list in the May, 1921, elections, Gramsci was not elected to Parliament. Clearly, many Communist voters had deserted him. No more vivid example of his isolation in the party could be given. Gramsci was the victim of the new party's factional struggles in which he had sought to maintain an independent position. His struggle for a new politics put him on a collision course with both Bordiga's mechanistic brand of Marxism and Angelo Tasca's cultural humanism. Gramsci attempted to bring together economic and cultural change in a new synthesis. In his view, Bordiga and Tasca abstracted one or the other term of the revolutionary equation and then gave the reified abstraction ("economics" or "culture") primacy. Al-

15. Gramsci to Togliatti, January 27, 1924, in *Formazione,* 180.
16. Gramsci to Togliatti, February 9, 1924, in *Formazione,* 192.
17. Giuseppe Fiori, *Antonio Gramsci: Life of a Revolutionary* (New York, 1970), 146–47.
18. *Il primo anno di vita del Partito Comunista d'Italia: Circolari interne riservate e riservatissime del comitato centrale della commissione esecutiva January–March, 1921* (Milan, 1966), 38. Typescript available in the library of the Istituto Feltrinelli, Milan.

though the ostensible reason given by some opponents of Gramsci was that in October, 1914, he had been in favor of Italy's intervention in the war, it is more likely that the attempt to pin an "interventionist" label on him was motivated by disagreement with Gramsci's views on the nature of Marxism and the revolution referred to above. As Giuseppe Fiori has pointed out, during the war Togliatti had actually served in the Italian army, and no similar accusation had been leveled against him. It was always possible that some party members thought the party image would suffer if they presented a hunchback as a candidate for public office. For whatever reason or combination of reasons, the fact is that in the fall of 1920 and the spring of 1921 Gramsci found himself completely isolated in his own Communist constituency in Turin. Indeed, Angelo Tasca recalled that at the Socialist party's general meeting to propose candidates for the elections of October 31–November 7, 1920, "there was a great outburst of protest" when Gramsci's name was put forward. This incident makes Gramsci's failure to be elected to Parliament in May, 1921 (even though he was put on the Communist party list), less surprising.[19]

The Consolations of Journalism

Although he found himself to be virtually alone at first in the Italian Communist party, Gramsci remained active as a journalist. At a substantially increased salary, he was now editor-in-chief of the new daily edition of *L'Ordine Nuovo*.[20]

Gramsci's journalism in the period following the foundation of the Italian Communist party centered on four themes: (1) improving the Communist party press and beginning leadership schools for the workers; (2) exposing the antirevolutionary character of the PSI leadership; (3) commenting on national and international developments relevant to the Italian political situation; and (4) analyzing the nature and rise of fascism. Gramsci's analysis of Italian fascism from a grassroots perspective, which remains gripping reading even today, will be discussed in chapter 8.

Gramsci's article entitled "Caporetto and Vittorio Veneto," of January 28, 1921, proclaimed the Livorno congress to have sounded the death

19. Angelo Tasca, as quoted in Fiori, *Gramsci*, 141.
20. Caprioglio, "Cronologia," xxiv.

knell of the PSI and its dominant doctrine, maximalist socialism. With its empty revolutionary rhetoric and false promises of an easy victory, the PSI under the maximalists resembled General Cadorna, who had led Italy to her greatest defeat at Caporetto. Maximalist socialism has led the proletariat to "the Caporetto of verbal and verbose revolutionism," declared Gramsci.[21] If its most advanced elements were to make common cause with the Communist party, however, the results would be analogous to Vittorio Veneto, Italy's greatest victory in World War I.

Three days later, in an article entitled "War Is War!" Gramsci wrote to warn of how difficult the revolutionary struggle would be, given the emergence of private armies supporting the bourgeois order. Much of Gramsci's language in this article is grim:

> [There is] mortal danger for those who take away the worker's bread. . . . War is War! He who seeks adventure must feel the iron jaws of the beast that he has let loose. . . . [I]f bourgeois Italy happens to have acquired the sweet and facile conviction that . . . Italian revolutionaries are not to be taken seriously, let the die be cast. We are convinced that more than one fox will leave both his tail and his cunning in the snare.[22]

Gramsci's dire warning here was directed at the Fascist "action squads" in the region around Bologna. This article is one of many articles he wrote calling for organizing working class defense organizations capable of punishing the Fascists or preventing their violent attacks on "left-wing" or "red" organizations.

From January, 1921, until his departure for Moscow in May, 1922, Gramsci was often holed up in his office at *L'Ordine Nuovo* with a gun in his hand, prepared for an assault by Fascist "white terrorists." He took his turn at sentry duty, ready to sound the siren if any suspicious-looking people approached the building. Ever since February, 1918, when he had declared himself to be a "professional revolutionary" to his close friend Leo Galetto, Gramsci had been prepared if necessary to face prison or even death. In July, 1919, he was actually imprisoned in Turin for several days for participation in a solidarity strike with the Hungarian Revolution. During his brief stay he charmed the guards, who were fellow Sardinians.[23]

---

21. Gramsci, "Caporetto e Vittorio Veneto," January 28, 1921, in *SF*, 52, and *SPW*², 4.
22. Gramsci, "La guerra e la guerra," January 31, 1921, in *SF*, 59, and *SPW*², 9.
23. Caprioglio, "Cronologia," xxvi.

GRAMSCI REMAINS A "COUNCIL MAN"

Togliatti's description of Gramsci as a party man should not be interpreted as implying that at some point Gramsci ceased to be a "council man." On the contrary, in 1921 Gramsci remained very much involved in the struggle for workers' control of the factories, and he never ceased to view the councils as essential instruments in the revolutionary struggle.

When, in February, 1921, in accordance with the promise he had made in return for peaceful evacuation of the factories, Premier Giolitti submitted to Parliament his bill for workers' control, Gramsci bitterly attacked the measure as a propagandistic ploy. Giolitti's so-called concession to the workers occupying the factories had only one real merit—to demonstrate the organic weakness of the bourgeois ruling class (*classe dominante*). Gramsci asserted that the working class must convince itself that its future lies not in wringing concessions from the bourgeoisie but in its becoming the leading class (*classe direttrice*) that guides the emancipation of all productive forces. Accordingly, the Communist party and the most advanced part of the working class together must begin again the campaign for true workers' control in the form of a national system of factory councils. The struggle for workers' control, Gramsci insisted, is not an end in itself but the means of bringing home to the great mass of the population that even its immediate needs—for food, shelter, electric power, clothing—can be fulfilled securely only when all economic (and hence all political) power will have passed into the hands of the working class.[24]

Yet another indication that the workers' councils remained essential to Gramsci's architecture of a new politics is his comment in a February 25, 1921, article:

> We hold that the struggle for the creation and development of factory and enterprise councils is the specific task of the Communist party. . . . Through the struggle for the councils it will be possible to win the majority of the [General Confederation of Labor]. . . . This process has been verified by events in Russia.[25]

24. Gramsci, "Controllo operaio," February 10, 1921, in *SF*, 67, 68, and *SPW*², 10–11.
25. Gramsci, "La Confederazione Generale del Lavoro," February 28, 1921, in *SF*, 83, and *SPW*², 13.

In March, 1921, after the General Confederation of Labor's national congress, which he had attended as an observer, Gramsci wrote in total disgust that the congress's only concern was how to protect the "impotent power" of the Socialist party. The majority's delegates were men "with withered hearts and shriveled brains" who ignored the desperate plight of the masses, increasingly subject to fascist violence. "Between them and the masses an unbridgeable abyss has opened up," he wrote. The only contact between these union bureaucrats and the masses comes when they "collect their dues and compile membership lists."

Those in charge of the conference who had denounced *L'Ordine Nuovo*'s reporting of the congress as vicious and unfair "did not convey even the tenth part of our pessimistic judgment" on the inadequacy of the trade union bureaucracy. "Our pessimism has increased, [but] our will has not diminished," because these officials "do not represent the base" of the workers' movement. Sounding the conciliar theme once again, Gramsci concludes by declaring that the General Confederation of Labor

> will be replaced by the organization of the councils, the workers' parliaments whose task it is to scrape away bureaucratic sediments and transform old organizational relationships. Our pessimism has increased, but our motto remains . . . pessimism of the intellect, optimism of the will.[26]

On March 24 Gramsci returned to the subject of the councils, declaring them to be "the sole popular instrument capable of controlling and reducing the industrial and agrarian bourgeoisie to impotence." The system of councils, the people's most powerful weapon, is like an axe to cut down the revolution's enemies.[27]

Gramsci's columns in *L'Ordine Nuovo* on the May national elections reflected the internal debate in the newly formed Communist party over whether to participate at all. Predictably, Bordiga had favored abstention on grounds that the bourgeois elite manipulated the so-called free elections. While agreeing with Bordiga's grounds, Gramsci disagreed with his conclusion. In a column published in mid-April, Gramsci con-

26. Gramsci, "Funzionarismo," March 4, 1921, in *SF,* 89–91, and *SPW*[2], 17–19. *SPW*[2] blandly translates *funzionarismo* as "officialdom." "Functionary-ism" would be a more accurate translation, for Gramsci meant to convey the idea that the bureaucracy had transformed itself into an ideology, or "ism."

27. Gramsci, "Il parlamento italiano," March 24, 1921, in *SF,* 115–17, and *SPW*[2], 29–31.

tended that the elections should be contested in order to identify both the Communist party's present strength and the social forces with which it may ally itself in the future. Elections "are one among the many forms of political organization" in modern society:

> The party is the superior organizational form; and the trade union and the factory council are intermediary forms into which the most [class-] conscious proletarians are incorporated for the day-by-day struggle against [finance] capital. In elections, the masses declare themselves for the highest political end, for the form of the state, and for the working class as the ruling class [of the future].[28]

Returning a week later to the question of why a revolutionary party should participate in a bourgeois parliamentary election, Gramsci gave as his answer that, while the economic and social conditions for the proletarian revolution were present in Italy, the spiritual preconditions were not. The electoral campaign could be used to show the workers the need for a "central political organism capable of issuing rallying cries (*parole d'ordine*) that resound in the proletarian consciousness as . . . commands of history."[29]

The term *parole d'ordine* (literally, "words of order") sounds authoritarian in English but has a different resonance in Italian. It is scarcely comparable to commands issued by the party general staff. In fact, *parole d'ordine* might well arise spontaneously from the workers engaged in strikes or other agitation. Thus, in a May 4 article entitled "La parola della masse" (The word of the masses) Gramsci hailed the workers at Turin's Fiat plant, already in their second month of a strike, for having demonstrated by their actions that the will to resist was still present and that September, 1920, did not mean the irrevocable defeat of the proletariat.[30]

When a few days later the Fiat workers voted to return to work even though defeated on the issue of workers' control, Gramsci extolled them as "men of flesh and blood" who had made every possible sacrifice before finally yielding to the "steamroller of capitalist reaction":

> Nothing has been lost if the conscience and faith [of the workers] remain intact. . . . The workers of Fiat have fought strenuously year in and year

28. Gramsci, "I comunisti e le elezioni," April 12, 1921, in *SF,* 133, and *SPW*[2], 33.
29. Gramsci, "Parole d'ordine," April 19, 1921, in Caprioglio MS.
30. Gramsci, "La parola della masse," May 4, 1921, in Caprioglio MS.

out, they have bathed the streets with their blood, and they have endured hunger and cold; because of their glorious past, they remain in the vanguard of the Italian proletariat as faithful militants . . . of the revolution. They have done everything possible that men of flesh and blood can do.[31]

Gramsci's articles prior to the May 15, 1921, elections were noteworthy for their realism; he never exaggerated the chances of Communist electoral success in hopes of getting out the vote. How many seats the party gained was irrelevant. Quality was more important than quantity:

May 15 will not be a day of victory for the Communists . . . but a day when the Turinese proletariat shows itself always in the vanguard.[32]

In "Should You Bother to Vote?" written four days before the election, Gramsci declared that Italian Communists should direct their message only to the most active and revolutionary part of the producers, the workers, and the peasants. Unlike the Socialists, who hypocritically mask the reality of the class struggle with "sweet talk," the Communists openly proclaim their aims:

to defeat bourgeois society, to arm the working class for its defense and emancipation, [and] to *install the Republic of the Councils.*[33]

Interestingly, on the eve of the elections of 1921 Gramsci made an appeal to liberals to vote Communist on the grounds that they had been betrayed by their party and that they shared with the Communists the will to create "an ever more profound liberation of the world."[34]

Gramsci's fears that the Communists would not do well in the elections materialized. They obtained only 16 seats in the Chamber of Deputies at Montecitorio, compared with 123 for the PSI. The *popolari* (the liberal Catholic party led by Don Luigi Sturzo) had 110 and the Fascists (like the Communists, competing for the first time), 35. Commenting on the elections, Gramsci observed that they merely proved that "the PCd'I is not yet a party of the great masses." The Communists will become a mass party after the Socialist deputies show how they have become *imborghesiti* (bourgeoisified) through collaboration with the capitalist parties, he added.[35]

31. Gramsci, "Uomini di carne e ossa," May 8, 1921, in *SF,* 56.
32. Gramsci, "La lotta elettorale nella fase conclusiva," May 4, 1921, in Caprioglio MS.
33. Gramsci, "Andrai a votare?" May 11, 1921, in Caprioglio MS. Emphasis added.
34. Gramsci, "Liberalismo e blocchi," May 14, 1921, in *SF,* 164.
35. Gramsci, "Risultati," May 17, 1921, in *SF,* 167.

MORAL COURAGE: GRAMSCI FIGHTS AGAINST THE ODDS

As discussed previously, the election of May, 1921, was not only a set-back for the Communist party but a personal defeat for Gramsci as well. His total vote was less than that received by two relatively unknown comrades, Fortunato Misiano and Pietro Rabbezana, who were awarded the seats won by the Communist party in Turin according to the proportional representation system. Gramsci could only have felt the loss keenly, and he must have been aware of widespread speculation over whether any hunchback could effectively represent the party. In-deed, the Comintern's representative in Italy, V. Degott, noted that Gramsci's small stature and hunchbacked condition "affected audiences unfavorably."[36]

Under the circumstances, Gramsci had no alternative but to fall back on his "moral courage." As he had written shortly before the May 15 election in a column rich with autobiographical connotations and en-titled "Who Is a Communist?":

> To be a Communist means to have a great deal of moral courage. . . . A Communist is someone who acknowledges himself to be weaker physi-cally but not inferior intellectually and spiritually; his body may be im-prisoned, but not his mind. . . . [The Communist is someone who knows that] what makes a man is the spirit of liberty and revolt.[37]

In what appears to be an overstatement, Giuseppe Fiori has written that during this period (summer of 1921), Gramsci "sank into a state of extreme physical and nervous debility."[38] He learned that his younger brother, Mario, was active in the Fascist party and that his older brother Gennaro was in emotional and financial distress because he was the fa-ther of an illegitimate child and did not want to marry the mother. These developments served only further to depress him.

Despite his unhappiness, Gramsci continued to put in long hours at the newspaper. During this period he wrote some of his most penetrat-ing analyses of Italian fascism, to be discussed in chapter 8. As time neared for the October national congress of the PSI he renewed his at-tack on the failure of that party to offer any effective resistance to fas-cism. In particular, he denounced PSI's parliamentary delegation for

36. Fiori, *Gramsci,* 150.
37. Gramsci, "Chi è comunista?" May 10, 1921, in Caprioglio MS.
38. Fiori, *Gramsci,* 150.

having signed a so-called pact of pacification with Mussolini in early August, 1921. This agreement was broken by the Fascists almost as soon as the ink on it had dried. Gramsci regarded the pact as the ultimate symbol of the Socialist party leadership's intellectual and moral bankruptcy in the face of fascist intimidation.[39]

In several of Gramsci's columns written in the summer of 1921, he compared the Socialist party to the Barnum and Bailey Circus. The only difference between the PSI and the real circus was that the Socialist leaders were "clowns who did not know how to laugh."[40]

GRAMSCI BECOMES MORE ACTIVE IN THE PARTY LEADERSHIP

By October, 1921, Gramsci became more active in the Italian Communist party. He became especially interested in establishing leadership schools. The PCd'I needed a trained leadership corps. He made a sharp distinction between party "functionaries" and "mandarins," however. Whereas the recent Socialist party congress at Milan had revealed a group of leaders who believed in nothing except keeping their position, the Communist party must have leaders who do not set themselves apart from rank and file workers and who are equipped to help the latter coherently develop their revolutionary aspirations.

In one article, Gramsci sharply attacked the oft-repeated proverb "La practica vale più della grammatica" ("Practice is worth more than grammar") and insisted that the party establish fellowships for young people to take leave from their jobs and learn how to be trade union organizers. Gramsci argued that to be a good union organizer one must have knowledge of (1) Marxist doctrine, (2) social legislation, (3) the history of the trade union movement, (4) accounting, and (5) even *grammatica*! Workers need to acquire intellectual discipline. Most people need the stimulus of others to learn.[41]

Aversion to philistinism—a word used by Gramsci to signify a combination of stupidity, selfishness, pomposity, arrogance, an inability to discriminate what is important from what is not, and poor taste—was a

39. Gramsci, "I capi e le masse," July 3, 1921; "Tra le pieghe della bandiera bianca," July 13, 1921; and "Come un partito muore," August 13, 1921, in *SF*, 224–26, 235–38, and 276–80.

40. Gramsci, "Cronache di Barnum," May 28, 1921; "La politica estera del Barnum," June 30, 1921; and "Buffoni che non possono ridere," September 21, 1921, in *SF*, 172–74, 217–22, and 344–47.

41. Gramsci, "Pratica e grammatica," October 30, 1921, in Caprioglio MS.

consistent theme during the year May, 1921–May, 1922. Although Gramsci saw elements of positivism and reductionism in the thinking of some of his fellow Communists, his public ire was generally reserved for Socialists. In August, 1921, he labeled Giacinto Menotti Serrati, the head of the maximalist Socialists, a megalomaniac with a petty bourgeois caste of mind. Gramsci was especially angry with Serrati for having agreed to the pact of conciliation with Mussolini. Indeed, his attacks on Serrati were so severe that at the meeting of the Communist party's central committee in December, 1921, Gramsci felt called upon to defend the violent form of his journalistic polemics as a way of arousing the masses from the state of passivity into which they had sunk.[42] Later he attacked various revisionist Socialist and anarchist intellectuals for their dialectical incompetence and their total immersion in the "marsh of philistinism." Instead of soberly analyzing the effective relationship prevailing between forces at work in history and then choosing their course of action, the reformist Socialists, anarchists, and others choose to regard so trivial an event as the luncheon given for representatives of the USSR by the King of Italy on his yacht, the *Dante Alighieri*, in the spring of 1922 as a "turning point" (*svolta*) in world history, Gramsci observed. People who think this way may be proletarian in name, but they are petty bourgeois in spirit.[43]

GRAMSCI BECOMES THE ITALIAN PARTY'S DELEGATE TO THE COMINTERN

How did it come to pass that Gramsci, who had occupied a marginal position in the party at its founding in January, 1921, should have been elected to the important post of delegate to the Communist International (Comintern) at the party's second congress in March, 1922? Was it chiefly because Bordiga, to whom Gramsci posed an intellectual challenge, wanted to get the Sardinian hunchback out of the way by sending him to Moscow? The hypothesis has a certain plausibility. There must have been other factors at work as well, however, including Gramsci's ability to respond creatively to pressures on the Italian party by the Comintern to establish a united front (*fronte unico*, literally,

42. Gramsci, as quoted in the Archives of the Italian Communist party, Rome (APC fasc. 39/2, fol. 34–35).
43. Gramsci, "Piccoli borghesi," May 8, 1922, in Caprioglio MS.

"single" or "common" front) with the Socialists. In August, 1921, Lenin himself had rebuked Bordiga for having exaggerated the fight against the Socialists to the point where he had made it into a sport. In December of the same year the Comintern's executive committee issued a list of twenty-five theses calling on all Communist parties to establish an alliance, or common workers' front, against reactionary elements in their respective countries.[44]

Gramsci understood that it was impossible to make a formal alliance with the maximalist and/or revisionist Socialists so soon after the separation of the Communists from the Socialists at Livorno. Therefore he argued for an informal alliance of Communist forces at the trade union level. By the time of the Italian Communist party's second congress at Rome in March, 1922, Gramsci had become known as highly knowledgeable about how to deal with the Comintern. He also kept his substantial reservations about Bordiga's so-called Rome theses—a verbose and doctrinaire document that presented the party as a perfectionist sect that should not sully its hands with political forces outside its ranks—confined to private conversations with Togliatti, Umberto Terracini, and a few others.[45] Given that he was well known in the Comintern for his articles in *L'Ordine Nuovo*, Gramsci was the logical choice to be the Italian party's delegate in the Comintern. The severity of Gramsci's attacks on Serrati and other Socialist leaders during the months preceding the March, 1922, Rome congress had undoubtedly helped blur, if not entirely erase, the misgivings his enemies in the party had harbored against the Sardinian about his so-called voluntarism (meaning his critique of deterministic Marxism).

One of the last articles by Gramsci published before he left Turin for Moscow in May, 1922, was entitled "Economics in the Party's Work." In it he declared in part:

> It is not possible to make sense out of political events . . . if one does not keep in mind factors that determine those events, first of all the economic factor. . . . [T]here has never been a social transformation that has not been *determined and conditioned* by transformations that have already taken place in the society's economic structure.[46]

44. Quoted in Fiori, *Gramsci,* 153.
45. Gramsci, Remarks at Italian Communist Party Congress, Rome, March, 1922, in *SPW²,* 118–22. The "Rome Theses" proposed by Amadeo Bordiga are *ibid.,* 93–117.
46. Gramsci, "L'economia nel lavoro di partito," May 14, 1922, in Caprioglio MS. New attribution. Emphasis added.

Gramsci's casual combination of the words "determined" and "conditioned" in the above passage,[47] together with his use of the word "factors" (in the plural) underlying political events—of which the economic factor is only one—reveals a Gramsci as averse as ever to the view that Marxism is a science composed of iron economic laws affecting human behavior in a manner analogous to the way the laws of physics affect atoms. He later adds that "economic facts determine political events *as to their general direction* (*in linea generale*)." Gramsci never changed his view that while economic factors were of major importance in helping us understand what has happened in the past, they do not rigidly determine what happens in the present. In his *Prison Notebooks* he wrote that "a scientific understanding that the economic structure has changed radically" is significant only as a stimulus to political action. Only through human *action*—triggered by the will—are changes effected in society.[48]

Gramsci later wrote that he voted for Bordiga's Rome theses only for the sake of party unity. Verbose and doctrinaire, they went counter both to the letter and spirit of Gramsci's new politics of inclusion. They advocated a purist Communist party, and they reflected a passive attitude toward the growing fascist menace. The Rome theses were grounded on an unimaginative literal reading of some passages in Marx. Gramsci understood that Marx never claimed to be a "scientist" of the kind who could predict in detail what would happen tomorrow in human affairs. Such a person would have seemed to him to be a magician rather than a genuine scientist.

Marx notwithstanding, Bordiga proceeded in his Rome Theses to predict that Italy's next government would be led by reformist Socialists and their liberal allies.[49] That prediction was made in March, 1922. On October 28, 1922, the Fascists staged their "March on Rome," and Benito Mussolini was named premier by His Majesty Victor Emmanuel III.

Had Antonio Gramsci remained in Italy until December, 1922, he would scarcely have encountered the social-democratic government

47. In the Preface to his *Critique of Political Economy*, Karl Marx uses the verbs "determine" (*bestimmen*) and "condition" (*bedingen*) as if they were interchangeable. See Robert C. Tucker (ed.), *The Marx-Engels Reader* (2nd ed., New York, 1978), 4.
48. Gramsci, in *Quaderni*, 1253.
49. Amadeo Bordiga, "Rome Theses," in *SPW²*, 116.

predicted by the Rome Theses. His life might well have ended then and there, for his bodily frame might not have withstood the savage beating fascist thugs administered to his brother Gennaro, whom they had mistaken for Antonio.[50] As we shall see, Antonio Gramsci, then in Moscow, was by then already preparing himself to lead the party on a "new course."

50. Caprioglio, "Cronologia," xxxii.

VI 🖋 "Holding Your Nose" About the Comintern: Gramsci in Moscow, 1922–1923

Every time you write a letter [to a Comintern official] it is necessary that you hold your nose and remember all the rules of diplomacy.
—Gramsci to Umberto Terracini, December 23, 1923; in *Formazione*, 135

Gramsci left Turin for Moscow by train on May 26, 1922. He was exhausted physically and drained emotionally. For eleven years Turin had been his home. He left behind his close friends Alfonso Leonetti and Andrea Viglongo, as well as the woman with whom he had had a close relationship, Pia Carena. He left behind *L'Ordine Nuovo,* the newspaper he had led to prominence, as well as the many workers he had come to know in the great factories of the city that had become his second home.

In Moscow, Gramsci had a room in the Hotel Lux, main lodging place of Comintern representatives from abroad. From June 7 to June 11 he participated in the meetings of the Comintern's "Enlarged Executive," during which he was elected Italy's representative on that organization's smaller executive committee.[1]

The session must have been stressful in the extreme for Gramsci. The Italian party was pressed to fall in line with the "common front" doctrine, about which, as we have seen, he had a position shared neither by Bordiga nor by the Comintern. Gramsci's roommate at the Hotel Lux, Antonio Graziadei, was from the Tasca wing of the party. There was literally no one with whom he could feel companionship upon his arrival in Moscow. Bordiga himself was the third Italian Communist then in Moscow. He had accompanied Gramsci for the meeting and was soon to return to Italy.

Almost immediately after the June 11 session, Gramsci, by his own

1. Sergio Caprioglio, "Cronologia," in *LDC,* xxxi.

testimony, began to behave psychotically. Through the good offices of the Comintern President Gregory Ovseyevich Zinoviev, Gramsci was transferred to Serebranyi Bor (Silver wood) Sanatorium near Moscow, where over the following months he gradually recovered. For some time he suffered from nervous tics and paralysis of the legs. Despite the fact that he received many visitors, he suffered from acute loneliness.[2]

Once more Gramsci was on society's periphery, only this time his alienation was even worse; his experience of marginalization occurred in the capital city of the newly established communist society, the USSR. He lived isolated geographically as well as psychologically on the fringes of the "new order" itself.

In spite of the gravity of his psychosomatic disorder, Antonio Gramsci quickly recovered from its psychotic stage. In fact, on July 22, only five weeks after entering the sanatorium, Gramsci wrote a letter to Karl Radek, chairman of the Comintern's committee on Italy, asking Radek to revise his proposed "Manifesto to the Italian Workers" to omit any reference to PSI head Giacinto Serrati. Serrati, Gramsci wrote bluntly, "does not have a single worker from the masses behind him. All he has behind him is his faction of the party, and it is composed [only] of trade union and municipal functionaries." The Italian Communist party archives in Rome contain a letter to Zinoviev written on August 20, 1922, only two months after his admission to Silver Wood, in which he analyzed the prospects of an imminent Fascist takeover in Italy. This brilliant analysis shows unquestionably that Gramsci had fully recovered his intellectual powers. The letter prophetically stressed the dangers of a Fascist *coup d'état*:

> The situation is extremely serious. . . . In an interview, Mussolini, while denying *for now* . . . [his intention to stage] a Fascist military march on Rome, makes clear that all the technical means have been prepared should such a march be necessary. The [latest] Fascist manifesto warns of a great definitive action in the near future. In the Chamber of Deputies and the Senate voices are heard in favor of a dictatorship—but certainly not of the proletariat.[3]

Two months later, the Fascists staged their so-called March on Rome, bringing Mussolini to the premiership. While a full dictatorship

2. Giuseppe Fiori, *Antonio Gramsci: Life of a Revolutionary* (New York, 1970), 155.
3. Gramsci to Gregory Zinoviev, August 20, 1922, in Fubini MS.

was not established until two years later, Mussolini's ascent to power sounded the death knell of Italian liberal democracy.

In September, 1922, Gramsci wrote an article on the Italian futurist movement at Leon Trotsky's request. Trotsky, who had met Gramsci and who in his autobiography praised the Sardinian revolutionary as one of a very few people to foresee the ascent of fascism to power in Italy, published the article as an appendix to his book *Literature and Revolution* (1923).[4]

GRAMSCI ATTENDS THE COMINTERN'S FOURTH CONGRESS

Although not fully recovered from his illness, Gramsci was at least well enough to leave the sanatorium and return to the Hotel Lux in early November, after a period of nearly six months, to attend the Comintern's fourth congress, lasting from November 5 to December 5. As a member of the "Italian Commission," Gramsci had close contact with prominent world Communist leaders such as Karl Radek, Matyas Rakosi, and Clara Zetkin, as well as with Trotsky and Zinoviev. Gramsci never met Lenin, who lay partially paralyzed with a stroke.

Rakosi immediately sought out Gramsci and urged him to take over the leadership of the PCd'I from Bordiga. Gramsci later recalled one of these occasions in a letter to his Italian colleagues:

> The Penguin [Gramsci's code word for Rakosi], with that diplomatic delicacy that so distinguishes him, took me by siege once more to suggest that I become leader of the party, eliminating Amadeo [Bordiga]. . . .[5]

Gramsci's code words for prominent figures in the Comintern demonstrate how far he was from viewing the Communist International (or Comintern) as a body above criticism. For example, he referred to Dimitri Manuilski as "the Pelican" and to Henryk Walecki as "the Gorilla." As a critical Communist, he had a lively sense of the imperfections of the people who made up the party. He even went so far as to say that Jules Humbert-Droz had "no sense of reality."[6]

Gramsci goes on in the letter to describe how in November, 1922, he

4. Caprioglio, "Cronologia," xxxii.
5. Gramsci to Mauro Scoccimarro and Palmiro Togliatti, February 8, 1924, in *Formazione,* 228, and *SPW*[2], 472.
6. Giovanni Somai (ed.), *Gramsci a Vienna: Ricerche e documenti 1922–1924* (Urbino, 1979), 82n, 92–93, and 199.

was still not fully recovered from his nervous collapse; he had difficulty working because of insomnia and occasional attacks of amnesia. He cautioned Rakosi that unless the ground were well prepared, Bordiga could not be challenged successfully. If he (Bordiga) and his followers were expelled, the Italian party would be worth no more than a "handful of flies." Gramsci's only promise was to do everything that he could to "help the Comintern Executive resolve the Italian question."[7]

At the Comintern congress the "Italian question" that was discussed was whether the PCd'I and the PSI should reunite in view of the twin facts that Filipo Turati's reformist Socialists had finally been expelled from the party and that the PSI had renewed its application to join the Comintern, claiming adherence to the "21 points" laid down previously as a condition for membership.

The Communist International's fourth congress set up a joint committee of Italian Communists and Socialists to work out the details for reunifying the two parties. Gramsci, Mauro Scoccimarro, and Tasca represented the Italian Communist party on the committee. By the spring of 1923, however, Pietro Nenni had wrested the PSI leadership from Serrati on a platform opposed to "fusion." The joint committee was dissolved.[8]

Bordiga's fierce opposition to Comintern pressures to open up the Italian Communist party to possibilities for allying with the PSI to present joint electoral lists eventually forced Gramsci's hand. Bordiga, who had returned to Italy in January, 1923, was arrested by the Fascists and imprisoned in February. From prison, Bordiga smuggled out a provocative manifesto attacking the Comintern for allegedly impeding the Italian Communists' work of building a new revolutionary party to replace the "corpse" of the PSI.[9]

In May, Togliatti, who had sensed that Bordiga's arrest might have opened up the possibility of a dramatic change in party leadership, urged Gramsci to think seriously about leaving Moscow for a location closer to Italy, which could serve as a base from which he could influence the Italian party's affairs more directly.[10] In the summer of 1923, Gramsci, his health fully recovered, affirmatively answered Togliatti's request and began the task of giving the party a new foundation.

7. Gramsci to Togliatti and Scoccimarro, n.d., in *SPW*[2], 472.
8. *SPW*[2], 475 n. 72.
9. Togliatti to Gramsci, May 1, 1923, in *SPW*[2], 133.
10. *Ibid.*, 137.

Gramsci knew from his friends Terracini, Togliatti, and Scoccimarro of the desperate state of the party in Italy, where in a single week the Fascists had succeeded in rounding up five thousand Communists, or one-fourth of the party's total membership, including virtually all its trade-union organizers. Moreover, the Fascists had seized all the party's funds in Italy.[11] He was well aware of how difficult and arduous the rebuilding effort would be. Not only would he find Bordiga and his allies arrayed against him but the might of the Fascist state as well.

JULIA

By no means all of Gramsci's life in Moscow was taken up with party business. He had fallen in love with Julia Schucht, a Soviet citizen whom he had met three months after arriving in the USSR. In September, 1922, Julia had come to the sanatorium to visit her older sister Eugenia. There she met Gramsci. "Tall and fair with large, sad eyes and a beautiful oval face," Julia was five years younger than Antonio.[12] He appears to have fallen for her instantly and to have wooed her ardently.

Julia Schucht, who taught music at the Lycee in Ivanovo, near Moscow, had studied violin at Rome's famed Academy of Santa Cecilia from 1908 until 1915, when she returned to Russia with her father, a former political prisoner of the czar who had known Lenin personally in Switzerland. The Schuchts were ethnically Jewish, which had made their lot under the czarist regime all the more difficult. Julia's younger sister, named Tatiana, was living in Rome, where she taught science at the International Institute on the Via Savoy. Tatiana would be the most important person in Gramsci's life after his imprisonment in 1926. Eugenia, the older sister, would accompany Julia to Italy in 1924 and insist on her return to the USSR in 1926, two months before Gramsci's arrest.

Inevitably, speculation abounds in the literature about the nature of Gramsci's relationship with Julia, and someone has even written a play rich in Freudian overtones about the love each of the three Schucht sisters allegedly had for Antonio Gramsci.[13] I shall leave those speculations

11. Hoare and Nowell-Smith, Introduction to *SPN,* iv.

12. Fiori, *Gramsci,* 156.

13. "Nonostante Gramsci," in Adele Cambria, *Amore come rivoluzione* (Milan, 1976), 209–69.

aside, except to note that in his prison letters Gramsci himself frequently expressed contempt for a reductionist use—or abuse—of Freud.

Antonio Gramsci's 1923 letters from Moscow to Julia Schucht show
their author to have been a party man with a difference. For all his political commitment, Gramsci nourished a deep sense of privacy. He was
perfectly capable of chucking party business and, without telling anyone, leaving the city to spend a day or two with his beloved. On at least
one occasion his proclivity for spontaneity brought him embarrass-
ment. In Italy, the Fascists had issued a mandate for his arrest, and in
Moscow his Comintern colleagues sought to inform him of this development. They were alarmed that no one knew of his whereabouts and
scoured the city in search of him. When he eventually returned to the
Hotel Lux, he was welcomed as someone returned from the dead,
Gramsci wrote to Julia.[14]

In his letters to Julia, Gramsci unburdened himself of painful memories of his childhood in Sardinia, when he was made to feel like a freak
among normal human beings. He wrote to her of the wounds that still
bled in his heart from his feelings of having been excluded from normal
life because he was a *gobbo,* a hunchback.[15] He referred to his past as a
sewer of bitterness that had backed up into his consciousness. From the
age of ten, his parents had made him feel like an intruder in his own
family. With her help he would burn out the residue of the past and
move on to a new life.[16] For the first time he would then feel like a
whole being who is fully included in the circle of humanity.

In a particularly striking passage from these early letters to Julia,
Antonio Gramsci raised the question of whether it was possible to love
a collectivity if one had never loved concrete individual human beings.
His love for Julia had shown him the answer. Indeed, if he had not
learned to love her, his life as a revolutionary and a militant party man
would have become a sterile, coldly intellectual, purely mathematical
calculation.[17]

Gramsci's encounter with Julia was immensely important in that it
occurred after he had suffered his most severe emotional crisis. While
Giuseppe Fiori may have exaggerated when he wrote that before Julia

14. Gramsci to Julia Schucht, n.d., 1923, in *2000,* II, 25.
15. *Ibid.*
16. Gramsci to Julia Schucht, February 13, 1923, in *2000,* II, 23–24.
17. Gramsci to Julia Schucht, March 6, 1924, in *2000,* II, 33.

"Gramsci had never opened himself to any woman"[18]—there had been Pia Carena in Turin—there is no question that his deep love for the beautiful Julia helped him appreciate individual human beings. Julia helped him avoid the temptation to view human beings as impersonal abstractions. She helped him at least partially to overcome the terrible sense of isolation he had felt from childhood even in his own family. That so beautiful a woman as she could fall in love with him helped him feel less embarrassed about his "stump," as he referred to the hump on his back.

PREPARATION FOR A NEW RULING GROUP OF THE PCd'I

In an important letter written in 1923 Gramsci agreed that the time for confrontation, or for an open and definitive discussion, with Bordiga had come. Discussion was necessary on "certain questions which today seem, or may seem, intellectual bickering, but which . . . could . . . become the cause of internal crisis or decomposition of the party." To deal with that crisis "it is necessary to create within the party a nucleus—not a faction—of comrades who have the highest degree of ideological homogeneity."[19]

In this letter Gramsci proposed reconstituting "the old Turin group" in order to give the Italian Communist party a new direction. Bordiga's inflexibility had led to the separation of the party from the masses. While he had correctly resisted compromise with the present leadership of the PSI, Bordiga failed to recognize the Communists' potentiality for winning over most of the Socialists in Italy, just as the Bolsheviks eventually won over the Mensheviks. Italian Communists should have more self-confidence because they are "in the flow of the historical current and will succeed," if only they "'row' well and keep a firm grasp on the rudder." "If we can operate correctly, we should absorb the Socialist party and resolve the first and basic problem of the revolution—to unify the proletarian vanguard and destroy the demagogic populist tradition," Gramsci insisted. Gramsci went on to express two major specific criticisms of Bordiga's leadership: (1) He and his group had failed utterly to exploit the recent divisions within the PSI between Serrati, who favored the Comintern policy of fusion with the Italian Commu-

18. Fiori, *Gramsci*, 157.
19. Gramsci to Togliatti, May 18, 1923, in *SPW*[2], 136, 138.

nists, and Pietro Nenni, who strongly opposed the policy. (2) Bordiga and his followers had done nothing to encourage Catholic sympathizers to join the party. Bordiga's sectarian anticlericalism prevented the party from seizing opportunities to win support from parts of the Catholic left. To Antonio Gramsci, for the party to be fanatically anti-Catholic in a country that has an overwhelming Catholic majority was to commit an act of utter stupidity.[20]

In a memorandum written in June, 1923, on relations between the PCd'I and the Comintern, Gramsci also sharply attacked the equivocal attitude that the party under Bordiga had maintained toward the Comintern:

> While we [Italian Communists] have [at times] proclaimed the utmost formal discipline and have used language more appropriate for inferiors speaking to their superiors *than for use between equals,* [on other occasions] we have acted in such a way as to give the impression that we were ready to do anything effectively to evade the directives established by the international congresses and the executive committee.[21]

Gramsci goes on to argue for pressing the Italian party's differences with the Comintern as frankly and vigorously as possible in private, but expressing support for the Comintern's collective decisions in public. He leaves no doubt that he thinks that "the Russian comrades" have been mistaken in pressuring the western European parties to adopt a common front strategy. The failure of such a policy is clear from the fact that "*in no country*"[22] has it been followed. Gramsci does not dispute that the Comintern's policy "is bringing disintegration and corruption into the Communist ranks." Far from recommending submission to the Comintern's insensitive interference into the operation of the European Communist parties, Gramsci takes the approach that "if the Comintern too receives a few blows as we strike back, we should not be blamed for that; it is a mistake to ally oneself with untrustworthy elements."[23]

Quintin Hoare and Geoffrey Nowell-Smith have contended that "throughout 1923, Gramsci . . . continued to support Bordiga."[24] It

20. *Ibid.,* 140–42.
21. Gramsci, draft of memorandum presumably written June, 1923, in *SPW*[2], 154. Emphasis added.
22. *Ibid.,* 155. Emphasis added.
23. *Ibid.,* 155–56.
24. Hoare and Nowell-Smith, Introduction to *SPN,* iv.

would be more accurate to say that by the late spring and early summer of 1923 Gramsci was increasingly engaged in constructing a new course for the party independent of both Bordiga and the Comintern.

A fragment of a letter by Gramsci from Moscow to his allies in Italy, written in July, 1923, contains this remarkable paragraph:

> You think that the discussion here in Moscow has revolved around fusionism [with the PSI] and antifusionism. This is only apparently the case. *Fusionism and antifusionism were the "polemical terminology" of the discussion, but not its substance.* The discussion was [over] the following: whether the PCd'I has understood the overall Italian situation, and whether it is capable of giving a lead to the proletariat; whether the PCd'I is capable of developing an extensive political campaign, *i.e.*, whether it is ideologically and intellectually equipped for a specific activity; and whether the leading group of the PCd'I has assimilated the political doctrine of the Communist International, which is Marxism developed into Leninism, *i.e.*, into an organic and systematic body of organizational principles and tactical viewpoints. . . .[25]

The above letter highlights Gramsci's understanding that politics is much more than a matter of factional struggles and a contest of slogans. If one analyzes the relationship between the Italian party and the Comintern according to Gramsci's understanding, the conventional accounts of the period in terms of factional struggles between Left, Right, and Center are shown at best to have limited value. To maintain, as Hoare and Nowell-Smith do, that Gramsci "continued throughout 1923 to share the greater part of Bordiga's perspectives," therefore, is inaccurate.[26]

Gramsci's July, 1923, letter is a continuation of the argument of his May 18 letter to Togliatti, the implications of which are fully apparent in his important article of October of the same year, published in a Communist youth periodical *La Voce della Gioventù* of Milan. This letter, entitled "Che fare?" (What is to be done?), clearly shows Gramsci's fundamental disagreement with Bordiga on the nature of politics itself. As Renzo Martinelli has written, this letter constitutes Gramsci's "first open, public attack on Bordiga's ideology."[27]

Two other surviving writings by Gramsci immediately preceding his

25. Gramsci to Togliatti and others, July 3, 1923, in *SPW*[2], 159. Emphasis added.

26. Hoare and Nowell-Smith, *SPN*, lvi.

27. Renzo Martinelli, "Il 'Che fare?' di Gramsci nel 1923," *Studi Storici*, XII (October–December, 1972), 790–802 at 801.

"Che fare?" letter were his report of September 12 to the party's executive committee in Rome and his article on trade-union strategy published in October. The September report proposed that a new national Communist daily newspaper, to be named *L'Unità*, be founded. Within a year Italy's largest Communist party newspaper, which continues in publication even today, was inaugurated.

The most interesting passages in the September 12 report refer to the need to give other social forces such as republicans, anarchists, and above all dissident Socialists an opportunity to express themselves. Gramsci was basically uninterested in the abstract question of whether the Communist and Socialist parties should fuse, or come together, in face of the Fascist danger, because he thought the issue improperly posed. He was for action, not agreements on paper; and he knew that, regardless of the paper agreements, the Italian Communists and the official Socialist leadership could not cooperate effectively. This hardly made him a Bordigan purist, however. On the contrary, he insisted that the party be open to common action with receptive elements of both the Socialists and the *popolari* (liberal Catholics) as those elements detached themselves and became available. Gramsci specifically recommended that his old adversary, exparty leader Giacinto Serrati, recently expelled from the PSI, be asked to contribute both signed and unsigned material to *L'Unità*. Serrati was to be free to conduct a polemic in a political rather than a sectarian spirit in favor of his views. Soon thereafter Serrati joined the Communist party. (Serrati, as we know, had been the object of Gramsci's severe condemnation from 1921 on.) Gramsci's recommendation that the words "Federal Republic of Workers and Peasants" be inscribed on the masthead of *L'Unità* is also interesting. The new slogan would advance the concept of a regime of soviets, with the party providing the regime's political centralization and the local popular forces providing its administrative decentralization, he claimed.[28]

In an October 18 article in an Italian periodical, Gramsci attacked a proposal by an Italian Communist to create a new autonomous national trade-union system in Italy. Gramsci insisted that as a matter of principle he was opposed to the creation of new trade unions, because it is in the nature of trade unions to become coopted into the capitalist sys-

28. Gramsci, memorandum to the executive committee of the Italian Communist party, September 12, 1923, in *SPW*[2], 161–63.

tem. He gives as a prime example the American Federation of Labor headed by Samuel Gompers who, Gramsci declares, reduced the AFL to a level of abject, counter-revolutionary servility. Gramsci refers to reformist dictators of trade unions and insists that in Italy the internal commissions in the factories hold out the best hope of mobilizing the working class against capitalism and fascism.[29]

THE BEGINNING OF THE PUBLIC ATTACK ON BORDIGA: GRAMSCI'S "WHAT IS TO BE DONE?"

Perhaps the most important document from Gramsci's period of residence in Moscow is his letter entitled "What Is to Be Done?" written in October, 1923, and published in *La Voce della Gioventù* (The voice of youth) in Milan on November 1. This letter was signed with the pseudonym Giovanni Masca. The questions raised in the letter to *La Voce*, Renzo Martinelli points out, are "like a radiograph of Gramsci's thought at a crucial moment in the development of the party."[30]

Gramsci's letter to *La Voce* exposes the intellectual poverty of Bordiga-style Italian communism. The party was in disarray, Gramsci insisted, because it possessed neither a general conception of life nor an empirical knowledge of the Italian political situation. If it had possessed either, the party would have provided far more effective resistance to the rise of fascism.

To overcome its crisis, the party had to make a new beginning. It must use Marxism to analyze concretely the social forces and party alliances in different regions of the country. It must seek to make inroads among landless peasants, and it must overcome its sterile anticlericalism so that Catholics might feel welcome in its ranks.

As Renzo Martinelli has written, Antonio Gramsci understood Marxism to be "a method of concrete research into . . . social and political reality."[31] The "Che fare?" letter insists in effect that Italian Marxists must do for themselves what the founders of Marxism had done for their time. Italian Marxists must study empirically the conditions of the poor and the dispossessed in each region. They must have a thorough and detailed knowledge of both the forces of reaction and the forces for

29. Gramsci, "Our Trade Union Strategy," October 18, 1923, in *SPW*[2], 165–67.
30. Martinelli, "Il 'Che fare?' di Gramsci," 798.
31. *Ibid.*

liberation. Italian Communists must understand that they have no choice but to make a new beginning. They must face the reality that there is no specifically Italian Marxist tradition from which to draw insight and inspiration. It is up to the new generation to create an Italian Marxism worthy of the name.

"We [Marxists] do not know Italy," Gramsci proclaimed. "What is to be done?" First, the party must engage in self-criticism. To do that properly it must have criteria and principles for such a criticism. Second, it must not allow itself the luxury of pessimism about its situation. Although presently defeated by fascism, the party can expose the shallow superficial basis of Mussolini's strength. Fascism, Gramsci insists, is nothing but a house of cards waiting to be blown down by the winds of effective political resistance.[32]

Gramsci's brief letter written in Moscow in October, 1923, to an obscure Italian Communist youth publication, is extremely important not only for what it says about Marxism but also for what it says about Gramsci himself. It reveals a party man who is also very much his own man, a man who proclaims the importance of ideology but who understands ideology in a profoundly unideological way, a man who esteems Marx but wants to think for himself. The "Che fare?" letter, in sum, reveals an original mind at work.

WHAT GRAMSCI LEARNED IN MOSCOW

In August, 1919, Gramsci had written in *L'Ordine Nuovo* that "historical conditions in Italy were not and are not very different from those in Russia."[33] During his eighteen months in Moscow Gramsci changed his mind, concluding that radically different conditions prevailed in western Europe, making necessary a fundamentally different strategy for revolution in the west.

What else did Gramsci learn from his eighteen-month stay in Moscow? He studied Russian and German. He read extensively in Lenin's works, compiling a report on everything Lenin wrote about Italy.[34] He learned that one had to hold one's nose when writing Zinoviev and

32. Gramsci, "Che fare?" November 1, 1923, in Renzo Martinelli (ed.), *Antonio Gramsci: Per la verità* (Rome, 1974), 267–70; *SPW²*, 169–72.

33. Gramsci, "Operai e contadini," August 2, 1919, in *ON*, 22, 25; *SPW¹*, 83, 85.

34. Sergio Caprioglio, personal interview, Turin, 1982.

his unsavory cohorts at the Comintern.[35] As he wrote to Umberto Terracini, his successor in Moscow after he left for Vienna:

> The so-called centralism of the Comintern [does not exist] . . . because
> . . . it has been unable to bring about a situation in which parties exist
> that know how to conduct an autonomous, creative politics, a politics
> that centralizes itself automatically.[36]

He also began to learn about Josef Stalin. "I do not know how to explain [Stalin's] . . . attack [on Trotsky and his allies]," he wrote to Julia from Vienna in January, 1924. "This attack seems to me at once irresponsible and dangerous."[37] This personal observation turned out to be a prelude to his lengthy and courageous letter of 1926 rebuking Stalin and his allies for contemplating using police methods against his opponents within the Soviet Communist party instead of listening to them. (See chapter 8.)

Finally, he learned about the Byzantine factional struggles within the Communist party of USSR (CPSR) at first hand. He immediately saw through the Left, Right, and Center labels:

> As regards Russia . . . Trotsky and Bukharin occupy a "left" position and
> Zinoviev, Kamenev, and Stalin a "right" position, while Lenin was in the
> center as arbiter in all situations of grave tensions. . . . In truth, however,
> the so-called left faction is nothing but a band of Mensheviks who cloak
> themselves in revolutionary language but are incapable of evaluating the
> real relationships between effective [social] forces.[38]

What else Antonio Gramsci learned in Moscow we do not and at present, at least, cannot know, for the Soviet regime persists even today in refusing to permit access to the Comintern's files concerning Gramsci, despite the fact that sixty years have elapsed since the time when the great Sardinian, huddled in his gigantic Russian overcoat, trudged in the snow to the meetings of the Italian Commission and the Executive of the Third Communist International.

We do know what he chose *not* to learn, however—how to become an *apparatchik*. Gramsci left Moscow for Vienna in December, 1923, as

35. Gramsci to Togliatti and others, December 23, 1923, in *Formazione*, 135–36.
36. Gramsci to Umberto Terracini, March 27, 1924, in *Formazione*, 261.
37. Gramsci to Julia Schucht, January 13, 1924, in Fubini MS.
38. Gramsci to Togliatti and others, February 9, 1924, in *Formazione*, 186–87.

"critical" a Communist as he was on the day he arrived eighteen months earlier. Despite his disappointment in the Comintern, however, he also remained every inch an internationalist. As he put it, "the Communist International is a world party, even if that has to be understood with many grains of salt."[39]

39. *Ibid.*, 196. As Giovanni Somai has written in *Gramsci a Vienna* (Urbino, 1979), 10: "Gramsci participated in numerous meetings of the Comintern, and it would be of great importance to be able to read the transcript of what he had to say."

VII ✒ Closer to Italy: Gramsci Plans the New Course, 1923–1924

Why did Antonio Gramsci consent to leave Moscow, the center of world communist power and the home of the woman he loved, for Vienna? The answer is clear: because it was the first step toward rebuilding the Italian Communist party from the wreckage left both by the Italian Fascist dictatorship and by the party's first leader, Amadeo Bordiga.

The campaign to bring Gramsci into closer touch with the Italian Communist party had begun at least as early as Palmiro Togliatti's letter from Rome of May 1, 1923:

> You ought to come closer to Italy. . . . You need to be much better informed about everything . . . , just as we need again to sense the presence of your guiding hand. . . .[1]

Togliatti's letter was written in the wake of the arrest and imprisonment in February of Bordiga himself by the Fascist police, who had discovered the party's clandestine office in Rome. While Bordiga and several of his key allies languished in prison, Togliatti, Umberto Terracini, Mauro Scoccimarro, and other key party members were emboldened to approach Gramsci, who at once enthusiastically accepted their overtures.[2]

---

1. Togliatti to Gramsci, May 1, 1923, in *SPW*[2], 137.
2. In letters of May 17 and 21, 1923, Umberto Terracini informed Togliatti that "Antonio is very happy to return" to Italy. In Giovanni Somai (ed.), *Gramsci a Vienna: Ricerche e documenti, 1922–1924* (Urbino, 1979), 57, n. 12. Somai quotes APC, 187/18, 21.

The Comintern's bureaucracy ground slowly. In October, Vienna was chosen over Berlin or Switzerland as the place from which Gramsci was to plan his eventual reentry into Italy. Although his real mission was to begin the refounding of the Italian Communist party, his official duty in Vienna was to direct the party's relations with other European Communist parties.[3]

Antonio Gramsci arrived in Vienna from Moscow on December 4, 1923. In a letter to Julia Schucht he remarked that crossing the border from proletarian to bourgeois territory brought on "a very unpleasant feeling" and abruptly revived old memories he would have preferred to forget.[4]

At first, Vienna assumed a melancholic aspect to Gramsci. The cold of winter ate into his bones. His lodgings on the outskirts of the city required him to travel long distances by tram to meet his appointments. He had to endure the humiliation of appearing personally before the Viennese chief of police to promise not to "disturb public order" during his stay. Ironically, he had to depend on the good offices of the Social Democrats, the Austrian equivalent of Filipo Turati's reformist Socialists, to obtain his residence permit.[5]

There were other complaints. Some of his books appear to have been irretrievably lost in transit from Moscow. His roommate, an Italian named "Monti" (Angelo Codevilla) assigned to him by the Comintern, was an utter boor with whom one could exchange only the most banal conversation. Although his room was in the home of Joseph Frey, the secretary of the Austrian Communist party, Gramsci saw little of his host and instead had to endure the witless meanderings of Frey's wife, who, incredibly for the wife of a Communist official, yearned for the "good old days of the Hapsburg monarchy."[6]

Through the efforts of Guido Zamis, an Italian émigré and man of intellect, Gramsci's circumstances took a turn for the better. It was Zamis who in late February found a small apartment for Gramsci in the center of Vienna, near the Votivkirche. His life then improved considerably, to the point where he even consented to have his picture taken while smiling.[7]

3. Somai, *Gramsci a Vienna*, 55–60.
4. Gramsci to Julia Schucht, December 16, 1923, in *2000*, II, 26.
5. Gramsci to Julia Schucht, January 18, 1924, in *2000*, II, 30.
6. Gramsci to Julia Schucht, December 16, 1923, in *2000*, II, 26.
7. Somai, *Gramsci a Vienna*, 75.

Gramsci came out of his isolation in Vienna only gradually, however. His first letters to Julia were uniformly gloomy in tone. "I am always alone," he lamented. "I do not even go out of the house except to [eat at] the *trattoria* or to keep some scheduled appointment."[8]

COMBATING BORDIGA'S MANIFESTO

A turning point in the struggle to refound the Italian Communist party occurred when on January 5, 1924, Antonio Gramsci for the first time composed a detailed critique of Bordiga's anti-Comintern manifesto. Smuggled out of prison in April, 1923, the manifesto in essence had declared (in Togliatti's paraphrase) that "the action pursued by the Communist International towards the PSI ha[d] prevented . . . [the leadership of the Italian Communist party] from carrying out successfully the historic task that it had set itself—the task of destroying the old pseudo-revolutionary tradition represented by the PSI, clearing this corpse out of the way and at the same time founding a new tradition and a new organization of struggle."[9] Bordiga wanted all the original leaders of the Communist party to sign the manifesto and have it distributed to the Italian proletariat at large, even at the risk of the party's expulsion from the Third International.

Gramsci asked Mauro Scoccimarro to show his January 5 letter to Togliatti, Alfonso Leonetti, and Pietro Tresso, indicating thereby that he was forging an alliance to do battle. Calling Bordiga's manifesto "crazy and absurd," Gramsci declared that were he to sign it he would become "a complete clown." He opposed it not only tactically—because for the Italian party publicly to attack Comintern resolutions would make a mockery of communism as an international movement—but also substantively:

> I do not agree with the substance of the manifesto either. *I have a different conception of the party,* its functions, and the relations that should be established between it and the masses outside any party, *i.e.,* between it and the population in general.[10]

8. Gramsci to Julia Schucht, January 1, 1924, in *2000,* II, 27.
9. Togliatti to Gramsci, May 1, 1923, in *SPW*², 133.
10. Gramsci to Scoccimarro, January 5, 1924, in *Formazione,* 150, and *SPW*², 174. Emphasis added.

Gramsci went on to argue that it would be useless to try to persuade Bordiga to soften the manifesto, as both Scoccimarro and Togliatti were advocating, because

> one absolutely cannot make compromises with Amadeo. He is too forceful a personality and has such a deep conviction of being in the right that to think of ensnaring him with a compromise is absurd. He will continue to fight and at every opportunity will always reintroduce his theses unchanged.[11]

Gramsci thought Togliatti wrong to argue that the time was not ripe to begin to break decisively with Bordiga's leadership. Bordiga's "conception of the party's function" has led to a "crystallization [of the party] into purely organizational debates and hence to real political passivity."[12] To Gramsci, both the Left faction of Bordiga and the Right faction of Tasca conceived of the party inorganically, as if the only question that mattered was the issue of fusion with the Socialist party. The Communist party was imprisoned in internal factional polemic to such an extent that it neglected its *raison d'être*, which was to encourage new mass formations of the dispossessed and marginalized, lasting longer than just a few hours, to come into being.[13]

Gramsci then dramatically declared his intention to proceed alone if necessary to design a new role for the Italian Communist party:

> I will write a report in which I will combat both of them [*i.e.*, the Bordigian Left and the Tascan Right] in my capacity as a member of the CC (Central Committee) of the party and the Comintern Executive. I will accuse both of them of the same fault, and will take the doctrine and tactics of the Comintern as the basis for an action program . . . for the future. . . . I assure you that no arguments from all of you will succeed in shifting me from this position.[14]

With those words, written in January, 1924, Antonio Gramsci emerged as the *de facto* leader of the Italian Communist party. He also emerged as the architect of a new kind of party.

A few days later, in what was quickly becoming a thick pile of cor-

---

11. *Ibid.* I have changed "represent" to "reintroduce" as the proper translation of *ripresentare*. See *Formazione*, 150, for the original version.

12. *Ibid.*

13. *Ibid.*, 151, and *SPW²*, 174.

14. *Ibid.*

respondence to his party comrades in Rome, Gramsci conveyed his thoughts on how the Italian Communist party of the future should be organized. He wrote crisply and authoritatively about how to resolve the tension that would inevitably occur between those who had been Communists from the first hour and the mass of new recruits a re-founded party would bring into its ranks. In order to prevent the original party faithful from being submerged in a tidal wave of new members (as had happened in the PSI after the war), it was necessary to guarantee that for the first five years after freedom (from fascism) is re-gained, the party's top posts would be filled by those who had endured major sacrifices during the period of Fascist persecution. However, these early members could not assume that they would hold these posts by right; on the contrary, they were sedulously to prepare themselves to lead. He called for the creation of party schools sufficient to prepare three hundred members capable of directing work in an entire province, and three thousand who could be responsible for smaller units. He clearly thought that one of the party's chief tasks was to prepare a government in waiting.[15]

In the letter of January 14 referred to above, Gramsci made clear that the party must not sit by passively waiting for the revolution to happen, but must actively promote a new climate of ideas in Italy as an alternative to the existing one. His letter is brimming with ideas for the party to serve as educator of its members and any others it could reach. He called for establishing a party quarterly, the first issue of which he outlined in detail. Characteristically, the quarterly, to be named *Critica Proletaria,* would even have space reserved for Bordiga to write on problems of revolutionary tactics, provided that others might engage him in a debate "of an elevated character." Other articles would focus on Rosa Luxemburg's analysis of capitalist accumulation, the program of the Comintern, prospects for a workers' and peasants' government in Italy, school reform, the structure of Italian industry, and the politics of the Vatican. Gramsci assigned each leading party figure a topic regardless of whether they were in agreement with him or not. Thus, he assigned Angelo Tasca the job of proposing a reform of the public schools and universities.

15. Gramsci to the executive committee of the Italian Communist party, January 14, 1924, in Somai, *Gramsci a Vienna,* 167–68. The greater part of this letter was not included by Togliatti in *Formazione;* none of the letter is in *SPW*[2].

Functioning as a kind of prime minister-in-exile, Gramsci sought to fashion a collective leadership for the party; his objective was not to substitute one sectarian view for another, or one clique for another, but to tap *all* the party's creative energies, to liberate initiatives from the bottom up, to ensure that each policy be subjected to the most rigorous criticism, and above all to develop an alternative vision of the good society. As he was to put it in his *Prison Notebooks,* the party was to develop a complex of ideas and institutions capable of replacing the current capitalist hegemony.

Gramsci reveals himself in the Vienna letters once again to be a man who freely and impartially criticizes his friends and expects the same in return from them. He also reveals himself as a theorist-practitioner *par excellence* and as the creator of a new style of political theory that seeks to relate the general principles of Marxist social criticism to the most detailed knowledge of the local situation. Thus, in the same paragraph of his January 14 letter he calls on his comrades to prepare anthologies of the essence of Marxism along with detailed analyses of Italy's *questione meridionale* (Southern question), of how to organize a "red army," and how to assist the self-taught worker (*l'operaio autodidatta*).[16]

He advises Umberto Terracini, who took Gramsci's place as Italy's chief delegate to the Comintern, on how best to organize a cooperative for importing lemons to Russia from Italy and how to resolve the question of the proper wage scale for Italian workers in the USSR. No problem large or small escapes the grasp of his practice-oriented intellect. His conclusions on tactics are always put forward as provisional in character, always subject to revision in the light of new evidence.

Writing to Giovanni Germanetto in March to urge him to join him in "passing to the counteroffensive," Gramsci focused on the defects of Bordiga's politics. Bordiga and his allies must be kept in the party so that their undeniable virtues could be utilized, but they must be made to see that words must correspond to facts, that general panaceas do not exist, and that "all [preconceived] theories are destroyed in the fire of events." To accomplish this end a strong central nucleus had to be formed in the party.[17]

16. *Ibid.,* 171–72. The anthologies were to include Marx's *Eighteenth Brumaire* and *The Civil War in France,* as well as Engels' *AntiDuhring.*

17. Gramsci to Germanetto, March 19, 1924, in Somai, *Gramsci a Vienna,* 203–204.

GRAMSCI'S TACTILE EXPERIENCE OF POLITICAL REALITY

The aptness of Ruggero Grieco's previously discussed characterization of Antonio Gramsci as a thinker who "breaks his subject down into a thousand elements" and then "dissects, measures, and experiences them in a tactile way" is vividly borne out in the letters from Vienna.[18] In Vienna, Gramsci began to analyze the politics of other Communist parties and to interview their leaders whenever possible.

In his lengthy letter of February 9, 1924, Gramsci insisted that a new conception of Communist politics must transcend the banal and superficial distinction inherited from parliamentary factional politics of Right, Left, and Center. In the most lengthy and important of his Vienna letters—that of February 9, 1924, to Togliatti, Terracini, and others—Gramsci insisted that the conventional political nomenclature—which in the Russian case positions Radek, Bukharin, and Trotsky on the Left; Zinoviev, Kamenev, and Stalin on the Right; with Lenin occupying the Center—obscures the fact that the so-called Left resembles to an extent the old Menshevite party disguised in revolutionary language. Before 1917, Trotsky was politically to the left of the Bolsheviks, while on organizational questions he often made a bloc with or actually could not be distinguished from the Mensheviks.

Commenting on the controversy over the NEP (New Economic Policy) in the USSR and its effect on the power struggle to succeed Lenin, Gramsci wrote:

It is well known that in 1905 Trotsky already thought that a socialist and working-class revolution would take place in Russia, while the Bolsheviks [*i.e.,* Lenin] only aimed to establish a political dictatorship of the proletariat, allied to the peasantry, that would serve as the framework for the development of capitalism, which was not to be touched in its economic structure. It is [also] well known that in November, 1917, while Lenin and the majority of the party had gone over to Trotsky's view and intended to take not merely political but also economic power, Zinoviev and Kamenev . . . wanted a coalition with the Mensheviks and Social-Revolutionaries. They therefore left the Central Committee of the party . . . and came very close to a split. It is certain that if the *coup d'état* had failed in November, 1917 . . . Zinoviev and Kamenev would . . . probably

18. Ruggero Grieco, profile of Gramsci in the Bordigan journal *Promoteo,* March, 1924, p. 30.

have gone over to the Mensheviks. In the recent polemic that has broken out in Russia, it is clear that Trotsky and the opposition in general, in view of Lenin's long absence from the leadership of the party, have been greatly preoccupied about the danger of a return to the old mentality. . . . Demanding a greater intervention of proletarian elements in the life of the party and a diminution of the powers of the bureaucracy, they want . . . to prevent a gradual transition to . . . developing capitalism, which was still the program of Zinoviev and Co. in November, 1917. This seems to me to be the situation in the Russian party . . . ; the only novelty is the passage of Bukharin to the Zinoviev, Kamenev, Stalin group.[19]

Continuing his tactile thinking, Gramsci turned his attention to the Byzantine power struggle in the German Communist party, preoccupation with which had led to the disastrous attempt at a *coup d'état* in October, 1923. As with the Soviet case, the point was to illumine the inadequacy of abstract typologies such as Left, Right, and Center:

The two groups that are competing for the party leadership are both inadequate and incompetent. The so-called minority group (Fischer-Maslov) undoubtedly represents the majority of the revolutionary proletariat; but it has neither the necessary organizational strength to lead a victorious revolution in Germany, nor a firm, stable line that can safeguard it against still worse catastrophes than those of October. It is made up of elements who are new to party activity and who find themselves at the head of the opposition only because of the absence of leaders that is characteristic of Germany. *They represent the great masses in the same way that the foam on the top of the waves represents the ocean.*[20]

Turning to the group led by Brandler and Thalheimer, Gramsci characterizes them as "revolutionary Talmudists":

Wanting at all costs to find allies for the working class, they have ended up by forgetting the function of the working class itself. Wanting to win over the labor aristocracy . . . they have thought they could do so . . . by seeking to compete with the Social Democrats on the terrain of democracy.[21]

19. Gramsci to Togliatti, Terracini, and others, February 9, 1924, in *Formazione*, 186, 187, and *SPW²*, 191–92.
20. *Ibid.* Emphasis added. The last line was not included in *Formazione* and therefore is absent from *SPW²* as well. I have consulted the definitive manuscript of Elsa Fubini at the Istituto Gramsci in Rome.
21. *Ibid.*, 188, and 193.

"Which of the two groups is on the right and which is on the left?" Gramsci asks rhetorically. "The question is rather Byzantine. . . . In certain respects, Brandler is a putschist more than a rightist. . . . Radek and Trotsky made the mistake of believing the confidence tricks of Brandler and Co.; but in fact even in this case their position was not a right-wing but a left-wing one, laying them open to the accusation of putschism."[22]

Gramsci's main point in this complex analysis was to illustrate the disastrous results of making decisions and forming groups according to abstract Right, Left, and Center distinctions. Such distinctions serve only to paper over the banal reality of a power struggle on behalf of Comintern President Zinoviev. Thus, the Brandler group attempted a *coup d'état* in order to prevent the minority (Fischer-Maslov) from getting control at the next party congress. Radek and Trotsky were taken in by Brandler, believing that the latter was supporting Trotsky's doctrine of permanent revolution, condemned as leftist by Zinoviev in the Comintern, when in fact the Brandler group was rightist.

In a long letter of April 4, 1924, Gramsci gave further illustration of his hunger for detailed, concrete knowledge of the political realities. This time the principal subject was Yugoslavia. Gramsci began with an account of his recent interview with Stefano Radic, leader of the Republican party of Croatian peasants. Gramsci described Radic as very shrewd and able but as lacking the qualities that make up a great man of state. Radic was a tactician, not a strategist. He was a combination of the manipulator who knows how to make temporary compromises to stay in power and the utopian visionary who utterly lacks a knowledge of concrete possibilities:

> On general questions his views are utopian, ignoring the real relationships of competing forces and attaching excessive importance to ideology—and to a nebulous, democratic, humanitarian ideology at that.[23]

Turning to the Yugoslavian Communist party, Gramsci pronounced it a "metaphysical entity." Instead of there being a single Communist party, there seemed to be as many parties as there were regions. The

22. *Ibid.*, 188, and 193–94.
23. Gramsci to the Central Committee of the PCd'I, April 4, 1924. This is from a report entitled "Stefano Radic e la situazione in Jugoslavia," in Somai, *Gramsci a Vienna*, 110.

resulting paralysis of the Yugoslavian Communist party left the way open to someone like the opportunist Radic, who could detach himself in a definitive way from "bourgeois democracy."[24]

Gramsci's long letter of April 4 concludes with remarks about the Greek Communist party and, quite interestingly, on the need to establish a Communist party in Albania.[25] Gramsci's name was of Albanian origin; his ancestors on his father's side had immigrated to Sardinia in the last century.

GRAMSCI ANALYZES THE ITALIAN PARTY

Gramsci's analyses of other Communist parties reveal clearly that his opposition to Bordiga's stewardship of the party rested on other than personal grounds. Bordiga shared the same faults as some of the Russian, German, and Balkan figures described above. Like them, Bordiga conceived of the party as a metaphysical entity without roots in the soil of real social forces.

In one of his earliest lengthy letters from Vienna to Togliatti, Gramsci identified the Italian party's organizational problems as political in nature. After Bordiga's arrest it was discovered that there were at least two different party centers often working at cross purposes. The organizational mess in the party, wrote Gramsci, "is the consequence of a general political conception. The problem is thus a political one."[26]

Luciano Pellicani has written that Gramsci conceived of the Italian Communist party "according to the operative model of the Catholic Church." Party functionaries were bishops and priests (with Gramsci as pope?) ruling over masses of simple people (*i semplici*). According to Pellicani, the principles of "hierarchy, ideological unity, discipline, indoctrination, systematic eradication of heresy, and expulsion of deviants from the community" were the hallmarks of the Gramscian conception of the party.[27] In truth, Pellicani has described the very model of the party that Gramsci attacked and explicitly rejected.

---

24. *Ibid.,* 115.
25. *Ibid.,* 116.
26. Gramsci to Togliatti, January 27, 1924, in *Formazione,* 180, and *SPW*[2], 187.
27. Luciano Pellicani, *Gramsci: An Alternative Communism?* (Stanford, 1981), 51. Pellicani also claims astonishingly that Gramsci's "organic intellectual" is only "a variant of the traditional figure of the priest."

The conception of the party advanced by Gramsci was *sui generis*. His model was neither that of the Catholic Church (as portrayed by Pellicani) nor that of liberal democracy. In his letter of January 13, 1924, Gramsci made clear that the existence of different "currents" was a sign of the vitality of a revolutionary party. These currents were not to be confused with the factions in liberal-democratic parties. Factions have their origins in conflicting class interests. Currents, on the other hand, constantly form and reform because in the Communist party only one class is represented—the proletariat.[28]

In his letter of February 9, Gramsci rejected Bordiga's idea, expressed in his manifesto, that the party was a unitary collective organism independent of the consciousness and will of individuals. The idea that it is the party as a whole that counts, while individual members are nothing, amounts to treating the members as serfs who are supposed to obey the decrees and peremptory orders of the leadership. This Menshevik notion of the party endorsed by Bordiga led to the withering away of all individual activity. The resultant passivity of the mass of the members produced only a stupid confidence that somebody else is always taking care of everything, Gramsci insisted.

In an important passage, Gramsci described the party as a dialectical process in which the spontaneous movement of the revolutionary masses and the organizing and directing will of the center converge. The above passage is consistent with all that we have previously learned about Antonio Gramsci's vision of a new politics as dedicated to overcoming the contrast between the center and the periphery. If he had in truth embraced the hierarchical model falsely ascribed to him by Pellicani, Gramsci would have betrayed everything he had previously written about the need for a new politics of inclusion. He also would have betrayed his basic life experiences as a hunchbacked outsider from Sardinia.

Far from conceiving the party as something rigid and fixed along the lines of a hierarchical church, Gramsci roundly rejected the notion that there is any fixed and final form for the party. Indeed, the final destiny of the party is to disappear:

> Until it disappears because it has achieved the highest ends (*i fini massimi*) of communism, it [the party] will pass through a series of transitory

28. Gramsci to Togliatti, January 13, 1924, in Fubini MS. The date of this letter is incorrectly given as January 12 in *SPW*[2], 177.

phases and will absorb new elements . . . through the recruitment either of individuals or of groups, large and small. . . .

The Communist party, Gramsci insisted, should be thought of as the new revolutionary center only in the sense that its very purpose is to abolish the distinction between center and periphery. The party's mission is ultimately to abolish itself by expanding to include the entire population: "[The party] will have assumed its definitive form only when it has become the entire population; in other words, when it will have disappeared."

Pellicani's strange conclusion that Antonio Gramsci favored a party based on the "systematic eradication of heresy" flies in the face of Gramsci's exact words to his comrades:

> The error of the party [under Bordiga] has been to accord priority . . . to . . . organization, *which in practice has simply meant creating an apparatus of functionaries who could be depended upon for their orthodoxy towards the official view.* It was believed, and is still believed, that the revolution depends on the existence of such an apparatus; it is sometimes even believed that its existence can bring about this revolution.[29]

Far from beginning to root out heresy in the party, Gramsci attacked the very idea of an orthodox party line. As Ruggero Grieco, himself a Bordiga supporter and not someone to present Gramsci in falsely idealized colors, wrote, Gramsci was a man who desired to be contradicted.[30] This did not mean that he had a liberal view of truth as emerging from the marketplace of ideas. What it did mean was that full and free debate should exist in the party about the best means to achieve the final ends of communism, and that judgments of policy should be based on the quality of the arguments behind them rather than on the rank or personal prominence of the person proposing them. Just as Gramsci in the winter of 1924 felt free vigorously to advance to his friends a new orientation for the party, so he wanted them just as vigorously to criticize both his conception and his conduct. His remarks to Umberto Terracini, who had written from Moscow to express surprise over the sharpness of tone in Gramsci's letters on how best for Italians in the USSR to organize a lemon-importing cooperative, are reminiscent of

29. Gramsci to Togliatti, Terracini, and others, February 9, 1924, in *Formazione,* 195, and *SPW*², 197–98. Emphasis added. I have translated *i fini massimi* the "highest ends" instead of the "ultimate aims."

30. Ruggero Grieco, "Gramsci," *Promoteo,* I (February 15, 1924), 30.

how the members of the Club for the Moral Life in Turin had pledged each other mutual criticism:

> I have noted in you a certain attitude to look with disdain on the work of those who preceded you as being of small value. Either that is so or you forget completely what they did. I think this method is mistaken. I want to say this frankly because I believe that you will not be offended, since you are aware that I too will welcome all observations from you made in a friendly spirit to help me correct bad habits and prevent mistakes. If in my irritation I offended you, however unintentionally, I am truly sorry and ask you to forgive me.[31]

To conclude this analysis of Gramsci's understanding of the party, Pellicani's accusation that Gramsci favored expulsion of deviants from the community needs to be considered. Once again one must stress that Gramsci did not have a liberal-democratic view of the party and undoubtedly valued (outward) party unity more highly than did liberal capitalist political parties. As we shall see more fully in the next chapter, however, Gramsci's passion for mutual criticism led him not only to retain his principal rival (Bordiga) in the party, but even to include him in its highest councils. The whole idea of the Communist party as a small band of ideologues whose purity had to be safeguarded by frequent expulsions was anathema to Gramsci. Gramsci wanted to *include* more elements of the marginalized sectors of the population in the party rather than to exclude those already within its ranks who dissented from his views.

To sum up Gramsci's view of the party as revealed in the Vienna letters, he desired a party open to new initiatives and to new social elements, as opposed to a party based on secretiveness and intrigue. He spoke derisively to Terracini of those in the party who merely "know how to maneuver" and who "have a politically more 'Bolshevik' temperament than we do."[32] He was against Bordiga's affinity for mechanical and absolute positions. He was also against Bordiga's penchant for "throwing rocks into the dark," by which he meant the Neapolitan engineer's desire to have the party use public invective against the Com-

---

31. Gramsci to Terracini, February 16, 1924, in Somai, *Gramsci a Vienna*, 195. The letter urges Terracini to plan to return to Italy from Moscow to take part in "the organization of an opposition." He did so in August, 1924.

32. Gramsci to Terracini, February 24, 1924, in Somai, *Gramsci a Vienna*, 197.

intern without weighing the consequences.[33] He did not want a party "suspended in the air," without any roots in real social forces. He did not want a party of functionaries. He wanted a new generation of leaders in touch with newly emerging social forces at society's margins and dedicated to building a new culture of inclusiveness.

One can detect in the February 9 letter the origin of the great distinctions, to be elaborated in the *Prison Notebooks,* between "political society" and "civil society" and between "the war of position" and "the war of manuever." Typically, Gramsci arrived at these theoretical constructs via his involvement in the detailed, concrete struggle against Amadeo Bordiga and his followers over the shape, form, and future of Italian communism:

> Amadeo . . . thinks that the tactic of the International reflects the Russian situation, *i.e.,* was born on the terrain of a backward and primitive capitalist situation. For him this tactic [of a common front with the PSI and other "progressive" elements to overthrow fascism and begin the revolution] is extremely voluntaristic and theatrical, because only with extreme effort of will was it possible to obtain from the Russian masses a revolutionary activity that was not determined by the historical situation. He thinks that for the more developed countries of central and eastern Europe this tactic is inadequate or even useless. In these countries the historical mechanism functions according to all the approved schemes of Marxism. There exists the historical determinism that was lacking in Russia, and therefore the overriding task must be the organization of the party as an end in itself.[34]

For Gramsci, Bordiga's argument is flawed both in principle and in detail. Bordiga is wrong in principle because there is no such thing as an objectively revolutionary economic situation that will automatically cause capitalism's collapse. The element of will is indispensable to achieving victory in the revolution wherever and whenever it occurs. One must have a party with the ability to raise the consciousness of the workers and provide a new conception of life, inspiring the mobilized masses to make a revolution, as distinct from merely seizing power.

Gramsci maintains that Bordiga is wrong in detail because he does not understand that, while in Europe the proletariat in 1924 is much

---

33. Gramsci to Terracini, March 9, 1924, in Somai, *Gramsci a Vienna,* 199.
34. Gramsci to Togliatti, February 9, 1924, in *SPW²,* 199.

more developed than it had been in Russia in 1917, Western capitalism has also created additional political superstructures capable of retarding the advent of communism. The existence of these political superstructures

> requires the action of the masses to be slower and more prudent, and therefore requires of the revolutionary party a strategy and tactics altogether more complex and long-term than those that were necessary for the Bolsheviks in the period between March and November, 1917.[35]

Gramsci points out, then, that Bordiga is utterly deluded in thinking that Italy is on the brink of a proletarian revolution. On the contrary, if fascism collapses or is overthrown, in the immediate aftermath the majority of the working class will go with the reformists (with Turati's Socialists), and the liberal-democratic bourgeois will still have a great deal to say about what is to be done. The Italian Communist party must be ready to win over the majority of the working class by demonstrating superior understanding of the crisis and by making alliances with newly emerging social formations.

The Italian party, asserts Gramsci, must also reject Bordiga's dogmatic insistence that Soviet hegemony in the Comintern is ephemeral and will shift to the West. Bordiga had insisted that Marx would be vindicated in Bordiga's prediction that the real revolution would occur first in the countries where capitalism is most fully developed, that is, in western Europe. Gramsci's rejoinder was that the October Revolution did not take place in a vacuum but is indissolubly related to the worldwide communist movement. As the first Communist party to take power, the Soviet Communist party will retain indefinitely the status of first among equals in the world revolution. Bordiga's call for the Italian party to work to contain Soviet influence in the Comintern until "the revolution in western and central Europe deprives Russia of the hegemonic position it holds today"[36] is nothing short of madness and would result only in the PCd'I's expulsion and consequent loss of influence.

Ever distrustful of slogans and simplistic schemes and ever open to the concrete specifications and nuances of the historical context, Antonio Gramsci reveals himself in this remarkable treatise-letter of February 9, 1924, to have been a "critical Communist" who argued *both*

35. *Ibid.*, 199–200.
36. *Ibid.*, 200.

for the hegemony of a genuinely creative Soviet party in the Comintern *and* for the recognition that the revolution in each country will be achieved in ways indigenous to that country's history, economic and social structure, and party efficacy. To Gramsci, the revolution, while conditioned economically, will have to be achieved politically. This meant finding and educating Communists who would know exactly what was going on and what is needed to be done. The revolution in Italy would occur only through the application of political will—not the political will of one individual and his clique, but of an active, well-organized *party*, open to the masses. The name Gramsci was to hit upon in the *Prison Notebooks* for such a party was the "Modern Prince."

Gramsci advanced four modest proposals for beginning the transformation of the PCd'I into a party capable of leading a revolution: (1) the whole Central Committee should be given more work instead of leaving everything to a small party executive; (2) a stricter division of labor and allocation of responsibilities should be established between the various party offices; (3) a commission made up predominantly of old workers should be created to adjudicate administrative disputes and to keep an accurate membership list; and (4) an agitation and propaganda committee should be organized to study local situations and propose varied forms of agitation.

Gramsci closes his letter by calling for greater attention to be paid to the *mezzogiorno*, or Italian south. Here one can see the Sardinian in him, even—or especially—while trapped in the depth of a Viennese winter. Continued exploitation of the south by northern capitalism and the emergence of a southern industrial bourgeoisie raise the possibility that the south will become the "grave of fascism." On the other hand, the *mezzogiorno* could become the "marshaling-ground for national and international reaction if, before the revolution, we do not adequately study its problems and are not prepared for everything." [37]

Gramsci's theme of a new politics of inclusion is written all over this important letter. Bordiga's tragic flaw, Gramsci argues, is his purist mentality leading him to exclude the masses from meaningful participation in the national party and the national party from meaningful participation in the International. Above all, the party must overcome its doctrinaire exclusion of the southern peasants from its calculations.

37. *Ibid.*, 203.

(Bordiga regarded them as irretrievably reactionary.) Bordiga's caste of mind will not permit him to move toward a politics of inclusion: it will only permit him to seek to substitute a Communist politics of exclusion for the existing capitalist structure.

In the February 9 letter Gramsci wrote that "the Statute of the International gives to the Russian party *de facto* hegemony (*egemonia*) of the world organization." He also argued that the "material basis" of the Soviet state gave "its supremacy (*supremecizia*) a permanent character difficult to impugn"[38] by any party that had not made a successful revolution.

Gramsci's affirmations of deference to the Soviet party need to be interpreted in the specific context of the polemic against Bordiga. They were not intended to mean that the Soviet party, through the Comintern, was in a position to give orders to the other parties, as if those parties had no indigenous politics of their own. This point needs to be borne in mind when, as secretary-general, Gramsci carried out the so-called Bolshevization policy of the Comintern. In his letter to Terracini of February 24, 1924, Gramsci spoke ironically of the term *Bolshevik* when he wrote of his fear that the PCd'I might fall "into the hands of the Socialists, who know how to maneuver better than we do and who have a more 'Bolshevik' political temperament than we do."[39]

In the Vienna letters Gramsci repeatedly inveighed against the puerile idea that the success of a revolution is guaranteed "only because at the head of the proletarian party there are specific persons named Tizio and Caio instead of Sempronio and Vegezio."[40] The last sentence, of course, dramatically illustrates Gramsci's aversion to the cult of personality. While no Stalinist, Bordiga encouraged the kind of discipleship that made Ruggero Grieco tell a Comintern official that Bordiga was not the kind of man who submitted to discipline but the kind who imposed it.[41] Gramsci on the other hand always saw himself as a party man. In a letter of March 27 he emphasized to Togliatti that he did not present his ideas as directives but as suggestions.[42] Gramsci's proposals in the Vienna letters for a new course for the Communist party stress

38. *Ibid.*, 194. I have revised the *SPW*[2] translation on the basis of *Formazione*, 190.
39. Gramsci to Terracini, February 24, 1924, in *Formazione*, 217.
40. Gramsci to Scoccimarro and Togliatti, March 1, 1924, in *Formazione*, 226.
41. Laurana Lajolo, *Gramsci: Un uomo sconfitto* (Milan, 1980), 82.
42. Gramsci to Togliatti, March 27, 1924, in *Formazione*, 256.

dispersing and multiplying power through progressively greater inclusion of members in the real life of the party. Far from exalting "Tizio"
or "Sempronio" as *capo* (leader) of the party, Gramsci's politics of inclusion called for *every* member to be called a leader insofar as was possible.
"I do not agree with what you say about discipline," Gramsci wrote to
Pietro Tresso in April. "You appear to conceive it a bit too mechanically
and soldierlike (*soldatescamente*). To impose discipline one needs a
strong center *that follows an adequate politics*."[43]

In the Vienna letters, then, there begins to emerge not only a new
theory of the party but also the profile of a new style of leadership.
Gramsci was able to develop and embody this new style after his election to the newly created post of secretary-general of the PCd'I in August, 1924.

JULIA'S PREGNANCY

In late February, 1924, just as his historic campaign to engender a new
type of Communist party in Italy was in full swing, Antonio Gramsci
received a letter from Julia Schucht announcing that she was pregnant
with his child. Gramsci was elated. He, a hunchback, was going to be a
father! "Your love has strengthened me, has truly made a man of me,"
he wrote to her.

Julia's reaction was utterly different. She was thrown into a severe
depression over this unexpected pregnancy and ceased writing him for
weeks. Finally she let it be known that she was offended by Gramsci's
rather clumsy attempt to send her money through a party comrade in
Moscow.[44]

At the time, Antonio Gramsci and Julia Schucht were not married.[45]
Rather, Gramsci was registered as the father in Moscow when their son
Delio was born in August, 1924. Because of repeated complications in
Julia's emotional life, she was a long time in joining Gramsci. He did
not see the child until he returned to Moscow for a Comintern meeting
in March, 1925.

43. Gramsci to Pietro Tresso, April 1, 1924, in *Formazione*, 336. Emphasis added.
44. Gramsci to Julia Schucht, letters of March 25 and 29, 1924, in *2000*, II, 38–40.
45. Adele Cambria, *Amore Come Rivoluzione* (Milan, 1976), 95, n. 39. "Julia and Antonio were not married."

GRAMSCI ELECTED DEPUTY

Despite his concern for Julia's emotional condition, Gramsci became a much happier man in Vienna in the spring of 1924. Not only was he a new father; he was also one of the nineteen Communist party candidates elected to the Italian Chamber of Deputies in the April, 1924, general elections. Now at last he could return to Italy because his election gave him parliamentary immunity from arrest by the Fascist police. Writing to Julia, he observed that when he considered how many workers had endured Fascist persecution to vote for him, he realized that for once, to be a deputy has value and significance. To Togliatti he wrote of the opportunity the elections gave their nucleus of opponents to challenge Bordiga's predominance in the party.

THE "INDUSTRIOUS BOHEMIAN" RETURNS TO ITALY

Sergio Caprioglio has recently discovered a photograph, presumably taken on the May 1 holiday, of a smiling Gramsci. The group, including the German Communist writer Victor Serge, Serge's wife and child, and a French Communist posed near Vienna's Votivkirche, not far from Gramsci's rooms on the Florigasse.

In his memoirs Serge describes Gramsci as an "industrious Bohemian, late in going to bed at night and even later getting up in the morning." Despite his tendency to get lost on the tram, Gramsci was "intelligently of this world," Serge concluded.[46]

On May 12, 1924, Gramsci, the "industrious Bohemian," reentered Italy after an absence of over two years. He was now to face his greatest challenge—to rebuild the Italian Communist party in the shadows of the developing Fascist dictatorship.

46. Sergio Caprioglio published the photograph of a smiling Gramsci, together with Victor Serge's comments on Gramsci as an "industrious Bohemian," in *Rinascita*, April 19, 1986, p. 32.

VIII ✌ Politics Among the Ruins:
Gramsci in Rome, 1924–1926

In early June, 1924, a diminutive, hunchbacked figure trudged lamely through Rome's Stazione Termini (Station of the Baths). Antonio Gramsci had arrived in Rome. He could not know that he would be buried there in a cemetery for exiles and foreigners.

Gramsci went immediately from the station to his rented rooms in the home of a German family on the Via Versalio, just off the Via Nomentana and, ironically, not far from the Villa Torlonia, residence of his principal adversary and future jailer, Benito Mussolini. His hosts did not learn that Gramsci was either a Communist or a member of Parliament until the night of his arrest twenty-nine months later. They took him to be "*un professore serio-serio*" and treated him with great deference.[1]

Appropriately, Rome's train station was located then just as it is today in the midst of the ruins of the gigantic public baths erected by Emperor Diocletian. Since his reign the Eternal City had seen many regimes come and go. Now it was presided over by the man who claimed to embody *Roma Terza,* the Third Rome of Italian fascism, successor to the First Rome of the emperors and the Second Rome of the popes.

In the two and one-half years from his arrival until his arrest and imprisonment, Antonio Gramsci was often to return to the *piazza* in front of Termini station to take coffee in his favorite bar. He and his companions would sometimes walk down the *Corso* as far as the Roman Forum

---

1. Camilla Ravera, in *GAR,* 83.

and the Coliseum, where they would conduct party business sitting on a bench listening to the itinerant musicians.[2]

In 1924 Rome was unfamiliar territory to Gramsci. He had visited it only for brief periods while he resided in Turin. As a Roman resident, he now had ample opportunity to breathe the city's air, take in its architecture, and directly observe the principal actors in the Italian political drama. In Rome more vividly than anywhere else, Gramsci could sense how imperfectly Italian unity had been realized.[3]

In a sense, one could say that at age 33 the former "provincial boy three or four times over"[4] had completed a journey from the periphery to the center, not only of Italy, but also of the Western world. Rome was the seat of the Vatican, a museum of ancient, medieval, and modern history, and the inspiration of poets and philosophers of every land. From his own personal perspective, however, Gramsci remained a Sardinian to the last. In Rome he was a stranger in a strange land. Isolated from Julia, who until October, 1925, refused his entreaties to join him with their new son and who remained there only until October, 1926, when she returned pregnant with Giuliano to Moscow, Antonio Gramsci was engaged in a battle royal on two fronts during most of the period that he resided in Rome as a free man.[5]

As we know from the last chapter, one front of the battle was in his own party against Amadeo Bordiga and his allies on the Left. (Angelo Tasca and his group on the Right gave Gramsci no problems of any significance.) Already at the Como conference, held clandestinely in mid-May, to which he had repaired immediately upon crossing the Italian border on May 12, Gramsci had confronted Bordiga directly and at length, telling him bluntly that his sectarian and passive view of the party should be replaced with a fundamentally new orientation. "Our party," said Gramsci at Como, "must become the party of the great masses of the Italians; it must become the party that realizes the hegemony of the proletariat in the larger framework of alliances between the working class and the peasant masses."[6]

As Leonardo Paggi has shown in meticulous detail, Gramsci had

2. *Ibid.*, 86.
3. Mario Mammucari, Introduction to *GAR,* 9.
4. *Quaderni,* 1776.
5. Caprioglio, "Cronologia," in *LDC,* xxxiv–xxxviii.
6. Gramsci, Remarks at Como Conference, May, 1924, in *CPC,* 459–62, and *SPW*[2], 250–54.

worked out the essentials of his famed idea of hegemony well before he put pen to paper in the *Prison Notebooks*.[7] By the time he reentered Italy in 1924, Gramsci already understood that western Europe in general and Italy in particular needed a strategy for revolution different from that followed by Lenin in October, 1917. A revolutionary strategy adequate to the Italian situation must accomplish three goals: (1) develop a new political culture adequate to the economic power of the proletariat and the peasantry; (2) forge an alliance between the party and other social forces with similar economic interests responsive to the appeal of the new culture; and (3) create for the first time an Italian state worthy of the name, a state in which the proletariat and the peasantry, hitherto at history's margins, were the predominant force.

Gramsci gradually won his battle with Bordiga, and he did so in an open, aboveboard fashion. Disdaining the politics of intrigue, he used his new office as secretary-general of the Communist party, to which he was unanimously elected in August, 1924 (while Bordiga was sulking in his tents), as a platform from which to propagate his new strategy of revolution. In October he went directly to Naples and took on Bordiga on his home ground. (To say that Gramsci spoke with Bordiga at length would be a considerable understatement: the two adversaries conferred for fourteen hours at one sitting.) Gramsci caused to be published in the communist press his own detailed objections to Bordiga's position, along with Bordiga's response.[8]

As a result of his indefatigable activity and the unforgettable impression he made on the various local and regional party groups that he addressed, as well as of the assistance given him by his old *L'Ordine Nuovo* group, Antonio Gramsci firmly established himself as the undisputed leader of the Italian Communist party. In the summer of 1925 he had a definitive showdown with Bordiga and his allies, who had formed a "Committee of Understanding" (*comitato d'intesa*) in opposition to the Comintern's so-called Bolshevization policy supported by Gramsci. After an open confrontation with Gramsci in the party press, Bordiga dissolved his faction and at the next party congress (held in secret in Lyons, France) agreed once more to serve on the Central Committee.[9]

7. Leonardo Paggi, *Le strategie del potere in Gramsci* (Rome, 1984), 215.

8. *Ibid.*, 223.

9. Gramsci versus Bordiga in Minutes of Lyons Congress, January 21–26, 1926, in *SPW*[2], 313–34.

"Bolshevization" Gramsci-Style

Gramsci's attempt to implement the Comintern's policy of "Bolshevization" has often been interpreted anachronistically and out of context.[10] In 1924–1926, the Comintern was scarcely the monolithic juggernaut it became after Stalin's unquestioned ascendancy. We will recall Gramsci's own assessment that the Comintern could be taken as a world party "only with a great deal of salt" (*con molto sale*).[11] Then there was Gramsci's loose and informal leadership style, which depended far more on persuasion and example than on formal orders issued from the center. As Paolo Spriano has pointed out, Gramsci did not attempt to be the head (*capo*) of the party in any military sense. To have done so would have meant to violate everything he had written against looking at the party *soldatescamente* (in soldier-like fashion).[12]

Bolshevization *alla Gramsci*, then, was an altogether different matter from what the word tends to imply to Western non-Communist readers. To Gramsci, Bolshevization meant increasing the capacity of each party member to act autonomously in the light of a shared interpretation of the world calling for a new politics of including the excluded and abolishing the distinction between the center and the periphery. It meant using the works of Marx and Lenin, not as holy writ, but as indicators of how the party members should go about analyzing and taking advantage of the opportunities for revolution contained in the concrete circumstances in which they found themselves.[13]

Above all, Bolshevization in Italy meant to Gramsci prudent but fearless and uncompromising resistance to fascism and preserving party unity in the face of persecution. It did not mean a closed party or an ideologically pure sect. The party was only the means of attaining the "highest ends" of communism as he saw them—abolishing the distinction between center and periphery.

10. See Joseph Femia, *Gramsci's Political Thought: Hegemony, Consciousness, and the Revolutionary Process* (Oxford, 1981), 5, 151, and 158, n. 5, for a particularly egregious example of anachronistic misinterpretation of Gramsci as a heavy-handed "Bolshevist."

11. Gramsci to Togliatti and others, February 9, 1924, in *Formazione*, 196, and *SPW*², 199.

12. Paolo Spriano, *Gramsci e Gobetti* (Turin, 1977), 152–53. See also the entire section "Gramsci dirigente politico," 137–67.

13. To be a Bolshevik means "to have brains as well as lungs and a throat," wrote Gramsci in *L'Ordine Nuovo*, April 15, 1924, in *SPW*², 227.

The second front of the battle facing Gramsci when he arrived in Rome was, of course, fascism itself. He eventually lost this battle, but not until he had left a legacy that deserves to endure long after the intellectual and spiritual nullity called fascism has been forgotten and the silent tomb has heaped mold upon its perpetrators.

GRAMSCI LOOKS AT FASCISM IN DIACHRONIC PERSPECTIVE

Antonio Gramsci had learned early from his training in linguistics to view political and social life from a diachronic perspective, and he brought that perspective brilliantly to bear on Italian fascism. Residing in Rome, where the past was always massively present, only strengthened a tendency he had already established from 1919 onward to view the fascist present in the light of the Italian past.

With remarkable consistency in scores of articles and analyses, Antonio Gramsci had described Italian fascism as a continuation of the aimless corruption and ruin produced by the Italian petty bourgeoisie. As he wrote in his January, 1921, article "The Monkey People"—the title taken from Rudyard Kipling's *Jungle Book,* wherein the "Bandarlog," or "Monkey People," believe themselves superior to all other inhabitants of the jungle—the ruination of the petty bourgeoisie began in the last decades of the nineteenth century. The chief defect of the Italian lower middle class and its representatives such as Agostino Depretis and Giovanni Giolitti, both masters of the parliamentary game called *trasformismo,* was that it had lacked the will to found a state. Intent only on acquiring political prestige and power for themselves in order to compensate for the loss of their economic power to the large industrialists and landowners, the leaders of the lower middle class had corrupted the entire state structure from Parliament to the bureaucracy and the courts. Now, with fascism, the petty bourgeoisie was proceeding to the corruption of the streets by wresting control of them from the workers after the "Red Biennium" of 1919–1920.[14]

Ruin, ruin, and more ruin was Gramsci's characterization of the postwar Italian political and judicial order. The elections of November, 1919, in which the PSI won 156 seats compared with only 52 before the war, had offered some hope that a new state based on the power of all

14. Gramsci, "Il popolo delle scimmie," January 2, 1921, in *SF,* 9–10, and *SPW*[1], 372–73.

the people might be created. Through widespread strikes and demonstrations in support of the decision by deputies to walk out on the king as he arrived to deliver his opening address to Parliament, and in other actions, the working class forced the petty bourgeoisie (*piccola borghesia*) to beat a retreat. This retreat was only temporary, however, as increasingly numerous and important segments of the lower middle class shifted their allegiances from the official state, weakened by the war, to fascist local and regional bosses who were richer and more reliable than the official state. It soon became apparent to everyone with eyes to see that after all its ultrapatriotic rhetoric (in favor of D'Annunzio's temporary seizure of the city of Fiume awarded to Yugoslavia by the Peace Treaty and the like) was peeled away, fascism's solid core was the direct defense of industrial and agricultural property from the assaults of the revolutionary class of workers and poor peasants.[15]

The above insights, all taken from Gramsci's January, 1921, article "The Monkey People," were deepened and developed over the next three years. In March of the same year Gramsci described fascism as the movement that believes that the problems of production and exchange can be solved "with machine-guns and revolvers."[16] In April he defined fascism as "the unchaining of elemental forces that the bourgeois system of government cannot restrain." Fascism is a synonym for the far-reaching decomposition of Italian society that inevitably accompanied the decomposition of the state, which in turn was the result of the low level of civilization achieved by the nation in its first sixty years of existence. While initially the Italian state made some headway in reeducating the "semibarbaric" part of Italy to civilized conduct, with fascism there had been a resurgence of those elemental (*i.e.,* primitive) forces as a result of a long process of decomposition of the state through a succession of corrupt lower and middle bourgeois parliamentary leaders. The goal now, wrote Gramsci, was to extirpate fascism by restoring the state. A restored state would be in the hands of the proletariat, the only class capable of reorganizing production and, as a consequence, all the social relations dependent on the relations of production.[17]

The marriage of civility and revolution evident in the above passage was a hallmark of Gramsci's new politics that would be celebrated in a

15. *Ibid.,* 10–11, and 373–74.
16. Gramsci, "Italia e Spagna," March 11, 1921, in *SF,* 101, and *SPW*², 23.
17. Gramsci, "Forze elementari," April 26, 1921, in *SF,* 150–51, and *SPW*², 38–40.

memorable passage in his *Prison Notebooks,* wherein he called for the creation of a "new integral culture that would have the mass character of the Protestant Reformation and the French Enlightenment along with the classical character of Greek civilization and the Italian Renaissance. . . ." [18] By contrast, fascism represented the union of corrupt petty-bourgeois barbarism and the pseudoclassicism of the cult of the Roman Empire, replete with its emperor (Mussolini). Mussolini was a reincarnation not of Hadrian but of Nero, however. Behind the "cynically pensive" face of Machiavelli lay the "loutish jeers of Stenterello." [19] Mussolini was a clown who amused himself with "trials of strength" and "verbal masturbation." [20]

In March, 1924, Gramsci returned to the theme of Mussolini as the farcical reincarnation of Roman emperors. This time the analogy was to the Holy Roman Empire. Gramsci began his article with a tribute to the recently deceased Lenin. Whereas Lenin strove to minimize any undue adulation of himself by conserving the spirit of a simple worker on the throne of the czars, Mussolini arrogated all power and acclaim to himself. Thus, with fascism "we have an official ideology that deifies its leader, declaring him to be infallible and extolling him as the inspiration for a reborn Holy Roman Empire." Whereas in 1917 Lenin had inaugurated a new epoch in history in which meaningful participation in politics had been extended to untold millions of ordinary people hitherto excluded from power and prestige, Mussolini in 1922 had come to power to exclude everyone from such participation except himself. Lenin's doctrine was Marxism; Mussolini's had none except that "contained in his physical mask, in his eyes rotating in their sockets, and in his fist always clenched" to threaten an adversary. [21]

MURDER INCORPORATED

In June, 1924, only a few days after Gramsci arrived in Rome, Mussolini's clenched fist struck again. This time the victim was Giacomo Matteotti, a reformist Socialist deputy who had risen in the newly convened Parliament to denounce the fraud, intimidation, and downright

18. *Quaderni,* 1233.
19. Gramsci, "I capi e le masse," July 3, 1921, in *SF,* 225, and *SPW*², 53.
20. Gramsci, "Sovversivismo reazionario," June 22, 1921, in *SF,* 206, and *SPW*², 47.
21. Gramsci, "Capo," March 15, 1924, in *CPC,* 14–15, and *SPW*², 211–12.

murder committed by the Fascists in the April 6 elections. A few days after making his speech, Matteotti was kidnapped and assassinated by Fascist criminals. Eventually the assassination order was traced to the office of Mussolini's press secretary, who in turn identified Mussolini himself as its source.

Indignation over Matteotti's murder was so widespread that, momentarily at least, the Fascist regime seemed shaken to its foundations. Joining with other anti-Fascist parties, the Communists, led by Gramsci, decided to abstain from attending Parliament until justice was restored. Soon this combination of opposition parties was called the "Aventine Secession."

Gramsci immediately grasped the significance of the situation and proposed a general strike. Instead, all of the other parties—PSI, reformist Socialists, republicans, some liberals, and the *popolari* (liberal Catholics)—rejected his appeal and opted to trust the king either to remove Mussolini from the post of prime minister or to induce him to accept legal reforms and guarantees. Gramsci knew that there could be no legal resolution of the crisis; fascism could be defeated only by taking away its control of the streets. The Matteotti assassination had forced the Fascists temporarily to withdraw their militia from public view.[22]

Gramsci was in no way surprised by the killing of Matteotti. Gramsci had spent many hours in Turin, siren in hand, taking his turn as sentinel to warn the others in the building where *L'Ordine Nuovo* was published if one of the Fascist action squads had come to put it to the torch. As early as December, 1919, he had predicted that the lower middle class, its ranks swollen because of demobilization, would produce a movement whose mission would be to defeat the working class through violence. The war, he wrote, had collected together a huge mass of "social debris." These lower middle class elements "from the back of father's store, from benches warmed in vain in the middle and upper schools, and from the editorial offices of blackmailing newspapers" returned home ripe for remobilization in an antiproletarian movement.[23] Terrified by the spread of the workers' council movement and determined

22. Quintin Hoare, in *SPW*[2], 489, n. 154.
23. Gramsci, "Gli avvenimenti del 2–3 dicembre," December 6 and 13, 1919, in *ON*, 61–62, and *SPW*[1], 135–36.

to preserve their status as small businessmen or landowners against any threat of a Communist revolution, these members of the *piccola borghesia* were easily incited by Fascist bosses who organized them into private armies. Especially in the Po River valley region, Fascist action squads went on punitive expeditions against the so-called reds. While the police and the courts of a state supposedly based on the rule of law often looked the other way and even at times provided assistance, these Fascist armed gangs had set out on a regular basis to burn down Socialist, Communist, and even some anti-Fascist Catholic (*popolari*) party headquarters, newspaper offices, and the like. So widespread were these punitive expeditions that the distinguished English historian Dennis Mack Smith has called Italian fascism "Murder Incorporated."[24]

Fascist squads killed approximately 100 people in the month of May, 1921, alone. Renzo De Felice estimates that in the first six months of 1921 alone, Fascist armed gangs destroyed 17 Socialist newspapers, 59 workers' cooperatives, and 110 "chambers of labor" (recreation centers).[25]

Gramsci, who had exposed Fascist violence in several vividly written articles, had no patience with those leaders of the PSI who had signed a pact of conciliation with Mussolini in the summer of 1921.[26] Now, three years later, the same leaders still thought one could reach an accommodation with fascism and even had their trade union issue a call to the workers to remain calm in the wake of Matteotti's brutal murder. The failure of the parties in the Aventine Secession to agree on any remotely effective strategy against fascism angered Gramsci to the point where he used some of his strongest and most controversial language against some of their leaders. He called Giovanni Amendola and other prominent Socialist leaders "semi-Fascists" and, after Matteotti's body was discovered in a remote wood, called Matteotti himself "pilgrim of nothing" (*pellegrino del nulla*).[27]

To Gramsci, Matteotti's personal courage was insufficient in light of his refusal to see that fascism could be overthrown only by creating an organization for combat for the destruction of the bourgeois and parasitical state that had produced it. Despite his heroic sacrifice, Matteotti

24. Dennis Mack Smith, *Mussolini* (New York, 1982), 74.
25. Renzo De Felice, *Mussolini il fascista* (2 vols., Turin, 1966), II, 22–23.
26. Gramsci, "Bonomi," July 5, 1921, in *SF,* 226, and *SPW²,* 54.
27. Gramsci, "Il destino di Matteotti," August 28, 1924, in *CPC,* 40.

failed to see that compromise with the bourgeois state was impossible, that there was no way to create a new world without destroying fascism.[28]

During his residency among the ruins of Rome, Antonio Gramsci authored two particularly significant analyses of fascism, one an anonymous open letter published in a journal for "independently minded" Fascists and the other a speech delivered in the Chamber of Deputies. Gramsci sent the letter through the good offices of his liberal friend Piero Gobetti to Curzio Malaparte, eccentric editor of a new Fascist journal called *La Conquista dello stato* (The conquest of the state). Intrigued by the new journal's title, Gramsci began by observing that the Italian bourgeoisie had repeatedly demonstrated its incapacity to found and administer a state. He agreed with the editor that no alternative existed except to found a new type of state to be run by the nation's most creative and vigorous elements. These elements could scarcely be drawn from the petty bourgeoisie, the very class that had held political power since 1860.

What was needed, Gramsci's prominently displayed and elaborately introduced letter continued, was the creation of a new state that will be both strong and national because it will have the consent of the great majority of the population. It will be a state for all (*tutto*) the Italian people and not just for the restricted class of owners of the land and the factories. As soon as they learned to reject the lies of official Fascist propaganda, according to which communism is either the idiotic and brutal revolt of starving plebeians who favor the nationalization of women or the diabolical work of a Jewish conspiracy for world domination, disillusioned young Fascists will turn toward the Communist party.

Gramsci's letter, which appeared in the December 7, 1924, edition of Malaparte's periodical, argues that far from conquering the Italian state, fascism had allowed itself to be absorbed by that very state, just as had every other political force in power since the *risorgimento*. Gramsci's word for fascism's absorption was "normalization."[29]

Gramsci's interpretation of fascism as the latest phase of Italian liberalism was developed further six months later, this time in the presence of Mussolini, Roberto Farinacci, and other Fascist leaders, who gath-

28. *Ibid.*, 43.
29. See Sergio Caprioglio, "La conquista dello stato per Gramsci e Malaparte," *Belfagor*, XII (May 31, 1986), 256–60. Gramsci wrote the letter in November, 1924.

ered around, the better to hear and harangue him. The occasion was Gramsci's maiden—and only—speech as a member of the Chamber of Deputies.[30] In the interim, Mussolini had delivered his intransigent speech of January 3, 1925, accepting full responsibility for his handling of the Matteotti crisis and announcing the beginning of an era of one-party dictatorship. The occasion of Gramsci's speech was to oppose one of fascism's many new laws presented to Parliament to root out and silence "subversive" political forces. This particular law outlawed Italian Masonry. Gramsci attacked it, not because he esteemed Masonry, but because he saw the law as a cover for persecuting any so-called secret association, the Communists first and foremost among them.

To Gramsci, Italian liberalism had to be studied from two perspectives: (1) the economic *interests* it served and protected and (2) the *doctrine* with which it sought to legitimate those interests. The interests were those of the large industrialists and landowners; the doctrine was that of free speech, free trade, individual civil liberties, and lay (unconfessional) culture. The doctrine, however, was highly expendable and could be ignored and violated whenever it was necessary to protect the economic interests of the privileged and powerful. With the development of proletarian class consciousness during the Red Biennium of 1919–1920, the bourgeois ruling class, especially in the rural areas, welcomed the rise of the Fascist squads that terrorized the rural areas and burned down Socialist and Popular (Catholic) party meeting places, newspapers, and the like. The highest levels of the bureaucracy, judiciary, and military of the liberal Italian state were permeated with Fascist sympathizers. Liberal doctrine on civil liberties was simply ignored or interpreted to apply only to the property-owning classes.

Gramsci scarcely contended that there was no difference at all between liberalism and fascism. Indeed, from the liberal point of view, fascism had gone too far and was threatening some of liberalism's key social formations, including Masonry. What he did contend in his speech, insofar as he was permitted to deliver it by Fascist hecklers, was that, despite its harassment of some individual liberals, fascism had made its peace with the class that had brought Italian liberalism into being. Fascism represented no qualitative change with respect to the earlier liberalism of Giolitti and Facta. Gramsci's rejection of fascism's claim to be a

30. Gramsci, "Origini e scopi della legge sulle associazioni segrete," May 16, 1925, in *CPC*, 75–85.

revolutionary movement is dramatically underscored in the following exchange:

> *Gramsci:* The Fascist revolution is nothing more than the substituting of one set of administrative personnel for another.
> *Mussolini:* Of one class for another, as happened in Russia, as normally happens in all revolutions, as we are doing—methodically!
> *Gramsci:* Revolution can only be based on a new class. Fascism does not base itself on any class except the one that has already been in power . . .[31]

Gramsci was convinced that fascism would collapse because it had no program worthy of the name. Fascism's "consent" was attained through the blows of the nightstick (*bastone*). Essentially, fascism is the last gasp of the corrupt Italian liberal regime. The law, ostensibly aimed at Italian Masonry, will in truth be directed against dissident *popolari* (Catholic) deputies like Guido Miglioli and, of course, against the Communists. The Fascists will not succeed in suffocating the organized protests of the oppressed in Italian society. The truly revolutionary forces will conquer fascism, Gramsci concluded.[32]

Given the luxury of hindsight, it appears that in 1924–1926 Gramsci severely underestimated fascism's durability. He did not anticipate that the institutions of a totalitarian dictatorship—the single party, the secret police, the state-controlled economy—would give such staying power to a regressive system that it would last for over twenty years. Would he have acted differently had he known that result?

While no sure answer can be given to such a hypothetical question, I assume that he would have acted the same way even had he been given a glimpse of the future. Secure in his faith in fascism's eventual defeat, Gramsci was prepared to endure imprisonment and even death if necessary. As "captain of the ship," he could not abandon it while it was sinking with passengers aboard.[33]

A man of Gramsci's political faith had little or no room to maneuver in the Italy of the midtwenties. He had no alternative but to go down to defeat, as defeat is measured pragmatically. Gramsci's scale of measure-

31. *Ibid.*, 80.
32. *Ibid.*, 85.
33. *Quaderni*, 1762.

ment was a longer one, however, and he never lost his faith in the human capacity to shape a political order qualitatively different from all previous historical regimes. From the first line of his high school essay "Oppressed and Oppressors" to the last line of the *Prison Notebooks,* an impressive continuity of inspiration exists proclaiming that, given the political will, a periphery-centered society is feasible.

Even though he and his party comrades suffered grievously from Fascist persecution, Gramsci did not condemn fascism primarily for its violation of the civil liberties supposedly guaranteed by the *Statuto* of 1848. Rather, he condemned fascism primarily for its having acted systematically to reduce the masses to passivity and to continue in power the same parasitic, unproductive ruling class of the old order. Through the cult of the *duce* and the mobilization of the youth, fascism was the ideal instrument to channel mass energies away from meaningful action for social change.

Antonio Gramsci never wavered in his conviction that Italian fascism was the logical result of a corrupt Italian liberalism and that the only sure way to defeat fascism was to replace the system that had allowed fascism to develop. Italian liberalism, furthermore, was the ally of Italian capitalism. Thus, in one of the last articles he wrote before his imprisonment, Gramsci insisted that capitalism, not fascism, was the particular "corpse" that the Communist party had to bury. Socialists and republicans who make up the "Republican Concentration"—a group of anti-Fascists led by Pietro Nenni and Carlo Roselli—were never so engrossed in their battle against fascism that they would refuse to permit the bourgeoisie to lead them. The result would be capitalism's preservation. There is "one road that we have to open up—that which leads to socialism; this is our specific duty, and nothing else. As we proceed along this road, we [also] shall attend to the secondary tasks and questions of detail." [34]

As Agostino Del Noce has written, Gramsci's opposition to Mussolini's fascism "had nothing in common with liberal-democratic anti-fascism." [35] Postwar defenders of liberal democracy have understandably severely criticized Gramsci for his refusal to make common cause with the Aventine Secession. Their criticisms fail to take seriously that, as

34. Gramsci, "Noi e la concentrazione repubblicana," in *CPC,* 352, and *SPW²,* 423.
35. Agostino Del Noce, *Il suicidio della rivoluzione* (Rome, 1976), 275.

Giuseppe Fiori has written, Gramsci was "one of the few who were able to grasp the real novelty of fascism." [36]

Giuseppe Tamburrano, Christian Riechers, and others have accused Gramsci of extreme naivete or myopia regarding the staying power of fascism. Tamburrano notes that even after Mussolini's famous speech of January 3, 1925, taking responsibility for everything that happened and announcing new restrictions on civil liberties, Gramsci continued to write as if fascism soon would collapse, to be replaced by a brief liberal-democratic restoration, to be followed almost immediately by the proletarian revolution. [37] Christian Riechers has sharply attacked Gramsci's August, 1926, report to the party predicting that a democratic-republican coalition would bring down fascism, now weakened by defections from the lower bourgeoisie. This democratic phase "would be as short as possible." Riechers then sarcastically adds, "What happens three months later is scarcely a democratic phase but a genuinely and openly totalitarian fascist *intermezzo* that would last until 1943." [38]

Was Gramsci naive about fascism's power to repress its opponents? That is not the way he saw himself. On the contrary, he had repeatedly attacked Italian liberals for having been naive in thinking that they could stand back and let fascism do its dirty work for them against the Communists and left-wing Socialists, and then expect to continue in power. There is some justice to Gramsci's claim, made during his speech to the Chamber of Deputies:

> We [Communists] were among the few who took fascism seriously even when it seemed only a bloody farce . . . [and] when all the other parties tried to put the working class population to sleep by presenting fascism as a superficial phenomenon of very brief duration. [39]

One objection to the Tamburrano-Riechers thesis that Gramsci was naive about fascism is that its proponents overlook the fact that many of Gramsci's writings were meant to rally his own forces and give them hope. Even if intellectually he perceived the odds in favor of fascism and against his own party, his abjuration of predestination still led him to resist according to the principle "pessimism of the intellect, optimism of

36. Giuseppe Fiori, *Antonio Gramsci: Life of a Revolutionary* (New York, 1970), 159.

37. Giuseppe Tamburrano, *Antonio Gramsci* (Milan, 1977), 179–80.

38. Christian Riechers, *Antonio Gramsci: Marxismus in Italien* (Frankfurt am Main, 1970), 89.

39. Gramsci, "Origini e scopi," May 16, 1925, in *CPC*, 75.

the will." In truth, Antonio Gramsci did understand the implications of Mussolini's January 3, 1925, speech. As he wrote two days later to Mauro Scoccimarro in Moscow, the speech meant that "free Italy has been dissolved."[40] Nonetheless, he was never a defeatist and undoubtedly believed that fascism, having come to power in such a volatile political environment, might as easily fall from it. The same letter continues:

> Naturally, an attack or a chance conflict can precipitate everything. We are working to reap all the fruits [from these events] and possibly to enlarge the movement through a mass action.[41]

Gramsci theorized that the greater the Fascist repression, the greater the likelihood of a mass shift of social (not parliamentary!) forces toward a new kind of democracy involving active participation by the working classes. From the Viennese letters onward he had argued for the creation of a constitutional assembly (*la costituente*) to draft a new plan of democratic government as a rallying point against fascism.

The accusation that Gramsci was naive in the face of the Fascist danger smacks of what C. Wright Mills called "crackpot realism." The "realists" and "prudent" people in Italy in the midtwenties were either Fascists and supporters of a program of accommodation with fascism that had little if any chance for success, for the reasons Gramsci noted. What else was there to do? One could of course withdraw from the political arena, but to Gramsci such a withdrawal would itself be a political (and pro-Fascist) action. The only alternative he saw was, against all apparent odds, to try to build up a mass opposition to fascism even in the shadows of the police state. Even though he failed, he was there, on the line, pressing his strategy, giving and risking everything he had.

In a recent book, Leonardo Paggi has criticized Gramsci for having undervalued fascism's capacity to produce a new political class with technical competence. By overvaluing the purely military, or police, aspect of fascism, argues Paggi, Gramsci failed to recognize fascism's staying power by virtue of its real political strength. Paggi also claims that Gramsci failed to appreciate fascism's resilience because he interpreted the Fascist party as a reactionary version of Amadeo Bordiga's paramilitary concept of the Communist party.[42]

40. Gramsci to Mauro Scoccimarro, January 5, 1925, in Fubini MS (APC 309/8).
41. *Ibid.*
42. Paggi, *Le strategie del potere*, 242.

Paolo Spriano has also written:

The [Italian] Communists, *and Gramsci first among them,* failed accurately to perceive the gravity of the moment when fascism realized the terroristic, repressive dictatorship that opened the way to the transformation of the . . . state. . . .[43]

If even so sympathetic an observer as Spriano has rendered this judgment, one is at first inclined to accept it. Interpreters too numerous to note agree that Gramsci never understood fascism's totalitarian, or quasi-totalitarian character after January, 1925. It seems more probable, however, that Gramsci did understand fascism's totalitarian potential well before 1925 and that he refused to accept its victory as inevitable. The knowledge that something is presently the case was for Gramsci never a sufficient argument for resignation. Resistance was always better than passivity. The resistance should be intelligent to be sure, but since it took Mussolini twenty-two months after his January 3, 1925, speech to arrest Gramsci, who today can say that he was wrong in pursuing his motto "pessimism of the intellect, optimism of the will"? Would the Italian Communist party command the allegiance of one-third of Italy's voters today had Gramsci chosen to go into hiding and then into exile in 1925?

Piero Pasolini once observed:

Marxism has never adequately confronted the problem of irrationality. One can [rationally] explain to me everything about the thought and action of Gramsci, for example, except that "sentiment," that "faith" that allowed him to endure prison and death.[44]

Gramsci's own explanation for his failure to leave Italy or go into hiding in time to escape his imprisonment was provided in a passage entitled "autobiographical notes" in his *Quaderni,* wherein he endorsed the principle that "the captain should be the last to leave the sinking ship." These remarkable pages of the *Quaderni,* coupled with the prison letters explaining his refusal to ask for a pardon, are more than sufficient to explain why Gramsci chose to stay and fight fascism even against overwhelming odds. Thanks above all to Gramsci's leadership, Domenico Zucaro could write:

43. Paolo Spriano, *Antonio Gramsci and the Party: The Prison Years* (London, 1979), 20.
44. Piero Pasolini, *The Ashes of Gramsci* (Peterborough, 1982), 11.

The only party remaining in 1926 truly to challenge fascism was the Communist party; even the other forces of the left . . . were tied to the Aventine wagon.[45]

GRAMSCI ON THE RUINATION OF THE SOVIET COMMUNIST PARTY

Gramsci's most important political act before his imprisonment in November, 1926, was his October letter in the name of the Italian Communist party to the leadership of the Communist party of the Soviet Union (CPSU), the background of which is as follows. In the spring of 1926 the Soviet party was racked by factional strife. The Stalin-Bukharin majority clashed with the so-called Joint Opposition led by Trotsky, Zinoviev, and Kamenev. On the eve of the party congress in October, the Joint Opposition called for a truce, promising in return to cease organizing as a faction.

Gramsci's lengthy handwritten letter, mailed in haste to Togliatti for editing and translation into Russian, made a number of points, chief among them that the Stalin-Bukharin majority should refrain from winning a crushing victory or from imposing excessive measures. "Comrades Zinoviev, Trotsky, and Kamenev have at times contributed significantly to educate us about the revolution. They have been among our teachers and at times have severely and energetically corrected our errors." Gramsci's letter of early October, 1926, concludes with the following declaration:

The unity of our brother party in Russia is essential for the growth and triumph of world revolutionary forces. . . . The harm done . . . by a schism . . . could be irreparable and mortal.[46]

Gramsci's letter aroused great alarm in Togliatti, who considered it inexpedient.[47] It is uncertain whether he ever transmitted it despite Gramsci's insistence in a second letter that he do so. In any event, the letter is very revealing about Gramsci's style and concept of party leadership. Even though the Italian party had only about thirty thousand

45. Domenico Zucaro, *Il processone* (Rome, 1958), 29.
46. Gramsci, "Al comitato centrale del partito comunista sovietico," October 14, 1926, in *CPC*, 130–31.
47. Togliatti to Gramsci, October 18, 1926, in *CPC*, 133.

members at the time, Gramsci saw the Communist International not as a place where the Soviet party majority wreaked its will on the world's other parties, but as a forum within which even the great Soviet party could be instructed and corrected by a "brother party" if necessary.

As in the autumn of 1926 he surveyed the world around him, Antonio Gramsci can only have seen ruin everywhere. In Italy every day brought news of more comrades killed or imprisoned by the Fascist dictatorship. Abroad in the USSR, the specter of what in the *Prison Notebooks* Gramsci referred to as Stalin's "statolatry" reared its ugly head. In chapter 6 we noted that, at least as early as January, 1924, in a letter from Vienna to Julia Schucht, Gramsci had declared that he did not know how to account for Stalin's most recent attack on Leon Trotsky. "This attack seems to me at once irresponsible and dangerous."[48] That he scented Stalinism and witnessed against it before it became a reality is evident from his October, 1926, appeal to the CPSU.

In the *Prison Notebooks* Antonio Gramsci proclaimed his motto to be "pessimism of the intellect, optimism of the will." Even though his intellect told him in a thousand ways that he could not build a new politics in the middle of the ruins of Rome, and that even in Moscow the October Revolution was on the verge of being reduced to rubble by Stalinism, Gramsci refused to give up his quest to construct a new political architecture.

THE PARTY AS THE ANTECHAMBER TO THE NEW POLITICS

Antonio Gramsci was justly proud of what he had been able to achieve as party leader in a brief period of time. Thus, at the meeting of the executive committee of the Comintern in Moscow in the spring of 1925, he delivered an impassioned defense of the Italian party against a Soviet delegate who, thinking it still under Bordiga's control, had accused the PCd'I of *Carbonarismo*. (The *Carbonari*, or "Charcoal Burners," were an ineffective secret society in Italy in the early nineteenth century.) Gramsci detailed the many mass meetings and demonstrations around the country sponsored by the party, its activity in numerous factories, and the recent tripling of party membership—all achieved in the face of

48. Gramsci to Julia Schucht, January, 1924, in Fubini MS.

increased Fascist terror. He was at pains to show that the party's influence extended far beyond its ranks to a large number of sympathizers.[49]

Camilla Ravera, Gramsci's principal administrative assistant in Rome,
has written of the extraordinary openness and informality of Gramsci's
leadership style:

> He put great store in acting in such a way that there was never any idea of
> a leader-follower relationship. . . . [He was not a leader who] commands
> you to do something; you had to show first you believed it was right.
>
> He listened with great attention to everyone. . . . I never saw him display
> a lack of respect for anyone, even those who contradicted him in an offen-
> sive way.[50]

Specifically referring to the way in which Gramsci prepared the party
for the congress at Lyons in January, 1926, Ravera recounted that every
provincial congress elected its own delegates to the national congress.
Gramsci chaired several of these provincial congresses, including those
of Sardinia, Tuscany, Puglie, and the Veneto:

> In all the provincial congresses he always presented a document; the first
> part began with a note on the state of the party, with the objective of
> securing the contributions of all those who participated. . . . The [pro-
> vincial] congress itself, it is well to remember, was organized on the basis
> of cells and was generally held in a comrade's house, so limited was the
> number of members [who could be present under clandestine condi-
> tions]. Or it was held outside in a remote place. . . . The majority of
> those present were party members, but there were many who were not
> members. In many places the meetings were open to the ranks of all the
> so-called sympathizers (*simpatizzanti*). . . . In fact, some young people
> participated.[51]

> While voting was restricted to party members, the discussions were open
> to the sympathizers, including even some Socialists. Gramsci always
> wanted the party to be open to debate and uninhibited discussion. Cer-
> tainly one had to be prudent because of the situation in which we found
> ourselves. The [national] congress, however, was prepared after many

49. Gramsci, Report to the fifth annual meeting of the enlarged executive committee
of the Communist International meeting in Moscow, March 21–April 5, 1925, in *CPC*,
43–48.

50. Camilla Ravera, reminiscences of Gramsci, in *GAR*, 109.

51. *Ibid.*, 94–95

meetings . . . of cells. *I repeat, the meetings were open.* In a meeting of a cell in a factory, one could not exclude workers even if they were not party members. . . . They [the nonmembers] had a right to know what we are saying and what as Communists we were proposing . . . said Gramsci. Thus the meetings were open to everyone we knew to be a sympathizer.[52]

As Camilla Ravera noted, Gramsci made the party much more flexible than it had been under Bordiga.

[Bordiga tended to] see the party as an army, as a very rigid military mechanism that ought not to have contact with anyone not inscribed in the party. This attitude was the opposite of Gramsci's views, who *wanted the party to be as open as possible,* compatible with the security of its members. Bordiga instead *wanted blind and total obedience of the components of the party to himself as the center, which made decisions binding on everybody.*[53]

Whereas Bordiga had emphasized memorization and regurgitation of Marxist doctrine conceived of as a sacred text, Gramsci recognized that a greater elasticity in the conception of what it meant to be a Communist was needed, especially regarding the youth:

"You cannot ask a young person only sixteen years old who wants to join the Communist youth group, 'Have you studied Marx? Do you know his doctrines well?'" Gramsci correctly observed. "You cannot ask him because he possibly does not even know who Marx was. He may still want to work with the Communists because he has seen what they [the workers] do in the factory, what they say in diverse circumstances and in response to specific events, and he finds himself in agreement with them. Then you should say, 'Fine, join the Communist youth group.'"[54]

Gramsci's emphasis on direct experience did not lead him to neglect the importance of study, however. As party secretary, he set up party schools for young people. No doctrinal test was required (for enrollment) in the schools, and practicing Catholics in particular were welcomed:

"That young person over there goes to Mass every day," [said Gramsci to Ravera when they visited the Communist party school in Rome]. "I

52. *Ibid.*
53. *Ibid.*, 96. Emphasis added.
54. *Ibid.*, 105.

don't ask him anything about it. He comes to hear what we think, because what we say and what we write in our newspapers interests him."[55]

Although he wanted young party members to learn about Marx's analysis of capitalism, he did not exclude them because of their religious beliefs and practices. In a country that was 97 percent Roman Catholic, Gramsci expected many Communists to be Catholics.

A voracious reader, Gramsci never forgot that even in the 1920s huge numbers of party members were illiterate. They could not be reached through the language of resolutions at party conferences. As a consequence, Gramsci learned to speak directly, appealing to their ordinary experiences. When he addressed party meetings, he made the uneducated and illiterate feel included. Using simple analogies, he translated Marxism—or "critical communism"—into everyday life.

Unquestionably, Gramsci's Sardinian background helped him appreciate how an illiterate worker thought:

> The first time that I heard Gramsci was in a large room in the *camera del lavoro* in Turin. He spoke with his characteristic conversational tone, without ever raising his voice. Unless complete silence prevailed one could hear nothing. The room was full of workers. Some university professors were also there. Piero Gobetti was there also. . . . There was silence, as if the room were empty. If anyone coughed, one heard someone whisper "Leave!" They do not want any noise to prevent their hearing every word. The workers listened. For example, [Battista] Santhia, who was illiterate, came in the evening [with some fellow workers] to look for him [Gramsci]. . . . They had understood Gramsci's talk so well that they wanted to continue to speak with him. . . . I have never heard anyone else speak as Gramsci did.[56]

Camilla Ravera's recollections about Gramsci's style of leadership have been confirmed by numerous other party members and associates. Alfonso Leonetti, editor of *L'Unità* when Gramsci was secretary-general of the party, has written that Gramsci's understanding of what was meant by party unity had nothing to do with the false monolithism that arose in the Communist world under Stalin's ascendancy. Gramsci insisted always on the need for vigorous political debate in the party.[57]

55. *Ibid.*, 106.
56. *Ibid.*, 108.
57. Alfonso Leonetti, reminiscences of Gramsci, in *GAR*, 61.

The historian Paolo Spriano has noted that Gramsci's primacy in the Italian Communist party was of an intellectual, spiritual, and ideological character. He did not like to adopt disciplinary measures when leading the party.[58]

The best, most concrete illustration of what Antonio Gramsci meant by breaking with the old politics of hierarchy, secrecy, and exclusion can be found in his praxis as secretary-general from 1924 to 1926. The notion that party discipline consisted of a passive and supine acceptance of orders[59] was worthy of fascism and could never give rise to a flowering of a new politics on the ruins of the old.

58. Paolo Spriano, *Gramsci and the Party,* 24.
59. Gramsci to Pietro Tresso, April, 1924, in *Formazione,* 336.

IX 🖋 Cut Off from Tactile Reality: The Prison Years, 1926–1937

On October 31, 1926, in Bologna, a fifteen-year-old boy named Anteo Zamboni attempted to assassinate Benito Mussolini. On the same day, Antonio Gramsci rode the train from Rome to Genoa for a scheduled meeting with Jules Humbert-Droz, Comintern representative for Italy, about the factional struggles in the Soviet Communist party. They were to discuss Gramsci's October 14 letter, forwarded to Togliatti in Moscow for transmission to the Soviet party leadership.[1] When Gramsci reached Milan and attempted to change trains, he was met by a police agent who "advised" him immediately to return to Rome. At that moment, Gramsci was as good as imprisoned. Zamboni's assassination attempt gave Mussolini the excuse to turn the screw a little tighter in the machinery of subjugation he had set in motion on January 3, 1925; it was the next step in the elimination of all legal opposition to the Fascist regime.

By law, as a member of Parliament, Antonio Gramsci was immune from arrest. The Fascist authorities could not even claim, as they did with respect to other anti-Fascist parties in the Aventine Secession still absent from Parliament, that the Communists had forfeited their seats by abandoning them. Gramsci had led the Communist delegation back to Parliament in late November, 1925. Making a mockery of the rule of law, Mussolini, on November 8, 1926, ordered the arrest of most Communist deputies, including Gramsci. On the following day the Fascist

1. For a discussion of Gramsci's October 14, 1926, letter, see chapter 8.

rump legislature approved a new "law," retroactively depriving all arrested deputies, Communist and non-Communist, of their parliamentary immunity.

Arrested in Rome in his lodgings on the Via Andrea Vesalio, just off the Via Nomentana, at about 10:30 P.M., soon after returning from the Parliament building in Montecitorio, Gramsci was taken directly to Regina Coeli prison. His cell was filthy, his mattress swarmed with lice, and the light from the bare bulb above his head shone throughout the night. A few days later he was transferred to a cleaner and more comfortable cell. Kept in strict isolation, he had at first no idea of his fate.[2]

The Fascists had big plans for Gramsci. As early as November 10, 1924, they had become aware of his key role in the party:

> For your proper vigilance [read a circular issued by the Ministry of Interior to all prefects] we draw your attention to the propaganda activities that the Honorable Gramsci, now secretary of the executive committee of the Communist party, has been undertaking for some time past, especially in the Islands and the south, propaganda intended to attract peasants to the Communist party and invite young men to . . . penetrate the army. . . .[3]

Ironically, the Fascist police knew more than most Communist party members about Gramsci's role in the party. Given the party's semiclandestine position under the Fascist dictatorship, the principle of anonymity prevailed, so that most party members did not even know that Gramsci was party secretary.

After sixteen days of "absolute isolation" in prison at Rome,[4] Gramsci, informed that he had been sentenced to five years confinement (*confino*), was transferred to the tiny island of Ustica, off the northern Sicilian coast. At first told that he might be shipped to Italian Somalia in galleys, a journey he probably could not have survived, Gramsci was temporarily elated over such relatively comfortable conditions. He had his old arch-rival Bordiga as one of his roommates. The prisoners were free to roam the island during the day and could purchase small sup-

---

2. Caprioglio, "Cronologia," in *LDC,* xxxiii.

3. Quoted in Paolo Spriano, *Antonio Gramsci and the Party: The Prison Years* (London, 1979), 23.

4. Gramsci to Tatiana Schucht, December 19, 1926: "My stay at Regina Coeli was the worst period of my detention: sixteen days of absolute isolation in my cell, under the most rigorous supervision."

plies of cigarettes and other items from a government store. Gramsci sometimes amused himself by talking with the local inhabitants. Interested in local lore, he learned how to catch a pig (by the hind legs, pushing it forward).[5]

In a letter to Julia, Gramsci described his daily routine on Ustica as follows:

> In the morning I am generally the first to wake up. Engineer Bordiga says that at this moment my walk has special characteristics; it is the walk of a man who has not yet had his coffee and awaits it with considerable impatience. . . . Then our life begins. We go to school, either as teachers or students. If it is a day for mail, we walk to the sea, eagerly to await the boat's arrival. If, because of bad weather, the boat carrying mail does not come, the day is ruined and a kind of melancholy descends on all of us. At noon we eat together. . . . Today it is my turn to be waiter and to wash the dishes. . . . We must be in . . . [for the night] by 8:00 P.M. . . . In the house we play cards. I had never played before. Bordiga assures me that I have what it takes to be a good player of "scientific *scopone*." I have set up a small library and can read and study. Bordiga and I argue over how best to arrange the books and newspapers. He unjustly accuses me of being very disorderly, and he sneakily puts my things in order, with the excuse that he has made them architecturally symmetrical. In reality I can't find anything in this symmetrical muddle of his.[6]

Gramsci's charming letter, replete with good-natured digs at Bordiga—the engineer whose passion for neat, symmetrical schemes carried over even into his "scientific" card playing and book arrangements—was written only five days before he was abruptly transferred, by a harrowing nineteen-day train trip, from Ustica to Milan.

Writing to Julia six years later, Gramsci described the horror of the journey:

> Exactly six years ago, I passed, guess where?—through Ravisindoli, in Abruzzo, where you will recall once having spent a summer holiday. I passed through in a metal [railroad] car . . . after remaining there all night in the snow. I had to remain seated, unable to move . . . for lack of space. I trembled with fever, my teeth chattered, and it seemed I would not be in a condition to finish the journey because my heart would by then be frozen.[7]

5. Gramsci to Tatiana Schucht, December 9 and 19, 1926, in *LDC*, 17.
6. Gramsci to Julia Schucht, January 15, 1927, in *LDC*, 43–44.
7. Gramsci to Julia Schucht, January 30, 1933, in *LDC*, 739.

Chained to common criminals and enclosed in a cattle car, Antonio Gramsci was taken in midwinter by what the government called "ordinary transportation" almost the entire length of Italy. He slept overnight in filthy local prisons at Palermo, Naples, Cajanello, Isernia, Sulmona, Castellmare Adriatica, Ancona, and Bologna. Finally, on February 7 his train arrived in Milan, and Gramsci began his time in solitary confinement.[8]

The reason for Gramsci's abrupt transfer from interior exile (*confino*) on Ustica to a harsh condition of imprisonment in Milan was that the Fascists had just enacted a new "law" setting up the Special Tribunal for the Defense of the State. This "court," whose judges were officers of the Fascist militia (MVSN), had broad powers to arrest and imprison suspected subversives. The tribunal began to function on February 1. On February 9, Enrico Macis, the tribunal's investigator, began to interrogate Antonio Gramsci. Macis did not even give Gramsci, whose wrists and ankles still ached from the manacles taken off barely forty-eight hours previously, time to begin to recover from his brutal journey. For most of the winter Gramsci remained in frail health. He remained in Milan's San Vittore prison from February 7, 1927, to May 11, 1928. During this period the Fascist authorities prepared for their "show trial" against Gramsci, Umberto Terracini, Mauro Scoccimarro, and other key leaders apprehended on or after November 8, 1926.[9]

Gramsci read widely during the fifteen long months he spent at San Vittore. He obtained permission to receive some books, periodicals, and newspapers from outside, and to take eight books a week out of the prison library. He was allowed to write two letters a week. In March, six weeks after his arrival in Milan, Gramsci conceived a plan to write something *für ewig* ("for always"):

> I am assailed (and this is a phenomenon characteristic of prisoners) by this idea: I need to do something *für ewig,* according to a complicated conception of Goethe, which I recall much tormented our own Pascoli. I want to occupy myself intensively and systematically, according to an established plan, with some subject that can absorb me and centralize my inner life.[10]

8. Caprioglio, "Cronologia," xxxix.
9. *Ibid.*
10. Gramsci to Tatiana Schucht, March 19, 1927, in *LDC,* 58.

Gramsci proposed four subjects for his research: (1) the role of Italian intellectuals in the nineteenth century in forming the country's public mind (*spirito pubblico*); (2) comparative linguistics from the perspective of the neolinguists, as opposed to the neogrammarians; (3) Pirandello's plays and the transformation of Italian dramatic taste; (4) serial novels and popular taste in literature. These four topics are similar, he wrote, in that they all concern the creative popular spirit in its different phases and levels of development.[11]

Few passages in Gramsci have occasioned more commentary than this one, but commentators have rarely remarked upon the humor with which Gramsci treated his exposition. "Dear Tania, I will horrify you!" he exclaimed, after he listed the topic on comparative linguistics. After explaining all four subjects, he adds: "Have I bored you? You know, writing can take the place of conversation for me. I feel I am really speaking to you when I write you." He proposed to write her every Saturday.[12] Because he felt he could converse with Tatiana Schucht through writing—a feeling he did not have toward Julia, who wrote him only stereotypical letters—most of his prison letters are addressed to her.

On March 20, 1927, Enrico Macis questioned Gramsci again. A fellow Sardinian, Macis did his best to gain Gramsci's confidence and make him reveal the inner workings of the party. Instead, Gramsci stuck to his position that he knew nothing about the party's organization. According to their agreement, he and his prison comrades refused to admit that they ran the party.

In April Gramsci was transferred to a new cell. He began to suffer seriously from insomnia. In May Tatiana Schucht moved to Milan from Rome in order to be more helpful to Gramsci. On June 2 Gramsci was again questioned by Macis. During the summer of 1927, Gramsci's brother Mario, a Fascist, visited him. Gramsci wrote his brother Carlo a memorable letter in September. After recounting the material privations he had suffered as a youth in Sardinia and during his first year at Turin University, he wrote:

> Why have I written you all of this? In order to convince you that I have
> found myself in terrible conditions before, and I did not despair. . . . My

11. *Ibid.,* 59.
12. *Ibid.,* 58–59.

moral situation is excellent. . . . I do not wish to be either a martyr or a hero. I believe that I am simply an ordinary human being who has deep convictions he will not sacrifice for anything in the world.[13]

From September, 1927, to January, 1928, Gramsci received frequent visits from Tania. He continued to read voraciously. Publications in Sardinian, Machiavelli's writings, and Giulio Bertoni and Matteo Bartoli's *Breviary of Neolinguistics* aroused his special interest.[14]

The spring of 1928 was taken up mainly with preparations for his trial. He denounced to the authorities an undercover agent's attempt to make him admit to acts he never committed. Finally he was allowed to choose his own lawyer. Toward the end of April, he learned that his trial would begin May 28. He had no illusions about the trial's outcome.

THE STRANGE LETTER

In March, 1928, Gramsci received a letter postmarked Moscow and signed "Ruggero." The author was Ruggero Grieco, a former supporter of Bordiga and the author of a profile on Gramsci published in 1924.[15] For the remainder of his life, the suspicion haunted Gramsci that Grieco, possibly supported by others in the party, had written the letter with malevolent intent. Gramsci saw Grieco's letter as sabotaging his strategy of denying any role in the party leadership outside of Parliament. Years later Gramsci referred to "the famous letter about which the investigating judge spoke to me." The judge had implied that there were people in the Communist party eager to see Gramsci sentenced to a long prison term, Grieco presumably among them.[16]

Paolo Spriano has written that Grieco's letter cast a "dark shadow over Gramsci's heart." In his book *Antonio Gramsci and the Party: The Prison Years,* Spriano has reproduced all documentation relevant to this episode. He inclines strongly toward the conclusion that Grieco's letter, while irresponsible and imprudent, was not deliberately malicious. As Spriano points out, Grieco also wrote Terracini and Scoccimarro at the

13. Gramsci to his brother Carlo, September 12, 1927, in *LDC,* 126.

14. Caprioglio, "Cronologia," xxxiv–xl. See also Gramsci to his mother, October 3, 1927, in *LDC,* 132, requesting copies of the Sardinian literary review appropriately named *Il Nuraghe* after the ancient stone edifices atop the Sardinian hills.

15. Ruggero Grieco's profile on Gramsci, written on the eve of the latter's return to Italy in May, 1924, was published in *Promoteo,* I (February 15, 1924), 30, n. 2.

16. Gramsci to Julia Schucht, April 30, 1928, in *LDC,* 207; Gramsci to Tatiana Schucht, December 5, 1932, and February 27, 1933, in *LDC,* 710–11, 753.

same time. By writing Gramsci, Terracini, and Scoccimarro, and having the letters postmarked from Moscow (Grieco himself was in Switzerland and sent them to Moscow to be mailed), Grieco's intention was clear—to indicate that both the party and the Comintern were behind them at such a difficult hour.[17]

Regardless of how one interprets the motivation for Grieco's action, the action itself was unfortunate in terms of its effect. Grieco's letters discuss the factional struggles in the Soviet Communist party resulting in Trotsky's exile, as well as affairs of the Comintern. Given that the party had means of communication to political prisoners other than the postal system, the letters do indeed seem strange, as Gramsci said. Years later, Gramsci recalled the words of the prosecutor when he gave him the letter from Grieco: "Honorable Gramsci, you have friends who certainly want you to remain in prison for a long time."[18]

The episode of the strange letter helps explain Gramsci's almost fanatical insistence, in many of his prison letters, that one could count only on oneself alone and should not depend on others. These declarations again indicate that, even after he became a party man, Gramsci spurned the mystical or pseudoreligious view of the party so evident in totalitarian thinkers. For Gramsci, the party was a practical organization and was not superior to the individuals composing and leading it. Gramsci was fully aware that if a Communist party at a particular time produces a Ruggero Grieco in a leadership position, it will be a weak and ineffective tool of the revolution.

On the eve of his departure for Rome to stand trial, Gramsci wrote his mother. Without mentioning his father's name, Gramsci had previously tried to convince his mother of the difference between his imprisonment and that of his father. Shortly after his arrest in 1926 he had written her: "Reassure everyone that they should not be ashamed of me and that they ought to rise above the narrow, petty morality of the countryside."[19]

In February, 1928, he lamented to his sister Teresina that he and his mother were separated by a kind of abyss:

17. Spriano, *Antonio Gramsci and the Party*, 33–34, and appendices, 1–5, 149–65. The appendices reproduce Grieco's 1928 letters to Gramsci, Terracini, and Scoccimarro, along with Gramsci's October, 1927, letter to Scoccimarro and Terracini's reply of March 28, 1928.
18. Gramsci to Tatiana Schucht, December 5, 1932, in *LDC*, 710.
19. Gramsci to his mother, November 20, 1926, in *LDC*, 7.

For her my incarceration is a terrible disgrace. . . . For me, however, it is merely an episode in the political struggle . . . that will continue to be waged not only in Italy but all over the world for who knows how much longer. I have been seized in the same way that prisoners are taken during a war, having known all along that this, or even worse, might happen. I fear, however, that you are like mother and that my explanation seems like a riddle expressed in a foreign language.[20]

In March, 1928, Antonio Gramsci asked his mother to take into account his moral position when reflecting on his imprisonment, because it is only morality that confers strength and dignity. "Prison is a terrible thing, but for me dishonor through moral weakness . . . would be even worse," he wrote her.[21]

On the eve of his departure from Milan to stand trial in Rome, Gramsci made his greatest effort both to console his mother and to convince her that he had chosen a moral path:

Dearest mother, . . . I want you to understand, intellectually and emotionally, that I am a political prisoner, that I will be a political convict, and that I neither am nor ever will be ashamed of this situation. At bottom I have willed this detention and conviction on myself, in a sense, because I have never wished to change my opinions, for which I have been ready to give my life, to say nothing of going to prison. . . . Dear mother, I wish I could embrace you with all my might so that you could feel how much I love you and how I would like to console you because of this unhappiness I have given you; but I cannot conduct myself differently. That is the way life is—very hard. To preserve their honor and dignity as men, sons sometimes must cause their mothers much suffering.[22]

Il Processone (The Show Trial)

On May 11, 1928, fifteen months after arriving at Milan's prison, Antonio Gramsci was forced to take another painful and debilitating journey, this time by "extraordinary transportation." Although extraordinary transportation was faster than ordinary transportation, it was not less harrowing. Prisoners were locked in tiny metal cells with room enough only to stand or sit on a stool. The cells were not opened for the

20. Gramsci to his sister Teresina, February 20, 1928, in *LDC,* 176–77.
21. Gramsci to his mother, March 12, 1928, in *LDC,* 189.
22. Gramsci to his mother, May 10, 1928, in *LDC,* 211.

entire trip. The journey to Rome lasted twenty hours because the prison car bearing Gramsci and his comrades was attached to a freight train that stopped at many small towns between Milan and Rome. Umberto Terracini described the journey as a form of torture.[23] Arriving in Rome the following day, Gramsci and the other Communist defendants in what came to be called the *processone,* or show trial, were imprisoned in Regina Coeli, the same prison where Gramsci had spent the night after his arrest eighteen months earlier.

The defendants were tried before the Special Tribunal for the Defense of the State. The head of the tribunal was a general in the party militia, or MVSN; the other five members were colonels. Giuseppe Fiori has written of this first great Fascist show trial:

> [It] was framed with every sort of Fascist pomp and circumstance: a double cordon of militiamen with black helmets, daggers, and rifles with fixed bayonets, judges dressed to the teeth, and a complex and sinister court-martial ritual.[24]

Gramsci, the first to be interrogated, denied any "clandestine activities" and sardonically noted that the Fascist police themselves were his best defense against accusations of subversion because six of them had followed him about for years. The Fascists never found any evidence to support their indictment of Gramsci for instigating civil war and destroying property and life. The report of the Rome police department that he had been found in possession of arms and explosives in November, 1922, was rather difficult to substantiate, Gramsci explained, because at that time he was in Moscow, where he had been living for six months. When asked by the presiding judge about the many references to war and to the proletariat's conquest of power in his writings, Gramsci replied:

> I believe, General, that all dictatorships of a military sort end sooner or later by being overthrown by war. When that happens, it seems quite clear to me that the proletariat should replace the ruling class, take over the reins of power, and try to build up the nation again.[25]

23. Umberto Terracini, in Mimma Paulesu Quercioli (ed.), *Gramsci vivo* (Milan, 1977), 155–56.

24. Giuseppe Fiori, *Antonio Gramsci: Life of a Revolutionary* (New York, 1970), 229.

25. Gramsci quoted in *ibid.,* 230.

Provoked by the court's tolerance of the prosecutor's frequent inter-
ruptions of his testimony, Gramsci turned to the judges and declared,
"You will lead Italy to ruin, and it is we Communists who will have to
save her!"[26]

The contrast between Gramsci's statement at the trial and Martin
Luther's "Here I stand; I cannot do otherwise" is instructive. Luther
spoke in the name of himself alone. His message was directed at the
Church as corporate power structure. Gramsci could have used the trial
to draw attention to his physical deformity and frail health. He genuinely believed in collective leadership, however, and so he spoke not of
himself but of "we Communists." As he explained in his letters, he did
not want to be thought of as a hero or martyr. He wanted to show that
anyone was capable of suffering what he suffered and enduring what he
endured if inspired by a faith in the possibility of a new politics.

On the last day of the trial, the Fascist prosecutor pointed to Antonio Gramsci and told the judges: "We must prevent this brain from
functioning for twenty years."[27] In one way, the prosecutor got his
wish: Gramsci received a sentence of twenty years, four months, and
five days. In another, the prosecutor failed; for many more years, Gramsci's brain functioned quite effectively. His prison letters and notebooks
are proof.

Gramsci was never to see his old comrades again. At the last minute,
the authorities agreed to send him to a separate prison in southern Italy
where the climate was less rigorous. He had been condemned to Por-
tolongone Prison, one of the most severe in Italy. Had he gone there,
he could not have received the regular outside medical attention essential to his survival. His old comrade, Mauro Scoccimarro, has poi-
gnantly described how he came to be sent elsewhere:

> We marched in line. I found myself next to Gramsci. They handcuffed us;
> then they tied each of us together with a long iron chain, which made an
> enormous uproar when we moved. We were almost to the exit when sud-
> denly a [police] agent arrived who announced: "Antonio Gramsci, out-
> side! . . ." Gramsci was released from the chain and, still handcuffed, was
> taken to one side. . . . I tried to get near him to embrace him, but the

26. *Ibid.* Gramsci's complete statement is in Domenico Zucaro, *Il processone* (Rome,
1958), 135–46. For the transcript of the pretrial interrogations of Gramsci, see the same
author's *Antonio Gramsci a San Vittorio* (Rome, 1961).

27. Zucaro, *Il processone,* 146.

handcuffs allowed us only to touch hands. "Good-bye, Gramsci!" I
shouted to him. And that was truly the last good-bye. I never saw him
again.[28]

Even the Fascist regime could not entirely overlook his health problems. Gramsci lost twelve abscessed teeth during the weeks leading up
to the trial, and he still suffered acutely from a kidney infection. His
sister Teresina had petitioned for Gramsci's assignment to a prison hospital, but the regime turned down this request and sent him instead to
the prison at Turi, near Bari, in southern Italy.[29]

Gramsci left Rome on July 8, 1928, for Bari via ordinary transportation. The journey took twelve days, with long stops at Caserta, Bene-
vento, and Foggia. Arriving at Turi, he was given a tag to wear around
his neck; he became prisoner number 7047. At first he lived in a cell
with five other political prisoners. His brother Carlo helped him obtain
a cell of his own. To ensure constant surveillance, the cell was adjacent
to the guards' quarters. One guard appears to have enjoyed out of mal-
ice banging on the bars of the cell in the middle of the night to make it
more difficult for Gramsci to sleep. In December Gramsci suffered a severe kidney infection and for three months could not walk unaided. In
January, 1929, Gramsci obtained permission to write in his cell. He was
permitted to order books from a store in Milan through an unlimited
account set up by his old friend Pierro Sraffa. Gramsci used large lined
notebooks to record meticulous observations about his reading. Thus
originated the famous *Prison Notebooks*.[30]

Before he died, Gramsci had written 2,848 pages, or the equivalent of
4,000 typed quarto pages. Each page bore the stamp of the prison warden.[31] One can easily imagine the bafflement with which the warden
must have read most of the notes, partly because prison wardens are not
noted for their humanistic learning and, of more importance, because a
whole army of scholars has labored to make their meaning intelligible,
so complex was the language and thought that Gramsci committed to
paper.

Writing the *Prison Notebooks* required profound faith on Gramsci's

28. Scoccimarro's moving description of their last good-bye is in *GAR*, 121.
29. Caprioglio, "Cronologia," in *LDC*, xl.
30. *Ibid.*, xli.
31. For a detailed description of the *Prison Notebooks*, see Valentino Gerratana's Preface
to *Antonio Gramsci: Quaderni del carcere* (4 vols.; Turin, 1975), 2367–2462.

part that, if his writings perished, someone else would carry on the work. Again and again he denounced the messiah complex. He thought that he was part of a process of human liberation to which he had already made a contribution. In part, he hoped that work on the *Notebooks* would help him keep himself mentally alert against the day when he could take up the struggle again on the outside. As he became involved in the *Notebooks,* they stretched his creative powers. They were a pale substitute for direct political engagement, however, especially since Gramsci had to write in code to escape the eye of the prison warden.

THE *PRISON NOTEBOOKS:* ORGANIZATION AND CONTENTS

On February 8, 1929, Gramsci entered his first note in his careful, neat handwriting; in 1935 at a clinic in Formia he made his last entry. The title of the first note was "On Poverty, Catholicism, and the Papacy." In the guise of summarizing an article, Gramsci contrasted Church teaching on poverty with that of the philosophy of praxis (Gramsci's code word from Marxism). He reported a French trade unionist's response to a reactionary priest who quoted Jesus' words in the Gospels "The poor you will always have with you" to mean that society had no obligation to eliminate poverty. "Fine—that will leave at least two poor people [in the world], because Jesus was never wrong," replied the trade unionist. Gramsci's long-standing rejection of a politics of philanthropy is evident in the way he reports the argument of some Catholics that, because charity is a moral duty, poverty must always exist to allow its exercise. Gramsci regarded the Church's entry into the trade union field as primarily inspired by a concern for widespread apostasy among the workers rather than by a concern to improve their lot.[32]

Gramsci's last major entry in the *Prison Notebooks* concerns Dante's recognition of language itself as a tool for human liberation. By breaking with the "Latinizing mandarin intellectuals" and writing his great poem in the vernacular, Dante demonstrated dramatically how the "language question" has always been a major part of the political struggle.[33]

Some scholars have treated Gramsci's *Prison Notebooks* as a philosoph-

32. Gramsci, "Sulla povertà, il cattolicismo, e il papato," *ibid.,* 6, 2087.
33. Gramsci, "La cosi detta 'quistione della lingua,'" *ibid.,* 2350.

ical text in the manner of Hegel's *Philosophy of Right*. In truth, Gramsci's *magnum opus* was *sui generis*.

Through his reading and reflection on Benedetto Croce's writings, Gramsci was able to refine and deepen his understanding of all human activity as political. Even the most detached and speculative of Croce's writing had a political character, Gramsci insisted.

What Gramsci wrote of Croce he certainly intended for himself. He did not regard the *Notebooks* as exercises in pedantry or rarefied speculation. Rather, the *Notebooks* were to be judged in the light of their contribution to the struggle against the prevailing hegemony.

Gramsci's point of reference for all the topics discussed in the *Quaderni* is a question whether the scrutinized activity perpetuates or helps overcome the old politics, in which the prestigious center subjugates groups at the margin. Unless this question is kept in mind, the *Notebooks* will appear to be the intellectual hodgepodge that some commentators have found them.[34]

After World War II, Gramsci's literary executors first published selections of the *Prison Notebooks,* organized according to such topics as "Literature and the National Life," "The *Risorgimento,*" and "Notes on Machiavelli." Only in 1975, with the appearance of Valentino Gerratana's definitive edition, were the *Prison Notebooks* published in entirety and in the order Gramsci wrote them. The earlier appearance of selections organized around themes by the editor, Felice Platone, may have contributed to the impression that the full edition is disorganized and full of irrelevant material.

Renzo Martinelli, director of the Istituto Gramsci in Florence, with his collaborators compiled the first complete index of Gramsci's prison notes, numbering each consecutively and offering cross-references.[35] Gramsci often reworked earlier notes, and Martinelli's index enables one quickly to compare versions and see which notes he did not choose to revise. By attending closely to Martinelli's enumeration of the prison notes, one discerns their antisystematic character. Gramsci was not dis-

34. This is Joseph Femia's approach to the *Quaderni* in his book *Gramsci's Political Thought* (Oxford, 1981).

35. Gramsci, "Indice dei 'Quaderni del carcere,'" in *Antonio Gramsci: Mostra bibliografiche* (Florence, 1978), 33–111. This publication is a catalog of an exhibit organized by Renzo Martinelli, director of the Istituto Gramsci in Florence.

organized, however. He deliberately chose to leave his thought fragmentary and open to future development rather than to imprison it in a system of the kind he knew Hobbes, Spinoza, and Hegel had constructed.

THE *QUADERNI* VIEWED AS GRAMSCI'S SKETCHES FOR A NEW SOCIETY

Considered as a whole, the *Prison Notebooks* can be compared to a vast collection of sketches of a great artist who died before he could complete his work. As we know, Gramsci's own analogy is that of an architect prevented from erecting the buildings he had designed. The analogy with the architect is not to be taken literally. Gramsci never completed the details of the plan for his new structure. Of more importance, he rejected the rationalistic idea that anyone could "plan" political life in this way. Nonetheless, the *Notebooks* should be read primarily for Gramsci's vision of a new politics.

The incompleteness of Gramsci's notes written in prison make them all the more interesting because of that incompleteness. To Gramsci's way of thinking, no one person could ever complete the design for a new society because the new world must be a collaborative effort of many wills and minds.

The *Quaderni* are also the more fascinating for having been written under censorship. When one views the original manuscript,[36] one is immediately struck by the censor's stamp appearing on every page of Gramsci's carefully wrought calligraphy. For these and other reasons, the precise meaning of some of Gramsci's notes will always be subject to legitimate controversy. Gramsci himself warned (perhaps to protect himself from persecution?) that when and if he had the opportunity to do research under normal conditions, he might come to conclusions the opposite of those reached in the notes.[37] While these warnings themselves should not be taken literally, they do indicate at least frustration with his inability to use all available sources. Gramsci also warned against the pursuit of philological perfectionism, since disputes about

---

36. Elsa Fubini, of the Istituto Gramsci in Rome, showed me parts of the original manuscript.
37. *Quaderni*, 1365.

detail should not prevent readers from discerning his grand design, especially when taking into account the rhythm of his thought in the early writings. The *Notebooks* present a portrait of a new manner of thinking and living that was to be the foundation of a new politics. In the next and final chapter an attempt will be made to convey a sense of the richness of Gramsci's political architecture.

THE IMPORTANCE OF THE PRISON LETTERS

Antonio Gramsci's prison letters are important sources of his political thought. They display the fluctuations in his physical and mental condition over his eleven years in prison. They must be read to gain a sense of the context in which he wrote. In addition, the letters contain succinct expositions of many themes in the *Notebooks*. Finally, as we have seen in the first two chapters, the prison letters are especially valuable as a storehouse of Gramsci's recollections of his formative emotional and intellectual experiences in Sardinia and Turin. The extraordinary range of Gramsci's aptitudes and interests, the vividness and concreteness of his imagery, the richness of his relationship to nature, the intransigence with which he argued matters of principle, and the playfulness he manages to salvage despite his sufferings—all these qualities are displayed in the brilliant letters, written at top speed to make the most of the weekly half hour allotted to him for letter writing.

As to his physical condition, Gramsci reported that his first major crisis occurred in the early morning of August 3, 1931, when for three hours he coughed up a sizable quantity of blood.[38] A year later, Gramsci wrote of his psychological condition:

> I have arrived at the point where my forces of resistance are completely collapsing, with what consequences I cannot foretell. In these recent days, I have felt worse than I ever have before; for more than a week I have been unable to sleep more than forty-five minutes a night, and some nights I do not sleep at all.[39]

Whereas in December, 1930, Gramsci could remark of his then four years' imprisonment that he had "not lost the taste for life,"[40] in August,

---

38. Gramsci to Tatiana Schucht, August 17, 1931, in *LDC,* 464.
39. Gramsci to Tatiana Schucht, August 29, 1932, in *LDC,* 665.
40. Gramsci to his mother, December 15, 1930, in *LDC,* 388.

1932, he feared he was falling apart intellectually and emotionally. In January, 1933, he wrote that 1932 was the worst year of his life:

> The old year was not exactly full of pleasant memories for me; it was the worst year I have spent in prison. The next year does not hold out any different prospects either. . . . I am worn out.[41]

Still, Gramsci insisted that he could somehow hold on and resist; after all, he had surmounted his four previous "nervous exhaustions": 1911–1912, 1916–1917, 1922–1923 (in Moscow), and 1927 (after being taken from Ustica to Milan).[42]

In March, 1933, bureaucratic details were finally ironed out for Gramsci's physical examination by a prominent specialist from outside the prison system. Professor Umberto Arcangeli's report found that "Antonio Gramsci is suffering from Pott's disease; he has tubercular lesions on the upper lobe of the right lung that have provoked two hemorrhages. In one of these he lost a notable amount of blood, and it was followed by a high fever lasting several days. He has arteriosclerosis and hypertension of the arteries. He also suffers from aphasia. He has lost weight (7 kilos). He suffers from insomnia and cannot write as in the past."[43] Arcangeli warned the prison authorities that Gramsci could not live much longer in prison and recommended his release or transfer to a hospital. A copy of Arcangeli's report was smuggled to Paris and published. An international committee was formed to work for Gramsci's release.

All that the authorities would do initially was transfer Gramsci to a quieter cell. Even this small step took until July to accomplish. Finally, on November 19, 1933, Antonio Gramsci left the prison at Turi for a private clinic at Formia, south of Rome. He was still a prisoner; bars were placed at the window of his room, and 24-hour police surveillance was maintained. The police sent Gramsci's family the bill for installing the bars.[44]

Apparently Gramsci's final act before leaving Turi was to take off his tag, numbered 7047, and give it to Gustavo Trombetti, a fellow prisoner who helped care for him during the last months. Trombetti was also the

---

41. Gramsci to Tatiana Schucht, January 2, 1933, in *LDC*, 726.
42. *Ibid.*
43. The physician's report is quoted in *ibid.*, 763.
44. Caprioglio, "Cronologia," xliv.

man who helped ensure that Gramsci left the prison with the eighteen notebooks he had written during his five years there. While Gramsci distracted the guard with conversation, Trombetti hid the *Notebooks* in Gramsci's trunk under his clothes.[45] Gramsci continued to work on the *Notebooks* at Formia, but he wrote only a small amount of new material.[46]

Gramsci left Turi convinced that his health was irretrievably ruined. "Five months ago," he wrote in October, 1933, "to spend some time in a clinic would have had an importance that today, after five months of being further worn out, it can no longer have."[47] Beginning in February, 1930, he had sought some amelioration of his status as a prisoner, on the condition that under no circumstance would he ask the Fascist regime for a pardon.[48] He thought his brother Carlo had ruined any chance of early commutation of his sentence by bungling his request and prematurely (and falsely) announcing Gramsci's release from prison. Some of his letters to Tatiana Schucht ring with rage over what he regarded as her refusal or inability to follow to the letter his instructions about appealing his sentence. In perhaps the most memorable of these outbursts, Gramsci declared:

> The idea that I am some kind of football to be kicked by anonymous feet from one part of Italy to another as has happened in the past, that for four years and four months I have been number 7047, who is not allowed to have his own will and does not enjoy the rights of a citizen (however minimal these are) has not entered into your head; therefore you have not hesitated, accidentally, to give the football a kick of your own, reminding me that to you also I am just a number.[49]

Whether justly or not, Gramsci in prison often felt abandoned by those on whom he should have been able to rely. We have mentioned the abyss separating him from his mother and others close to him in Sardinia because of their failure to understand his status as a prisoner or

45. *Ibid.*, 832n.
46. Spriano, *Antonio Gramsci and the Party,* 96. At Formia, Gramsci for the most part mechanically copied earlier versions of the notes. Occasionally he would work in new material he had read. He did add something of substance to his notes on marginal groups of the earliest period.
47. Gramsci to Tatiana Schucht, October 24, 1933, in *LDC,* 823.
48. Caprioglio, "Cronologia," xli.
49. Gramsci to Tatiana Schucht, September 19, 1932, in *LDC,* 678.

the moral dimension of his resistance to fascism. Even Julia was unable to write him a meaningful letter or to mail it when she did.[50] Finally there was his feeling of having been abandoned by his comrades in prison. The facts in this case are tangled. Gramsci's surmise that the hostility and envy of a few Communist prisoners at Turi came from all imprisoned comrades was unfounded.

Was Gramsci Abandoned by the Party in Prison?

Putting all the sources together, what seems to have happened is as follows: When Gramsci was sent to the Turi prison in the summer of 1928, he was separated from Terracini, Scoccimarro, and other key leaders with whom he had worked in the party. The Communist party in exile, headed by Palmiro Togliatti, never ceased to work for the mitigation of Gramsci's prison conditions and his ultimate release. In July, 1928, Togliatti wrote to Nikolai Bukharin, president of the Comintern, proposing that the Soviet government urge Gramsci's release as a reward for the rescue of shipwrecked Italian explorers by the Soviet ship the *Krassin*.[51] Togliatti's plan was rather complicated: the rescued Italian crew would return to Italy and second the call by the crew of the *Krassin* for Gramsci's release on health grounds. Nothing ever came of this initiative, nor from the Italian party's demonstrations in Paris and Moscow urging Gramsci's release. Delio even wrote his father about having seen his picture on a poster at the Moscow demonstration. Paolo Spriano cites other evidence for the view that, as an organization, the Communist party did not abandon Gramsci. On the contrary, Gramsci's prodigious posthumous influence on the Italian Communist party suggests the opposite of abandonment.[52]

Togliatti kept in touch with Gramsci, principally through Piero

50. "From Piero's letter . . . it appears that when writing to Gramsci his wife sends letters to an office, which then has to forward the letters. This office held the letters for six months! Couldn't someone teach this blessed woman that in the walls of houses in modern cities (and in villages too) there are rectangular boxes with a slit at the top and that when letters are put in them one can be sure that they reach their destination in reasonable speed?" Palmiro Togliatti to Luigi Longo, August 27, 1930, quoted in Spriano, *Antonio Gramsci and the Party*, 58.

51. Palmiro Togliatti to Nikolai Bukharin, July, 1928, in Spriano, *Gramsci and the Party*, 167. How ironic that Togliatti's appeal went to Bukharin, whose popular book on Marxism Gramsci would tear to shreds in the *Quaderni!*

52. See Togliatti's fourteen speeches on the importance of Gramsci's legacy for the PCI in Palmiro Togliatti, *Gramsci* (Rome, 1965).

Sraffa, and in June, 1930, he sent Gramsci's brother Gennaro, a fellow Communist, to ask Gramsci his opinion of the expulsion of his old friend Alfonso Leonetti and two other prominent party figures, Pietro Tresso and Paolo Ravazolli. There are widely differing accounts of what Gennaro reported that Gramsci said. From what we have learned about his personality, the most likely answer Gramsci gave was that he had no opinion, because in prison he was out of touch with events.

As to whether Gramsci's party comrades in prison at Turi abandoned him, there is wide disagreement. In a 1980 preface to Laurana Lajolo's biography of Gramsci, Umberto Terracini went so far as to say that Gramsci's prison comrades at Turi "expelled" him in 1930 over a dispute about tactics for opposing fascism; he added that from 1930 to 1945 the party as a whole banned him from its discussions.[53]

However, Terracini was not in Turi prison and could only have learned about the matter at second hand. In 1982 in Sardinia I interviewed Giovanni Lay, who as a very young man had taken part in many of the conversations initiated by Gramsci in the courtyard during the common exercise hour. The discussions concerned the Comintern's reversal of its analysis of fascism in 1928–1929, when it abandoned the "united front" and predicted the imminent collapse of the capitalist order, to be superseded immediately by the dictatorship of the proletariat.

According to Lay, Gramsci expressed his opposition to the Comintern's new line. He was disturbed that the party would urge its members to take serious risks against the Fascist regime on the supposition that fascism was in its death throes and therefore their imprisonment would be short. To Gramsci the height of irresponsibility was to beat one's head against a wall, because "it is one's head that breaks and not the wall."

According to Giovanni Lay, the party group in prison neither turned on nor abandoned Gramsci; on the contrary, Gramsci himself decided to terminate the conversations about the *svolta*, or turn, in Comintern policy regarding fascism. The snowball incident, in which a prisoner is supposed to have hurled a snowball with a rock inside it at Gramsci during the exercise hour, was not the doing of the Communists, Lay insists.[54]

---

53. Umberto Terracini, "Prefazione" to Laurana Lajolo, *Gramsci: Un uomo sconfitto* (Milan, 1980), 8–9.

54. Interview with Giovanni Lay, Cagliari, Sardinia, May 1, 1982.

The historian Paolo Spriano concludes that at least two of the Communist prisoners, Enrico Tulli and Angelo Scucchia, disliked Gramsci strongly, partly because of an antiintellectual fear of any criticism of the party line and partly out of envy for Gramsci's prison privileges. "There was," Spriano writes, a "passionate feeling of egalitarianism" pervading Communist groups in prison. "To some members, it seemed that Gramsci did not defer to this feeling, since he clung to his few, but precious, privileges—a cell to himself, books, a special diet. . . . From all this Gramsci received insults and an ostracism that greatly embittered him."[55]

In a letter written in March, 1931, Gramsci himself refers to having broken personal relations with some other prisoners.[56] He could not have been anything but bitter over the resentment of his privileges by those in reasonable health and normal stature. What privilege had he sought but to continue the political struggle through other means—to leave an intellectual legacy for future generations? Whether justly or not, Gramsci came to feel himself to be among the *emarginati* even within his own party in prison.

THE USE OF THE PRISON LETTERS IN INTERPRETING THE *NOTEBOOKS*

A frequent theme in Gramsci's prison letters is that he was somehow "doubly imprisoned." A month after his arrival at Turi, he wrote Tania, who had proposed that he be transferred to a prison for the sick at Viterbo:

> I have felt doubly imprisoned, because even you will not recognize that I have a will, and you presume to order my life according to whatever idea enters your head, without waiting to listen to my view. . . . How can you delude yourself still about "extraordinary transportation" . . . when you have seen what has happened to me up to now?[57]

In November, 1928, Gramsci wrote that he felt the effect of prison all the more: "Ho sentito di più il carcere." He recognized that prison separated him from life's immediacy and concreteness:

55. Spriano, *Antonio Gramsci and the Party,* 70.
56. Gramsci to his brother Carlo, March 28, 1931, in *LDC,* 422.
57. Gramsci to Tatiana Schucht, August 6, 1928, in *LDC,* 227.

I read a great deal . . . , but reading has lost much of its zest. Books and reviews convey only general ideas; they cannot provide an immediate, direct, alive impression of Peter, Paul, or John, who are real, individual persons. *Without a knowledge of them one cannot understand universal and general concepts either.*[58]

From his Turin period he recalled a worker who had come to see him every week. Gramsci, then editor of *L'Ordine Nuovo,* said the worker wanted to know what was happening in Japan. He was obsessed with Japan because there were never any stories about it except when the emperor died or when thousands of people were killed by an earthquake. Wrote Gramsci:

Today I understand him. I also have my Japan: it is the life of Peter, Paul, and also Julia, Delio, and Giuliano. If I lack the molecular sensations, how can I perceive the life of a complex whole, even in summary fashion?[59]

The conventional interpretation of Gramsci elevates the prison writings above his earlier work. Is there justification for such a procedure, given that concreteness was everything for Gramsci and that he judged his prison writings unavoidably deficient in concreteness? Gramsci specifically says that his research into the history of Catholic parties, for example, was for him a new "Japan." Far from relishing the opportunity to write something *für ewig* in isolation from everyday events, Gramsci lamented the fact that his physical separateness also produced a psychological isolation.[60]

Only in August, 1929, or almost three years after his imprisonment, did Gramsci succeed in having Julia send him a full photograph of the children. Before she had sent only their faces. "Now I am persuaded with my own eyes that they have bodies and limbs," he wrote.[61]

Gramsci's tactile way of thinking and his zest for concrete experience made it impossible for him to adopt a disinterested perspective (as traditionally defined) or to seek knowledge for knowledge's sake. He needed a partner in dialogue, and for that reason, he said in December, 1930, that he would no longer write Julia because she did not answer his

58. Gramsci to Julia Schucht, November 19, 1928, in *LDC,* 235. Emphasis added.
59. *Ibid.*
60. *Ibid.,* 236.
61. Gramsci to Tatiana Schucht, August 26, 1929, in *LDC,* 296.

letters. (He authorized Tania to send Julia copies of his letters to her.) He did not wish to "throw rocks into the darkness."[62]

Gramsci did not cease writing Julia, however. In January, 1931, he wrote to thank her for several photographs of Delio. He urged her to write him so as to interrupt his isolation from life and the world even for a brief moment. He recounted the prison warden's having told him on November 19, 1926, eleven days after his arrest, that he would be sent to Somalia, passing over the equator, a two-month journey in chains. He had written her a letter, thinking it was his last will and testament. Only on November 26, in Naples, was he told he would be sent to Ustica instead. "That was a moral turning point in my life," he wrote, "because after that I was used to the idea I might soon die. After that, what could hurt me more deeply?"[63]

"The past has a great importance for me," Gramsci wrote Tania a few weeks later, because "the present and the future are outside of my will and do not belong to me." Thus, "the past has a great importance, as the only certain thing in my life."[64] During his pre-prison past Gramsci had made progress toward overcoming his youthful feeling of isolation by establishing a network of friends in Turin and later falling in love with Julia. He eventually became the head of a party dedicated to overcoming the very marginalization he had experienced in his youth. Now in prison he not only reexperienced the loneliness and isolation he had felt as a youth; he also was deprived of most of the meaningful contacts he had made over the years in Turin, Moscow, and Rome. His wife was incapable of communicating with him other than in a stereotypical way. Of necessity he received only the briefest, most clandestine news about the party and Comintern. Finally, in 1931 as we have seen, he felt compelled to break relations even with his fellow Communist prisoners at Turi.[65]

Gramsci's double isolation, physical and psychological, from real, live human beings and their problems took its toll on his political theory. Had he never been imprisoned, it is unlikely that he would have produced the seemingly abstract speculation one finds in parts of the

62. Gramsci to Tatiana Schucht, December 15, 1930, in *LDC,* 390.

63. Gramsci to Julia Schucht, January 13, 1931, in *LDC,* 398–99.

64. Gramsci to Tatiana Schucht, February 23, 1931, in *LDC,* 412.

65. Gramsci refers to his having clashed with other prisoners and broken personal relationships in a letter to his brother Carlo, March 28, 1931, in *LDC,* 422.

Quaderni. He wrote that imprisonment robbed him of his capacity to think concretely. By implication, he warned his readers to retranslate the abstract notions of the *Quaderni*—hegemony, civil society, the war of position, Caesarism, the passive revolution, the regulated society, and the rest—into concrete language. From everything we know about Antonio Gramsci, there can be no doubt that he would have been disgusted by purely academic discussions about his work. One should never forget that in the *Quaderni* Gramsci wrote under the eye of the censor and was isolated from the real life that had been the stimulus of his thinking. Reading books and articles about, for example, the history of nineteenth-century French social movements was his "Japan."

So powerful was his disposition to concreteness, however, that not even the brutality of prison could rob him of it completely. In a letter to his mother, written after four years' imprisonment, Gramsci wrote, "I have not lost the zest for life; everything still interests me, and I am sure that even if I can no longer 'munch roasted beans' I can still enjoy watching and feeling others munch them."[66]

Two long years later, on the other hand, Gramsci wrote his sister Grazietta that he had completely lost his capacity for image making "because when nothing happens in real life, nothing happens in the life of the imagination (*fantasia*) either."[67] But not even ten years of imprisonment could utterly destroy his imaginative capacities. Thus, in 1936 he wrote Julia a long letter distinguishing between abstract and concrete imagination and criticizing her for having too much of the former and not enough of the latter.[68] Three years earlier he had criticized Tatiana Schucht for lacking imagination in such a way as to show that he still possessed it. Gramsci told his sister-in-law that all the events of the past twenty years, including the war with all of its effects on the way human beings relate to each other and the value they put on individual human lives, seem to have swept past her unnoticed, so that she was still the "kind, sweet little lady of 1912–13–14."[69] On balance, then, Gramsci's letters reveal a man whose exceptional gifts for recalling the larger implications of tangible, immediate events in the everyday life of his preprison existence decline gradually yet without ever withering away.

66. Gramsci to his mother, December 15, 1930, in *LDC,* 388.
67. Gramsci to his sister Grazietta, December 13, 1932, in *LDC,* 716.
68. Gramsci to Julia Schucht, n.d., 1936, in *LDC,* 875–77.
69. Gramsci to Tatiana Schucht, October 24, 1933, in *LDC,* 825.

THE TENSIONS IN GRAMSCI'S POLITICAL THOUGHT

Much has been written about the tensions and contradictions in Gramsci's thought in the *Prison Notebooks*. Much of that writing comes from scholars immersed in the dialectic of Hegel and Marx. To interpret the tensions in Gramsci's thought as the result of the faulty application of the dialectic is to reveal oneself to be a prisoner of one's own intellectual system. The tensions in Gramsci's thought between discipline and spontaneity are rooted not in the abstract idea of the dialectic but in the recollection of his concrete experiences. Gramsci held on to these experiences despite his physical imprisonment, evidence of his imperviousness to intellectual imprisonment in an abstract ideology.

Gramsci wrote his sister Teresina in reference to her daughter Mea that above all else, it was important that she acquire "strength of will" and a "love of discipline and work . . . without repressing her spontaneity." The necessary tension between discipline and spontaneity, so evident in Gramsci's personal development, is evident in his theories of the party, the revolution, and the regulated society.

Gramsci never lost his aversion to what he called the formulas of life. "Real life . . . is born from interior roots," he wrote. External influences and standardized slogans can never engender life. Slogans have their usefulness only as incitements to or justifications for dreams so that these dreams might become concrete realities.[70]

Gramsci wrote his mother that the only real paradise that exists is "the heart of her own sons." He did not want to offend her religious opinions, but he thought that she agreed with him more than she realized.[71] Gramsci repeatedly inveighed against reductionist positivist or vulgar materialist philosophizing, with a passion originating from his own concrete inner experiences. He insisted that the mind was not a passive receptacle upon which experience writes, but an active partner in a process taking place both within and without the individual.

The goal of giving form to a new politics, productive of new types of humanity, always remained central to Gramsci's thoughts in prison. Such a creation cannot take place automatically. Both the state and individual parents must play their role, even if it means that they exercise coercion in educating the new generations. He rebuked Julia for re-

---

70. Gramsci to Tatiana Schucht, May 8, 1931, in *LDC*, 434.
71. Gramsci to his mother, June 15, 1931, in *LDC*, 442.

maining tied to "certain spontaneitist and libertarian ideas" derived from romanticism. Rousseau's *Emile*, with its author's assumption of an innate natural goodness waiting to be liberated from social conformism, was a bad model for a critical communism to adopt. There is no escape from some measure of conformity.[72]

Several of Gramsci's most interesting letters of 1931 and 1932 concern Benedetto Croce. They explain more clearly than do the *Quaderni* themselves why Gramsci placed so much emphasis on the famous Neapolitan philosopher and literary critic. He saw Croce as the promoter of a movement of intellectual and moral reform, whose first point was that modern man can and ought to live without religion, meaning without a revealed, positivistic, mythological, or any other kind of religion. Gramsci calls Croce's insight "the greatest contribution to world culture made by modern Italian intellectuals" and "a civil conquest that must not be lost."[73] Care needs to be taken here to observe Gramsci's definition of religion, which includes not only revealed religion (traditional Christianity, Judaism, and so forth) but also scientific dogmas and irrational myths. Gramsci's own critical, skeptical caste of mind is apparent here. His own "critical communism" could never tolerate the idea that Marxism provided magical solutions to problems or that Stalin was a kind of god.

In the letters, Gramsci's first discussion of hegemony takes place in the context of a remark about Croce as Italy's "lay pope":

> The state is usually understood as political society (or dictatorship, or coercive apparatus to make the mass of the people conform to a given type of production and economy at a given moment) and not as the equilibrium of political society with civil society (or the hegemony of a social group over the entire national society exercised through so-called private organizations, such as churches, trade unions, schools, and so forth). The intellectuals work in civil society (Benedetto Croce, for example, is a sort of lay pope [*papa laico*], and he is an exceedingly efficacious instrument of hegemony, even if from time to time he happens to find himself in conflict with this or that government . . .).[74]

72. Gramsci to Julia Schucht, July 27, 1931, in *LDC*, 457. See also his letter to Julia of July 30, 1929, in *LDC*, 295: "Geneva and the environment saturated with Rousseau have left a great impression on you."

73. Gramsci to Tatiana Schucht, August 17, 1931, in *LDC*, 466.

74. Gramsci to Tatiana Schucht, September 7, 1931, in *LDC*, 481.

In the above passage one finds an important element of Gramsci's own prison program—to highlight the importance of dethroning Croce as Italy's lay pope. Gramsci most emphatically is not proposing to substitute himself for Croce as the new lay pope, however. Everything we have learned about Gramsci militates against such an elitist idea. In Gramsci's new politics there will be no papacy at all. Neither Gramsci's writing nor anyone else's should be taken as a gospel to be venerated. In the prison writings, Gramsci reveals himself not only as the architect of a new politics but as the creator of a new *concept* of architecture as well. No one great artist will draw a blueprint for the coming intellectual and moral reformation. Ultimately, the new society will be built by the people themselves. Popular impulses will not automatically produce a new society, however. A revolutionary movement, itself the product of national-popular, social, and intellectual forces, will give shape, form, and coherence to those impulses. The new party must not deteriorate into a mandarinate or priestly class, however. All of Gramsci's past experience, in which the moments of discipline and spontaneity coexist in fruitful, enduring tension, forms the basis of what could be called his "theory of social change," except for the detached and academic connotations of such language, alienated as it is from the concrete political struggle.

Despite Gramsci's profound, implacable aversion to the lifeless, detached, uninvolved culture then prevalent in the Italian universities, he was anything but a cultural philistine. If he had ever heard the dictum attributed to Hermann Goering that "When I hear the word *culture* I reach for my revolver," he would have rejected it with contempt. Not even if the "revolver" in question belonged to the proletariat would Gramsci have approved in any way of such an antiintellectual slogan. To Gramsci, what was needed was not the destruction of culture but the creation of a new culture. Such a new culture would be open to the richness of the high thought and great art of the past.[75]

Perhaps the cardinal tenet of Gramsci's political thought is that "there exists a general historical process that tends continually to unify the entire human race."[76] In that sense, the result of such a process will be the

75. "Philosophical and philological controversies are so boring that they put me to sleep, but the boredom they induce is so great that it forces me to wake up," as Gramsci paraphrased Heinrich Heine, to Tatiana Schucht, September 7, 1931, in *LDC,* 482.

76. Gramsci to Tatiana Schucht, October 5, 1931, in *LDC,* 501.

universalization of high culture through which everyone will be forced to wake up from his intellectual slumbers. In that respect *everyone* will become an intellectual, thereby obliterating the line now drawn around a small mandarinate of intellectuals and the rest of mankind. Then scholars like Guido De Ruggiero will no longer be able to conceive of humanity as a collection of national groups of intellectuals, intellectuals here being understood in the restricted sense used by Croce. Gramsci's decision to use the term *intellectual* in a very wide sense in the *Quaderni* grows out of his overall, inclusive vision of politics.[77]

Gramsci's commitment to the oneness of mankind at times evoked from him a language analogous to that of religion. Although he was not open to the experience of a world-transcendent God from whom each person derives his being and through whom he is related in essential equality, Gramsci did go so far as to write Julia that "God is none other than a metaphor to indicate the ensemble of human beings organized for mutual aid."[78] The context for this comment is Gramsci's tight-lipped lament that those closest to him (such as Julia herself) have de-nied him aid just when he needed it most. Organizations founded on a secular, anthropocentric concept of man and society ought to be un-usually attentive to their obligations to aid those in trouble, there being no God to help them. "In fact this does not happen," wrote Gramsci. "Individuals belonging to these organizations [presumably including the Comintern and the Italian Communist party] neglect their duties on purpose, . . . excusing themselves, pharisaically, with the thought that the afflicted person can support himself with his own means and moral strength."[79] Such a passage indicates that, despite Gramsci's enor-mous emphasis on the importance of organization, he always knew that there was nothing mystical about organizations, including political par-ties, and that they were no better than the particular individuals who made them up. The education of those particular individuals was cen-tral to any revolution worthy of the name.

In 1932, Gramsci wrote several important letters about Benedetto

77. Gramsci to Tatiana Schucht, October 19, 1931, in *LDC*, 511–12. Regarding Guido De Ruggiero's famous *History of European Liberalism*, Gramsci wrote that the author "tends to conceive of humanity as an aggregation of national groups of intellectuals" (in the traditional elitist meaning of the word *intellectual*). *Ibid.*

78. Gramsci to Julia Schucht, December 7, 1931, in *LDC*, 537.

79. *Ibid.*

Croce, praising his "scientific prose," at once simple and sinuous. Croce's literary style, conveying an attitude of "Goethean serenity," is appropriate for the moral life.

> While many people lose their heads and waver between apocalyptic sentiments or intellectual panic, Croce becomes a . . . [source from which his readers can] draw interior strength through his indestructible certainty that, metaphysically, evil cannot prevail and that history is rationality.[80]

Croce's enormous influence on Italian and European thought (especially in Great Britain and Germany) stems from his ability to express his conception of the world in a series of brief, unpedantic writings capable of reaching a wide public. His replies to philosophical questions are clear enough for any educated person to understand. Croce's reflections are accepted as good sense by countless intellectuals in Italy, Germany, France, and Great Britain.[81]

There are so many common elements between Gramsci's description of Croce and Gramsci himself that one sometimes wonders whether Gramsci is not using Croce to describe himself. Gramsci always kept his head as party leader and abjured apocalyptic sentiments and intellectual panic. He saw to it that his thoughts circulated anonymously by writing brief, unsigned essays. Like Croce, Gramsci also had faith in modern civilization that does not need transcendence and revelation, but contains in itself its own rationality and origin.[82]

Gramsci broke with Croce precisely over the issue of whether politics should remain the preserve of restricted groups. Gramsci describes Croce as one of the avenues used by the ruling group to co-opt and absorb elements from below for the ruling group's advantage. Since 1815, Italy had been run by a small ruling group that succeeded methodically in absorbing into its circle all the political personnel produced by mass movements of subversive origin. Gramsci then relates the familiar story of *trasformismo* as a technique of co-optation worked out by various prime ministers after Italy's unification.[83]

Although Gramsci attaches enormous importance to Croce in promoting and maintaining hegemony for Italy's "small ruling group," his June, 1932, letter describes Croce as only one of the weapons used to

80. Gramsci to Tatiana Schucht, April 25, 1932, in *LDC,* 612–13.
81. *Ibid.*
82. Gramsci to Tatiana Schucht, June 6, 1932, in *LDC,* 632.
83. *Ibid.,* 633.

promote the ruling group's hegemony. The absorption into the elite of potentially troublesome elements from society's rank and file occurs through many avenues and by diverse methods.[84] In reading the *Quaderni,* one should not forget this statement: without it Gramsci will be misinterpreted. Gramsci wrote extensively about Croce, in part because he had earlier identified Croce as one of the most active reactionaries in the whole of Italy and a leader in forming the ruling block in the south, and in part because he believed that serious ideas have a greater effect on the disposition of material forces in a society than is generally believed. Throughout the *Quaderni* he also emphasized the importance of organized institutional activity, including that exercised by the Church, in maintaining the position of the ruling elements. In no sense did Gramsci think that a new politics could be created through one's study and writing a book—even a great book. The new politics, unlike the old, would not be produced by great intellectuals writing about specialized epistemological or philological questions. The new politics would result from the collective effort of the *emarginati* and the support of those at the center fed up with the banality and futility of life based on prestige and power.

What will the man of the new politics look like? Gramsci's prison letters are perhaps more revealing than the *Quaderni* on this point. As he wrote Julia:

> Modern man should be a synthesis of . . . the American engineer, the German philosopher, and the French politician, recreating, so to speak, the Italian men of the Renaissance; [he should be] . . . Leonardo da Vinci having become mass or collective man while still retaining his strong personality and individual originality.[85]

While the first part of the above citation is quoted frequently, the latter part is less frequently noted in the Gramscian literature. The Renaissance man, "having become mass or collective man while still retaining his strong personality and individual originality"—that is Gramsci's view of the new man of the new politics. As with the antinomy of discipline—spontaneity, so with that of collectivity—individuality, Gramsci asserts the primacy of experience over logic.

Liberal-democratic or collectivist-Communist interpreters who seek to divorce his political theory from his experience will never understand

84. *Ibid.*
85. Gramsci to Julia Schucht, August 1, 1932, in *LDC,* 654.

Antonio Gramsci. He knew from his own life that it was possible at once to live as a vividly distinctive individual and as a part of the national-popular collective will. His manner of thinking integrated moments said by good sense to be irreconcilable opposites into a new style of life.

Similarly, the logical antinomy between political content and aesthetic worth, or the problem of ideology versus art, never existed experientially for Gramsci. "I can admire Tolstoy's *War and Peace* aesthetically," he wrote, "and not share the book's ideological substance. . . . The same can be said for Shakespeare, for Goethe, and also for Dante." [86] Gramsci's many admiring comments on the great literary classics of the past reveal a rejection of the idea that advances in science and technology necessarily bring progress in the quality of a society's art and literature. As one of the rubrics of the *Quaderni*, "Past and Present," suggests, the new politics hardly implies forgetting civilization's achievements of the past. The past lives on in the present, which can either creatively use the past or submit to a form of "Shintoism," resulting in a fossilized culture. As for rejecting the past altogether and constructing an order oriented exclusively to material production, Gramsci recoiled at such a prospect with horror. His notes on Henry Ford's "Taylorization" of production in the "Americanism and Fordism" section of the *Quaderni*, often misinterpreted as praise, is a relentless exposure of the dehumanizing effects of the industrialization process left to itself. [87]

DEATH

Antonio Gramsci died at 4:10 A.M. on April 27, 1937, at the Quisisana Clinic in Rome from complications resulting from Pott's disease. He was forty-six years old. He had been in poor health for at least two years. Only his sister-in-law, Tatiana Schucht, followed the hearse to the English Cemetery, where his ashes were deposited in an urn. It is appropriate that he who had given his life for those outside the pale of power and prestige should have been buried in a cemetery reserved for exiles and foreigners. [88]

86. Gramsci to Julia Schucht, September 5, 1932, in *LDC*, 670. On Tolstoy, see also Gramsci to his son Delio, n.d., 1936, in *LDC*, 858–59.

87. For the places where Gramsci discusses "Americanism and Fordism," see the Index to *Quaderni*, 3164.

88. Fiori, *Antonio Gramsci*, 290.

X ⸘ The Political Architecture
of the *Prison Notebooks*

In this final chapter, I will attempt to show that, for all their fragmentariness, Gramsci's *Prison Notebooks* possess a unifying theme, or *leitmotif*. (In Italian, the word is *impostazione*.) My purpose is to convey at least something of the work's unifying vision as it emerges from the discussion of an astonishing variety of topics. As a political architect, Gramsci was gifted both at analysis and synthesis, and, despite his having been cut off from tactile reality (as we saw in the last chapter), he continued in the *Quaderni* to exhibit a remarkable feel for concreteness.

A SEEMING CHAOS OF TOPICS

Anyone who opens Renzo Martinelli's excellent Index to the *Quaderni* encounters a seeming chaos of topics. Here are some of the topics discussed by Gramsci in a section of his *Notebooks* chosen at random:[1]

> The Italian *Risorgimento* and the Puzzle of 1848–1849
> Fr. Bresciani's Offspring: Ugo Ojetti and the Jesuits
> Catholic Action
> State and Church
> The Nature of the Lateran Accords of 1929
> The Cosmopolitan Function of Italian Intellectuals
> The Crisis of 1898 (Rise in the Price of Bread)
> Garibaldi's Passage Through Calabria in 1860

1. "Indice dei *Quaderni del Carcere*," in Renzo Martinelli (ed.), *Antonio Gramsci: Mostra bibliografica—catalogo* (Florence, 1977), 53.

Medieval Monasticism and the Feudal Regime
Red Clubs During the Paris Commune (1870)
Sorel and the Jacobins
The 1921 Italian Census Reveals Shift in Population from Countryside to City
Influence of Dante and L. B. Alberti on the Modern Conception of the
    World
Demand for Italian Jurists Outside of Italy in the Twelfth Century
Popular Literature: H. G. Wells
Development of the "Bourgeois Mentality" in Italy
The Importance of "Invisible Exports" to the Post–World War I British
    Economy
Insufficiency of Italy's Industrial Apparatus in World War I
Sicilian Regionalism as Obstacle to the *Risorgimento*
Brief Notes on Islamic Culture
Resistance to British Rule in India
Contradictions in Sixteenth-Century Italian Culture
A Diplomatic Incident Between Italy and France in 1911
The Decadence of Eighteenth-Century Italian Culture
The Negative Popular-National Character of Italian Literature
The Man of the Renaissance and Reformation
The 1892 Italian Referendum on the Most Popular Books

The topics listed above are for some of the notes comprising only 30 out of a total of 2,345 printed pages of Gramsci's *Quaderni*. These pages appear to have been composed during 1929–1930, the first year after Gramsci, having finally received permission from the authorities to write in his cell, began what proved to be an enormous enterprise. They reveal a Gramsci intent on analyzing the way major social transformations occur, including the rise of Christianity and Islam, the emergence of the modern conception of life and society, and the creation of a unified national state in Italy. While material factors (population shifts, fluctuations in the price of basic commodities, "invisible exports," the insufficiency of the industrial apparatus) are scarcely neglected, Gramsci's emphasis in these pages is definitely on what Marx and Engels had identified as the intellectual and organizational superstructure. The competence or incompetence of political and military leadership is for Gramsci a significant factor in determining the efficacy of political change, as is the presence or absence of political will in the masses who need to be awakened from the slumbers into which "Jesuitical" serial novels and other popular cultural forms have seduced them.

Many of the entries concern modern and contemporary Italian history. Gramsci's conviction that one cannot understand the Italian present in isolation from the European past is evident from his fascination with late medieval, renaissance, and early modern European history. His notes on the medieval symbiosis between Catholicism and feudalism, on the cosmopolitan (European-wide rather than Italian) perspective of most renaissance Italian intellectuals, and on the development of a modern conception of man beginning with Dante in the early fourteenth century and culminating with Leon Battista Alberti in the early sixteenth century, combine to suggest how modern Italy was modern in name only. Dante was still too bound to the medieval order and Alberti addressed too narrow an audience for them to serve as true fabricators of the modern Italian imagination.

One of the conclusions to be drawn from the list of topics cited above is that Gramsci sought to know Italian political reality intimately as the basis for concrete, revolutionary action. (Recall that in his October, 1923, letter from Moscow he had deplored the fact that "we [Italian Communists] do not know the terrain.") To achieve that goal, however, one had to situate the Italian reality in the larger European and even worldwide reality. Hence the reference to the French Revolution, the Paris Commune of 1870, the dependency of the United Kingdom on "invisible exports," the strength of forces of resistance to British imperialism among the indigenous Indian population, and observations about Islamic political culture.

Anyone approaching the *Prison Notebooks* with an attitude of regret that Gramsci saw fit, as it were, to "clutter up" his text with detailed historical references will end up misinterpreting Gramsci in the most fundamental way. For Gramsci, creative political theory lived in the interstices between the details of actual life. The task of theory was to connect those details into a meaningful pattern to serve as the basis for concrete practical action rather than merely speculative understanding. Gramsci himself is a theorist-practitioner combining armchair philosophy and the street smarts of a hard-boiled politician into a novel character type.

To build a new order one first had to understand the mistakes of the old one. A true revolutionary had to grasp genetically how his particular corner of the worldwide political reality had come into being and, insofar as possible, how it was related to the rest of the world. The empty cosmopolitanism of the traditional Italian humanist intellectual should not be fought with the philistine parochialism of the modern social engineer, however. A new culture of concrete universalism had to be forged before the birth of a new world could occur.

The *Notebooks* record the action of a mind determined to continue the struggle for a new, inclusive politics, a struggle begun over three decades before in Sardinia. Gramsci had empathized with the excluded: with the retarded boy chained in a hovel in the vacant countryside, with the workers in the mines who had to boil roots for nourishment, and with shepherds who could not afford to buy shoes. The author of the *Quaderni* was the same person who had refused to climb the ladder of prestige afforded to the distinguished scholar of linguistics he certainly could have become, but who turned himself into a revolutionary ready to endure any sacrifice to work for a new order dedicated to erasing the margins separating the prestigious few from the powerless many. He was the same person who left the Socialist party to form the Italian Communist party, who spent eighteen months in the USSR as Italian representative on the Comintern, and who returned to Italy under conditions of grave danger to refound that party after it had sunk into a quagmire of passivity and paranoid infighting.

The Antonio Gramsci who authored the *Quaderni* was the same man who in 1923 had warned the party that it had suffered a disastrous defeat at the hands of fascism, a defeat for which it had been partially responsible. Like Dante in the Inferno, who could not proceed directly to the hill of earthly happiness because of the ferocious beasts surrounding it, the forces that Italian communism aspired to lead would have to "take another way," arduous, painstaking, and roundabout if they were to prevail, Gramsci had concluded. Bit by bit and stone by stone, these forces would have to build a new culture from the ground up through an unprecedented intermingling of power and art, strength and spirit, work and wonder. His *Prison Notebooks* were his last contribution to such an effort.

In the section that follows, I propose to extract what I consider to be a representative sample of passages that convey not only the work's diversity but also its rhythm and intellectual coherence. I am asking the reader to join in the search for that coherence first by wading through a thicket of passages. Then and only then will I offer a commentary on the passages from the perspective of the work's political architecture.

To assist the reader to follow my commentary, I am appending a symbol to each passage selected. As a result, I hope that my thesis that the fragments of the *Prison Notebooks* intimate an architecture for a new politics will have been demonstrated.

Code of Symbols for Themes Treated in the Selected Passages that Follow

A	Autobiographical Remarks	L	Leadership
AF	"Americanism and Fordism"	LI	Liberalism
		LOR	Lorianism
AR	Art	M	Marx or Marxism
ARCH	Architecture	MACH	Machiavelli
C	Croce	MAR	Margins of History
CI	Categorical Imperative	NP	New Politics
CS	Civil Society	OP	Old Politics
CUL	Culture (Integral)	OS	Open Society
D	Dante	P	Party (Revolutionary)
E	Education	PHIL	Philanthropy
F	Fascism or National Socialism	PI	Pirandello
		PL	Plato
G	Goethe	R	Revolution
H	Hegemony	RS	Regulated Society
HB	Historical Block	TH	Theory and Philosophy
HO	Hobbes	TR	Transition Period
I	Intellectuals	W	War
INT	Gramsci's Own Principles of Interpretation	WP	War of Position

Index of Representative Passages in the Quaderni
in the Order in Which They Appear

Page Number in Gerratana Edition (1975)	Symbol (see Code)	
13	L	Gramsci opposes a permanent hierarchy between professors and students.
48	HB	Croce and Fortunato form a reactionary intellectual block in the Italian south.

57	M	Marx had a "feel for the masses."
80	A	Gramsci expresses empathy for a young fellow prisoner who cries out in the night, "I want to die."
120	W	The analogy between war and politics is not to be taken literally.
122	H WP	Gandhi is master of different forms of nonviolent political struggle: boycott, strike (what is later to be called the "war of position").
130	H	*Permanent* hegemony is always bad; *temporary* hegemony of one group or region may be beneficial to all. Hegemony of north over south in Italy has been bad but need not have been so.
205–207	A	There are contradictions between the poet Giovanni Pascoli's Marxist internationalism and his parochial rationalism. In this context Gramsci questions Pascoli's claim to be writing "for always" ("*für ewig*").
222	OP	The political hypocrisy of a contemporary publicist on land reform.
236	L	On Roberto Michels' iron law of oligarchy as a mere sociological schematism: The orchestra does not believe that the conductor is an oligarchical *padrone,* for example. Leadership does not necessarily imply oligarchy.
274–75, 289	AF	"Taylorism" is a new form of psychic control over some American workers, creating a new caste of highly paid workers indistinguishable from the lower middle class (the Ford experiment).
297	MAR	The need for understanding messianic movements at the "margins of history" instead of automatically condemning them as pathological.
311	TR	"The [current] crisis consists precisely in the fact that the old is dying and the new is unable to be born. In this interregnum one observes morbid phenomena of the most varied kind."
369	I	The importance of the rediscovery of Roman law in the twelfth century for the development of the modern state.
406	A ARCH	"An architect can be judged a great artist by his plans, even if he has never built anything materially."

407	A ARCH	"A great architectonic art can emerge only after a transitional stage of a [practical] nature in which one seeks to achieve the greatest possible satisfaction of the people's elementary needs. . . ."
438	A	The context is Gramsci's withering criticism of Nikolai Bukharin's philosophical naivete in *The ABC of Communism:* "In general, one must remember that all of these notes are provisional and written at top speed. . . ."
562	OS	On Western prejudices in studying Chinese culture: It is not true that there is no philosophy in traditional Chinese culture.
566, 630	LOR	On the "Brescianism" of Enrico Corradini: It produces neither art nor great politics but simply ideological rhetoric.
580	OS	The effect of the introduction of Buddhism into Japan is the successful interaction between a transnational religion and the national culture.
585	M	Nicholas of Cusa is important as a medieval precursor of German idealism and of Marx through his doctrine of the *coincidentia oppositorum* (the coincidence of opposites).
621–23	OS	It is necessary to study the theological universities of Islam and Catholicism (especially Cairo); the gulf between the learned clergy and the people; and the role of periodic displays of popular fanaticism in both religions.
658	MACH H	"Machiavelli leads everything back to politics, which is the art of governing men, of procuring their permanent consent, of founding 'great states.'"
662	CS P H RS	On the "modern prince": The revolutionary political party is head (*capo*) of a new type of state, which is not exclusive, as was the old absolutist, monarchical state. Rather, the party exercises the hegemonic function in civil society. The party, however, is so intertwined with political society [that] all the citizens sense that it (the party) reigns and governs. This new type of state has its own disappearance as its goal through the reabsorption of political society (government) into civil society.

693	RS	"Complete and perfect political equality cannot exist without economic equality." Utopianism consists in the belief that one can introduce economic equality with arbitrary laws or as a simple act of will. So long as the state based on classes exists, the "regulated society" (*società regolata*) cannot exist, save as a metaphor.
700	NP	"In the politics of the masses, to tell the truth is a necessity."
703	H CS	"Civil society . . . is the political and cultural hegemony of a social group over the entire society; [as with Hegel] it is the ethical content of the state."
705	PI CUL	"Pirandello's . . . importance is more of an intellectual and moral [cultural] than an artistic character: he sought to introduce into popular culture the 'dialectic' of modern philosophy in opposition to the Aristotelian-Catholic manner of conceiving the 'objectivity of the real.' Pirandello does not always overcome a tendency to solipsism, however, and as a result, his dialectic is at times more sophistic than 'dialectical.'"
708	R TR	Not everyone who wants to destroy something succeeds. "To destroy is very difficult—just as difficult as to create." This is because one is not dealing with material things but with invisible, impalpable relationships even if the latter are concealed in material things.
733	R TR	Ideologies and superstructures do not reproduce themselves parthenogenetically; for historical change to occur, "the 'masculine' element—revolutionary activity that creates the 'new man'—that is, new social relationships, must intervene."
758–60	D	The study of Dante's political thought reveals the following: (1) Dante was a defeated person whose political ideas had no direct influence on Machiavelli and modern thought generally. Political thought can be reduced to a mere element in Dante's biography. (2) Dante's problem was that he became isolated from everyone and produced a mere political utopia oriented toward the past, calling for a revived Ro-

		man emperor to arise and serve as arbiter in the war between the classes.
760–62	NP	Politics should not be confused with diplomacy. Diplomacy tends to conserve situations created in the collision of state politics. The diplomat by habit is narrowly conservative. Politics can be revolutionary *and* realistic at the same time. Not Guicciardini but Machiavelli should be the model for the politician. The (conservative) diplomat who wants to preserve the status quo despite the emergence of new forces is the true utopian. Skepticism ("pessimism of the intellect") needs to be linked to the "optimism of the will" in order for all the possibilities of politics to be recognized.
763–64	CS RS H LI	"The state = political society + civil society." It is hegemony armed with coercion. One can imagine the element of state coercion gradually exhausting itself, as elements of the regulated society (or ethical state or civil society) become more conspicuous. The regulated society should not be confused with the "nightwatchman state" as conceived by liberalism. The regulated society will begin an era of organic liberty and should not be confused with a new liberalism.
771	L A	Ambition ought not automatically be condemned; there is great ambition in contrast to small ambition. The latter may be called opportunism.
771–72	L A	Every leader worthy of the name is ambitious in the sense that he seeks to exercise state power with all his might. "An unambitious leader is not a leader." The authentic leader with great ambition differs fundamentally from a charismatic or "Bonapartist" demagogue (such as Mussolini). Whereas the latter makes a desert around himself, the former builds a bridge between himself and the masses, whose will he represents, raising up those capable of replacing him even if they are his competitors. Above all, the leader with *grande ambizione* elevates the level of capacity of the masses.
799	H	The serial novel in Italy substitutes (and favors at

	CUL	the same time) an imaginary man of the people in place of an authentic man of the masses. It is a narcotic that deadens the sensibilities of the readers to the social evils around them.
801–802	WP R	The passage from the war of maneuver (or of frontal attack) to the war of position also in the political field is the most important question for political theory posed by the postwar period. Trotsky ("Bronstein") did not deal with it adequately. The war of position demands enormous sacrifices from the beleaguered masses. In politics the war of position is everything; once won, it is definitively decisive. The war of position is comparable both to siege war and underground (guerrilla) war.
808	F LI	In the civil war between socialism and fascism in Italy, the so-called liberal state aligned itself with fascism.
821	OP PHIL	Every government, no matter how reactionary, does something to benefit the masses. However, "a desert with a group of tall palm trees is still a desert; indeed, it is in the nature of deserts to have small oases with groups of tall palm trees."
854	HB	On the need to turn Croce on his feet (just as Marx did to Hegel): "In historical materialism, the concept of the historical block (*blocco storico*) is the philosophical equivalent of 'spirit' in Crocean philosophy." (See 1321.)
863	H R CUL	On the individual versus the mass man: The problem is not *whether* an individual conforms but *to what* he conforms. The battle is not (as the reactionaries say) between civilization and mass society but between the *kinds* of civilization to favor—one that is inclusive and progressive or one that is exclusive and regressive. A new conformism from below will also create liberty for the individual.
866	R H CS	Lenin understood correctly that the war of maneuver, or of frontal assault, successful in Russia, could not be victorious in western Europe. In the East the state was everything, while civil society was primordial and gelatinous; in the West there was a correct relationship between the state and civil society and

behind the trembling of the state a robust structure of civil society emerged immediately. In the West, the state is the forward trench behind which there is a robust chain of fortresses and pillboxes.

867	C H	On Croce: "Croce is a kind of secular pope (*papa laico*)" for the bourgeois forces of reaction in Italy.
871–73	M TR R	Contra the simplistic economic determinism of Bukharin: Marx was a writer of concrete historical and political works and not a propagator of pseudo-philosophical abstractions. The tendency of some followers of historical materialism (Marxism) to regard every fluctuation of politics and ideology as if it were the immediate consequence of a change in society's economic base or structure must be fought theoretically, as a form of primitive infantilism, or practically, with the authentic testimony of Marx himself. Economic determinism is defective for at least three reasons: (1) the role of the structural (economic) factor in political change can be studied accurately only after a process of change has run its course and not while it is taking place; (2) mechanical historical materialism fails to consider the possibility of error by the ruling class as an explanation for changes, reforms, and so forth; (3) many political acts are attributable to internal necessities of an organizational character. For example, the ferocious medieval controversy over whether the Nicene Creed contained the words "and the Son" (*filioque*) that resulted in the schism between Roman Catholicism and Greek Orthodoxy can scarcely be attributed to a change in the society's economic structure.
882	M RS CUL	Marx was more than a great economist. No other economist produced an original and integral conception of the world. Marx is the person who intellectually begins a historical era that will probably last for centuries, that is, until the disappearance of political society and the advent of the regulated society. Only then will his conception of the world be superseded, in that a "condition of necessity" will be superseded by a "condition of freedom." The question of whether Marx or Lenin is greater is otiose.

		There would be no Marxism as a historical force without both of them, just as there would be no Christianity without both Jesus and Paul.
883–84	LOR	Feuerbach's statement "Der Mensch ist was er isst" ("Man is what he eats"), if taken seriously, would result in "kitchen history." The grain of truth in Feuerbach's reductionism is that reason and spirit—concepts beloved by Croce—cannot explain man. They are merely formal concepts. "It is not 'thought' but what one really thinks that unites or divides men."
885	OS	"'Human nature' cannot be found in any particular man, but in the entire history of the human species." Particular human beings display qualities that put them in a contradictory relationship to other human beings.
886	C M H TH	"Croce's merely speculative approach provokes one to affirm the equation between 'philosophy and politics,' between thought and action—that is, a philosophy of praxis. Everything is political, including philosophy or the philosophers . . . and the only 'philosophy' is history in act—that is, life itself." In this sense, the German working class was the heir of Hegel's philosophy, and the theorization and realization of hegemony achieved by Lenin was a great metaphysical event.
887	G A	Quotation from Goethe: "How can a man attain self-consciousness? Through contemplation? Certainly not, but through action."
903	NP	On the role of women in the *risorgimento:* Every innovative historical movement is mature only to the extent that old and young, men and women, participate in it.
926	P F	To be a party man is different from being a fanatic for a faction. The fanatic for a faction wants to destroy the adversary; the party man wants instead to create an equilibrium of parties within an organized whole, with hegemony going to the strongest party. "Party" signifies part of a whole; "faction" signifies an armed force that follows exclusivist military laws.
928	OS	On the need for *empathy* to understand foreign cultures (expressed as advice to foreign correspon-

dents): The greatest and most common error is not to know how to break out of one's own cultural shell. One tends to measure foreign cultures by one's own barometer. The result is not to see the differences beneath the same appearances and the identity under different appearances. Every political party has both a national and an international character.

937	LI	The intent of liberalism historically has been to make the entire society bourgeois. Far from promoting liberty, liberalism promotes conformity.
948	M OS A F	On Marx's inclusive attitude toward the past: In the *Communist Manifesto* Marx and Engels showed a generous attitude toward the achievements of the bourgeoisie. By contrast, Gramsci implies that Mussolini and the Fascists only ridicule their predecessors and boast about themselves. The Fascist's undervaluation of the past implies a spurious justification for the nullity of the present.
953	CI P	"Intellectual and moral reformation is always tied to a program of economic reformation." The political party, or modern prince . . . takes the place in men's consciences of the divinity and the categorical imperative. (See 1484 on categorical imperative as abstract.)
954	PL	"Plato's *Republic* is the precursor of medieval feudalism. . . ."
958–59	TH	The word *theorist* has a negative connotation in the present-day political vocabulary. In part, this is attributable to a healthy reaction of common sense against certain cultural degenerations. In its turn, common sense has overstepped its role and allowed intellectual laziness to produce a philistine and mummified view of theory and the theorist.
969	H CUL	An artificial and bookish view of the life of the poor is communicated not only by serial novels; Verdi's operas also serve to convey such a view.
970	HO	The expression *homo homini lupus* (man is a wolf to man) has had great success in "the political science of philistine pharmacists."
1004	OP	"The more extensive is the service sector of a society, the more is a society badly organized."

1050–51	L NP A	Every great political man must also be a great administrator, every great strategist a great tactician, every great fabricator of doctrines a great organizer. This should be the criterion of evaluation: one judges the theorist, or the fabricator of plans, by his quality as an administrator, and to administer means to foresee acts and operations called for by the plan in their most minute, molecular, detail. The reverse is also true: from particular actions one should be able to deduce the general principles on which they are based. The detailed application of laws translated into regulations is what indicates the true nature of a state.
1056	LI OP	In its most realistic and concrete signification, the word *democracy* means the molecular passage of ruled groups into the ruling groups. Democracy and medieval feudalism were inconsistent because the ruling groups were closed.
1063	TH	Neither common sense nor philosophy exists abstractly in and of itself; both are products of concrete historical process.
1108	R W	"A revolution is not achieved by killing as many people as possible on the other side. As a general has written, the destruction of an army does not mean the death of its soldiers but the dissolution of the tie holding them together as an organic mass."
1116	M R P	Fatalistic, deterministic Marxists help ensure that the party attracts those elements noted for their lack of initiative, perseverance, ability to concentrate forces, and so forth. Adherence to economic determinism helps produce an elite in reverse made up of the party's lowest tenth (*decimo sommerso*).
1126	A	"Prison is a file so sharp that it completely destroys thought; or it does as did the master artisan given a beautiful trunk of olive wood with which to carve a statue of St. Peter. (Trimming here and there, the artisan finally succeeded in carving only a meager handle.)"
1131	A R	The idea that one is free to overturn the present and project that overturning into the future is a dangerous illusion. Instead of dreaming with open eyes

and imagining you can do whatever you wish, you should direct your attention to the present as it is, if you want to transform it. "Pessimism of the intellect, optimism of the will."

1133	TH P	To treat so-called theoretical questions as if they were valuable in themselves, independent of any practical situation, is the essence of "Byzantinism." Bordiga's Rome Theses, presented to the second congress of the PCd'I in March, 1922, were a typical example of Byzantinism. Bordiga sought to apply the mathematical method of pure economics to practical reality instead of deriving his principles from that reality.
1145	LOR	Reductionist materialism ("Lorianism"), or economic determinism, is an easy target; witness Mussolini's article "Fascism" in the *Enciclopedia Italiana*. *Il Duce* offers "Lorianism in reverse," however, in the following statement: "Fascism believes . . . in saintliness and heroism, that is, in acts in which no economic motive—direct or indirect—is operative."
1191	A OP M	"Optimism is very often only a way of defending your own laziness, irresponsibility, and will to do nothing. It is also a form of fatalism and mechanicism. It counts on forces extraneous to your own will. . . ."
1211	C H	On Benedetto Croce's contribution to the struggle against economic determinism: "Croce's thought should be appreciated for its instrumental value. . . . He has called attention to . . . culture and thought as elements of political dominion, to the role of great intellectuals in the life of states, [and] to the moment of hegemony and consensus as the necessary form of the concrete historical block. Ethical-political history, then, is one of the canons of historical interpretation always to keep in mind . . . if one wishes to conceive of history in an integral instead of a partial and external way."
1216	C ARCH TH	Gramsci praises Croce's opposition to system building in philosophy after the manner of Hobbes, Spinoza, or Hegel. Croce shows that a philosophy can have a systematic character without being pre-

sented in a systematic form. The systematic character of Croce's philosophy "consists not in its architectonic structure but in the intimate coherence and fecund comprehensiveness of every particular solution it offers. Croce conceives of philosophical thought not as a development from one idea to another but as the thought of a [particular] historical reality."

1231

C
A

Despite his accomplishments in combating positivistic and vulgar materialist interpretations of history, Croce succeeds only in writing fragmentary history. His accomplishment is to have produced "the political masterpiece through which a given class succeeds in presenting and gaining acceptance of the conditions of its existence and development as a class, as a universal principle, as a conception of the world, as a religion."

1233

C
A
M
CUL
H
TH
OS

Just as Marx translated Hegel's speculative philosophy into historicist language, so Croce has retranslated Marx's historicist language into speculative philosophy. Gramsci makes the following autobiographical comment: "[In 1917] I wrote that, just as Hegelianism had been the premise of the philosophy of praxis [Marxism], the Crocean philosophy could be the premise for a revival of . . . [Marxism] for our generation. The question was then hinted at . . . in an inadequate way, because at that time the concept of the unity of theory and practice, of philosophy and politics, was not clear to me, and I was tendentially rather Crocean. But now . . . I can rephrase my position and present it in a critically more developed way; which is to say, the problem is to repeat for Croce's philosophical conception the same reduction that [Marx and Engels] had carried out respecting the Hegelian conception."

Using Croce as Marx used Hegel, Gramsci thought it possible to elevate a Marxism that had been vulgarized because of the necessity of practical life to the height it needed to reach if it were to solve the more complex problems posed by the present-day struggle in the West. Chief among the problems facing a new Marxism was "the creation of an integral culture that would have the mass character of the Protestant Reformation and the French Enlightenment and the classic character of Greek culture and the Italian Renaissance, a culture . . . synthesizing . . . Robespierre and . . . Kant, politics and philosophy in a dialectical unity intrinsic not only to a social group, not only French or German, but European and worldwide."

1234	C CUL R	To produce such a new integral culture it was necessary to come to terms with Croce, who is the present-day representative of classical German (Hegelian) philosophy. "An *Anti-Croce* having the same importance today as Engels' *Anti-Duhring* had in his time must be written." Significantly, however, Gramsci does not propose to write such an *Anti-Croce* himself. Instead, he proposes that a whole group of men dedicate ten years to such an activity.
1247	M	"In a certain sense . . . one can say that [Marxism] equals Hegel plus [David] Ricardo."
1257	R OP	The chief defect of French revolutionary political thought is that it deals in the formal abstractions of the jurist. Even the Jacobins lacked a dialectical and concretely revolutionary mentality. In a sense, their frame of mind could be described as conservative, because they sought to give a perfect and stable form to the innovations they achieved. In innovating, they thought always of conserving, of embalming their innovation in a legal code.
1284	L	There is no such thing as *homo oeconomicus* (economic man) in general. However, the very assumption that there is, is an important cultural weapon in capitalism's expansion. In reality, there is only the capitalist, the worker, the serf, the feudal baron, and so forth.
1287	M R	There is no such thing as an economic law independent of time and place. There are only laws (regularities, patterns of behavior) of a particular type of society. The cultural and psychological context in which a person is situated is of crucial importance in how he or she regards the force of economic laws.

1288	M	Marx's theory of surplus value ought not to be taken literally. It is a neologism of metaphorical significance, not an iron law.
1289	M LOR	"What passes in Italy for Marxism is really contraband made up of Lorian scientific trash."
1292	M LI TH	"It is an illusion of fossilized intellectuals that a conception of the world [Marxism] can be destroyed by rationalistic critiques." Marxism cannot be defeated by intellectual arguments because it expresses the contradictions of life and because it has spread throughout all sectors of society. Liberalism, on the other hand, has remained confined to restricted sectors of the population.
1293	C M H	Croce is wrong to say of Marxism what Erasmus said of Lutheranism: "Where Luther enters, culture dies." Marxism has the advantage over both Erasmus and Luther. Unlike the liberalism of Croce, confined to small circles of the educated and privileged, Marxism is an intellectual and moral reformation including all the people; but also, like Erasmus, it can bring culture, that is, philosophical depth and richness.
1301	M H NP	The richness of the new Marxist culture will not be measurable according to standards employed by class society: "A prejudice of intellectuals is to measure historical and political movements with the yardstick of intellectualism, originality, and geniality, that is, of polite literary expression and of great, brilliant personalities. . . ."
1303	C OP	Croce is the philosopher for those with prestige and power in current class society. Croce has produced an atheism for gentlemen, an anticlericalism that abhors the roughness and coarseness of plebeian anticlericalism.
1319	M TH R	Marxism is not just another ideology, but the unmasker of ideology as a form of dominion. "For the philosophy of praxis, ideologies are anything but arbitrary; they are real historical facts to be fought and unmasked in their nature as instruments of dominion . . . in order to render the governed intellectually independent of the governors, in order to

destroy one hegemony and create another, as a necessary moment in the overturning or reversal (*rovesciamento*) of praxis."

1320   M
       R
       NP

"Marxism . . . is not the instrument of government of dominant groups in order that they have consensus to exercise hegemony over the lower classes; it is the expression of these lower classes who want to educate themselves in the art of government and who want to know the truths, including the most unpleasant ones, and to evade the deceptions . . . of the upper class and even more of themselves."

1321   M
       HB

The saying that the economy is for society what anatomy is for the biological sciences does not mean what economic determinists think it means. "In the human body, the skin and general physical appearance are scarcely illusions, leaving the skeleton as the only reality." Gramsci adduces this example to support his view that between the structure (or base) and the superstructure (the realm of consciousness) there exists a necessary and vital nexus. For this nexus Gramsci uses George Sorel's term "the historical block."

1326–27   M
          NP
          TR
          ARCH

The new politics inspired by the philosophy of praxis is not aprioristic. It recognizes that life is a compound of rationality and irrationality, choice and necessity, strength and weakness. The new politics will not take the form of "history by design." Immersing itself in the everyday struggle, the new politics recognizes that history is not made or reconstructed according to mathematical calculations. "No innovative force realizes itself immediately." Gramsci's designs for a new politics are themselves of a new type in that they anticipate being revised in the process of building and perpetually rebuilding a new architecture for a new world.

1328   C
       LI
       NP

The new politics rejects the liberal contention (evident in Croce's historiography) that historical development is like an athletic contest with preestablished rules to be respected loyally by the participants. The idea that political life should be viewed as a game is itself an example of "history by design."

1329	TH P	The new politics knows that the philosopher and thinker cannot be detached from the political and party man.
1338	HB OS	The new politics recognizes that man himself is a "historical block" of both purely individual and subjective and mass objective or material elements with which as an individual he is in active relationship. The notion that ethical betterment is purely individual is an illusion and an error. A person develops his or her individuality only in relation to ever-widening circles of other men until one reaches the greatest relationship, which embraces the human species as a whole. Therefore one can say that man is essentially political, since the activity of transforming and conscientiously leading other men realizes his humanity, his human nature.
1345	R CUL	The new politics recognizes the need to remake the concept of man. Man should be conceived of as a series of active relationships, a process in which individuality has the greatest importance but is not the only element to consider.
1354	OS TR R NP	The new politics recognizes that it is mankind as such that comprehends and justifies all the pasts of the many social groups into which it has been divided. The great majority of human beings who have been at history's margins will come into their own and create a new history, which while still (inevitably) imperfect will contain more positive elements and exhibit fewer errors.
1365	A	Preface to *Quaderno* 11 repeats the warning given earlier (438) that "the notes contained in this notebook, as in the others, have been written off the top of my head (*a penna corrente*). . . . All of them should be reviewed and checked meticulously, because they certainly contain imprecise statements, false comparisons, [and] anachronisms. Written without having present the books mentioned, it is possible that after checking they should be radically corrected because precisely the opposite of what I have written is true." The warning is curiously phrased, because Gramsci seems meticulously to have written his

notes. He did have on hand many of the books to which he refers, and many "imprecise" comments were based on his own personal experiences which as his letters show he remembered vividly. It is possible that Gramsci may have feared the *Notebooks* would fall into the hands of Stalin's police had he been the beneficiary of an exchange of prisoners between Fascist Italy and the USSR.

1377	CUL P	The new politics recognizes that truth inheres not in the originality of propositions but in the practical conduct of life. To create a new culture means not to be "original" but to diffuse critically truths already discovered throughout the population.
1382–83	TH I	The new politics recognizes that philosophy is not a mere academic speciality but a way of life. Only if philosophy maintains contact with the ordinary people (*i semplici*) will it purge itself of merely individualistic, intellectualistic elements and come to life. The new politics recognizes the need for intellectual elites of a new type who emerge directly from the masses and who, by remaining in direct contact with them, constitute the "ribs of the corset" of the new society.
1397	M TR	In the new society the philosophy of praxis will not be a stagnant doctrine; it will always be expressed in polemical form and will be in perpetual struggle with lethargic elements. (Presumably such a philosophy will be free to criticize the government itself.)
1408	TR	The new politics will hardly reject the entire inheritance of the past. There will of course be instrumental values to be accepted, developed, and refined.
1439	M	Marx himself was not completely original. In Giordano Bruno, for example, there are many traces of what would become the philosophy of praxis.
1484	CI	Kant's categorical imperative "Act in such a way that your conduct can become a norm for all men in similar circumstances" is a truism that is not helpful in making concrete ethical decisions. Everyone tends to be indulgent with himself. For example, the peasant who kills his wife for being unfaithful easily convinces himself that any other husband

would do the same. Kant's maxim is a form of cosmopolitan intellectualism.

1505   I
CUL
H

The new politics recognizes that the true intellectual is someone who feels the elementary passions of the population, understanding, explaining, and justifying them in a determined historical situation, dialectically tying them together to the laws of history, in a superior conception of the world, scientifically and coherently elaborated. One does not make politics and history without this passion, this connection of sentiments between intellectuals and the people-nation.

1515   C
I

On the pretended disinterestedness of the "great intellectuals" in class society: "Croce . . . feels himself especially tied to Aristotle and Plato, but he scarcely conceals the fact that he is tied to Senators Agnelli and Benni. . . ." (Agnelli was head of the Fiat Works.)

1524   A

For the third time Gramsci warns that these observations ought to be checked and that they should be considered simply as stimuli for memory. (Here he is comparing the "gelatinous history of Russia" with the formation of Italian intellectuals.)

1543   E
H
A
I

The new politics recognizes that the school in class society has become detached from life and that one must have an educational system that encourages the active participation of the student in the school. The mechanical way in which grammar is taught must be discarded. This does not mean that the schools should become narrowly vocational. On the contrary, they should encourage the full range of human creativity, now repressed in varying degrees for both rich and poor pupils. To reform the schools, one might begin by reading *L'Ordine Nuovo* in its earliest period, when it was still only a weekly. Through that journal, the young Gramsci had labored to form a new intellectualism. The new intellectual will not excel in eloquence—the exterior and momentary motor of the passions—but in immersing oneself in practical life as builder, organizer, "permanent persuader" rather than pure orator. Above all, he or she will rise above the abstract mathematical frame of mind. From technique as work to technique as science, the new intellectual will progress to a humanistic and historical conception of life without which he or she would remain a mere specialist instead of becoming a leader (*i.e.,* a specialist plus politician).

1561	CI P	Gramsci returns to the passage on 953 about the "modern prince" having replaced God and the categorical imperative. Any intellectual and moral reformation must be linked closely to an economic reformation. Indeed, the program of economic reformation is the concrete way in which one presents an intellectual and moral reformation.
1568	W A	The new politics understands that what von Moltke said of military plans is true also of political plans; namely, "they cannot be elaborated and fixed in advance in all their details, *but only in their nucleus and central design.*" (Emphasis added.) (Gramsci again recognizes the limitations on his role as architect of a new politics.)
1571	RS CI	The new politics recognizes that law is only the repressive and negative aspect of the state's activity, which should be chiefly positive and concerned with civilizing its people.
1639	L P	Bordiga represents the antithesis of the kind of party leader required for the new politics. He believed himself to have an infallible recipe for solving the party's ills and would not cooperate with those members who disagreed. The result: he helped seriously to weaken the party just when it was engaged in a life or death struggle with fascism. The new politics knows that there are no infallible recipes for solving all problems.
1643	F P	The *Action Française* group led by Maurras was trapped into rigid intellectual schemes that ended with everyone thinking the same way because they could no longer think at all. The new politics knows to avoid such sterile uniformity.
1654	ARCH	Architecture aims both at the functional and the beautiful. The new politics is well aware that the

latter is not identical with the former. Perhaps both concepts can be united in the practical, provided that "practice" is broadly understood.

1656   ARCH   Modern architecture is usually equated with rationalism. Rationalism has always existed, however. It is simply the manner of expressing the beautiful according to the taste of the time. Architecture differs from other arts in its collective character. "A book or a small statue can remain in place . . . according to one's personal taste; not so for an architectonic construction." The new politics knows that architecture is the most reformable and discussable of the arts.

1666–67   AF   Observations on the United States: Although political and religious freedoms are guaranteed by law, in actuality they are severely limited by economic pressure and open, private violence. The judiciary leaves private armies free to prevent the formation of political parties other than the Republican and Democratic.

As to religious freedom, new sects are almost always financed by powerful economic groups in such a way that political-cultural compression is the result. By implication, the new politics would not use pressure or violence to coerce political or religious beliefs.

1682   D   On Dante and contemporary politics: In a note em-
M   bedded in his extended analysis of Canto X of the
P   *Inferno,* Gramsci compares Amadeo Bordiga to Don
F   Ferrante: "The 'Theses of Rome' reveal the same mental attitude of Don Ferrante." Both wanted to will away the disease they feared. In Bordiga's case, in 1921, he pronounced a Fascist *coup d'état* an impossibility. The new politics will not make wish father to the fact.

1690   MACH   Machiavelli was really on the side of the people, be-
NP   cause he made available to anyone who read his books knowledge formerly reserved to rulers as *arcana imperii.* In effect, Machiavelli "gave dog's teeth to sheep." The new politics will assist those at the margins of society to discover that they are not sheep at all.

1706	P A NP	The new politics knows that discipline is anything but a passive and supine acceptance of orders. Rather, discipline is a conscious and lucid assimilation of directives to be realized. Discipline in the new politics does not annul the personality but only limits the amount of arbitrariness and irresponsible impulsiveness, to say nothing of fatuous vanity displayed.
1724	ARCH NP	The new politics knows that architecture is for everyone. In class society, the other arts are necessary only to the intellectuals and men of culture, but in the regulated society those arts will exist for everyone. The boundary between so-called functional and decorative art is not rigid, and such an arbitrary distinction will not exist in the new politics.
1752	L RS NP	The cornerstone of politics and of any collective action whatsoever is that there are governors and governed, leaders and led. All the art and science of politics is based on this primordial, irreducible fact, obtaining in certain general conditions. While beginning with this primordial fact, the new politics concerns itself with *"how to attenuate this fact and make it disappear."* (Emphasis added.) According to the new politics, the division between leaders and led (in the manner that class society has known it) is historically conditioned fact rather than a perpetual feature of the human condition. Whether some form of division between leaders and led will always be necessary because of the division of labor is a question to be resolved in practice. The new politics recognizes that only technical requirements would justify extension of the division into leaders and led. Such a division, where it occurs, should not imply that the leaders are more worthy than the led. In the regulated society everyone will be a leader to some degree. (See 1762 for a continuation of this discussion.)
1762	A L P F RS	On the contrary, far from bringing prestige, leadership in the context of the new politics may bring extreme sacrifice and danger, at least in the transitional stage. Speaking autobiographically, Gramsci compares himself, as secretary-general of the Commu-

	NP	nist party, to the captain of a sinking ship. The captain's absolute obligation, in case of shipwreck, to be the last to abandon ship and to go down with it if necessary, is not irrational. Rather, the guarantee that no one will accept responsibility and then abandon those in his charge to provide for his own personal security is what makes collective life possible. Gramsci had frequently been asked why he had not left fascist Italy while there was still time and thereby avoided imprisonment. This is the answer—the captain does not abandon the sinking ship—that he gave in his prison letters and repeats here in the *Quaderni*.
1763	A	Autobiography (continued). The effect of imprisonment on the psyche: "One hears it said, 'He has resisted for five years, why not for six? He can resist another year and prevail.' The truth, however, is that the man of the fifth year is not the man of the fourth, or the third, or the second, or the first . . . ; he is a new personality, completely new, in whom the years spent [in prison] have demolished the moral checks, the forces of resistance that characterized the man of the first year."
1776	A OS	Autobiography (continued). Gramsci wishes to be remembered not for the deterioration inflicted on him by imprisonment but for the meaning of his life as a whole, which constituted a "continuing attempt to overcome a backward way of living and thinking proper to a Sardinian at the turn of the century in order to embrace a way of living and thinking no longer regional or local (*da 'villagio'*), but national, all the more national . . . to the extent that he sought a European way of living and thinking. . . . If it is true that one of the greatest needs of Italian culture even in the advanced . . . urban centers is to deprovincialize itself, how much more evident ought the need be in the experiment of a young Sardinian who was a "provincial person three or four times over?"
1840–44	A INT M	In discussing the best method for interpreting Marx's political theory, Gramsci either consciously or unconsciously indicates the best method to apply to

the study of his own writings. That method is none other than political and intellectual biography, or the method followed in this book:

"If one wishes to study the birth of a [new] conception of the world that its founder has never systematically expounded (and whose essential coherence is not to be sought in any single piece of writing [*scritto*] or series of writings, but in the entire development of the varied intellectual production in which the elements of the conception are embedded), . . . it is necessary first of all to reconstruct the process of the thinker's intellectual development and indicate the elements that became stable and 'permanent.' . . ."

"The search for the *leitmotif*, for the rhythm of the thought in development, should be more important than individual, casual affirmations and detached aphorisms. . . ."

"Among a given thinker's works . . . one should distinguish between those he has completed and published and those that remained unpublished because they were not completed. . . . It is possible in the case of the latter that the author decided never to complete them because he repudiated them in whole or in part or was not satisfied with them."

1874   RS   It has been said that the new politics of erasing the
        OS   circle between the few at the center and the many at
        TH   the periphery is against human nature. However,
        NP   the nature of man is the ensemble of social relationships that shape the consciousness of a particular historical epoch. This ensemble is in continual development; therefore the nature of man is not the same for all men in all times.

The new politics will form a block binding together technical developments making for the unification of the human species and the new conception of the world implicit in such unifying tendencies to produce a human nature that thrives on inclusion rather than exclusion, or on increasing the power of the powerless rather than on increasing the power of the powerful.

2012   H   A new politics requires for its catalyst a new type of

	R	intellectual, organically related to the society's mar-
	I	ginalized majority. "An independent class of intel-
	NP	lectuals does not exist, but every social group has its

own stratum of intellectuals." The marginalized majority that has never had its own groups of intellectuals is in the process of coming into its own. The
new politics will succeed not through force of arms
but through the hegemony of a new conception of
the world.

2043	L	Through specific knowledge of their respective
	A	terrains, each national group of the new type of in-
	H	tellectuals linked to their respective marginalized
	TR	majorities will indicate precisely the way to forge a

counterhegemony to the prevailing politics of privilege by forming alliances with the most exploited
groups and classes. Gramsci shows what local knowledge each national intellectual group would need to
supply by discussing the Italian situation in detail.
See the entire section on the Italian *Risorgimento*,
1959–2078, on *Catholic Action* and the Role of the
Papacy in recent Italian politics (2074–2103), and
on the problem of forming a national Italian culture
through a popular literature worthy of the name
(2107–35).

2139	AF	"Americanism and Fordism." Gramsci begins this
	MAR	section, put together in 1934, with an important
	TR	preface about the contradictory nature of modern

society, which is wracked by economic and moral
crises and tends toward catastrophe. He had already
commented (311) on the morbid symptoms of the
world of the interregnum between the old politics
that is dying and the new politics that is yet to be
born.

"Americanism and Fordism" is the rubric under
which Gramsci discusses the attempt by the world's
most advanced capitalist power to move from economic individualism to a programmed economy.
Such a transition is necessary to overcome various
forms of resistance encountered in the *societas rerum*
(society of things) and the *societas hominum* (society
of men).

Of necessity, Gramsci asserts, the drive toward a programmed economy in the United States has been resisted by the lower, or subordinate, forces (*le forze subalterne*) that must be manipulated and rationalized according to the new goals. What is noteworthy, however, is that some sectors of the ruling forces (*forze dominanti*) also resist. Prohibition, which had been necessary in the United States to develop the new type of worker required by a Fordized industry, fell to the opposition of marginal forces (*forze marginali*). It was these marginal and still backward forces that brought an end to prohibition, and not the opposition of industrialists and workers in the rationalized, assembly-line industries.

Despite his great distance of every kind from American political reality, with the inevitable result that his discussion of that reality seems abstract and schematic in comparison with his presentation of the Italian situation, Gramsci does show an understanding of the basic, fundamental difference between the American and European situation. He had read in the original German Werner Sombart's book *Why There Is No Socialism in the United States,* and he understood the consequences of the absence of a feudal tradition in American society. Thus, instead of speaking of social *classes* Gramsci speaks here of social *forces.* He knew that in America there were no "classes" in the European sense (bourgeoisie, proletariat), and he did not allow his Marxism to prevent him from recognizing this fundamental truth.

2145   AF   The absence of feudalism, of great historical and cultural traditions, allowed America to avoid the accumulation of parasitic sedimentations in the bureaucracy and in society generally.

2169–72   AF   Gramsci elaborates on his earlier analysis of the process of "Taylorization" (after the American industrial psychologist Frederick Winslow Taylor) and its dehumanizing effect on the new type of worker. Despite the payment of high wages (2172), many workers left because Ford employed these methods of psychological management more fully than any other firm. Gramsci read several books by and on Henry Ford.

2188–90	C I NP	Not Benedetto Croce but Federico De Sanctis is the model for a literary criticism worthy of the new politics. De Sanctis led the fight for a new culture and a new humanism in nineteenth-century Italy. What attracted Gramsci most to De Sanctis was the latter's ardent fervor and willingness openly to take sides. Unlike Croce, whose commitment to detachment made him come across as cold and unfeeling, De Sanctis recognized that a special bond exists between literary critics and the people. (He had made this point on 1739.)
2192	AR CUL H	"To fight for a new art . . . means to fight for a new culture, that is, for a new moral life that can only be tied ultimately to a new intuition of life, until that becomes a new mode of feeling and seeing reality. . . ." (Note the concreteness, the tactile quality, of Gramsci's language.)
2194	AR CUL	It is not true that the greatest art can be appreciated only by an elite group of cultivated minds. "A statue by Michelangelo, a musical excerpt by Verdi, a Russian ballet, a painting by Raphael . . . can be almost immediately understood by any citizen of the world, including a noncosmopolitan mind, even if he has not transcended the narrow circle of his native province." (Notice that Verdi, whose operas were dismissed as picturesque and quaint on 969 has now been brought back into the ranks of great artists.)
2266	A H E	Possible uses of autobiography in a new journalism: "Political-intellectual autobiographies, if well constructed with sincerity and simplicity, can be . . . of great formative efficaciousness. How one has succeeded in extricating oneself from a certain provincial . . . environment, and through what external impulses and inner struggles one has attained a historically higher kind of personality, in a vivid manner can suggest an intellectual and moral direction as well as be a document in the cultural development of certain epochs." (What an autobiography Gramsci could have written! This passage suggests

that had he survived prison he might well have written one. On the other hand, all his writing was autobiographical in a larger sense.)

2267–68   H
R
P
TR

The principal condition for overthrowing the hegemony of the politics of privilege and replacing it with the new politics of inclusiveness is the diffusion of a homogeneous mode of thinking and working from a homogeneous, or organic, center." (Presumably Gramsci, a Communist to the end, is speaking here of the party as an organized entity.) One must not think that such a diffusion can be accomplished after the manner of Enlightenment rationalism, however. Those who spread the new conception of the world must understand the society in which they work in all its diversity and complexity. They must understand that the same style of argument that may appeal to an intellectual in the city may have no appeal for the sharecropper or the worker in a mine or the inhabitant of a backward and "fossilized" region of the country. Therefore, every concept must be adapted to the particular intellectual environment in which one works. Every partial aspect of that concept must be gradually integrated into the totality of the new mode of feeling and seeing reality.

2268–69   H
R
CUL
P

The formulation and propagation of the new conception of the world must involve deduction and induction combined, identity and distinction, positive demonstration and destruction of the old. This must not be done abstractly but concretely, on the basis of real and effective experience. The literature most diffused and accepted by the people and the ideological currents of the past must be studied in order to detect which errors and sedimentations from the past are most common. (Gramsci does not need to add that the purpose of the new "organic center" is to help bring into being a centerless society because he has already said so countless times.)

2269   H
TR
R

The work of infusing society with the vision of a new politics will not be easy. Very rarely do changes in modes of thinking, in beliefs, in opinions come

	WP	about rapidly through cultural explosions that affect the whole society at once. Patient, detailed work over a long period of time is needed to win the war of position in the West.
2279–94	MAR	Some of the last notes written or collected by Gramsci in his *Notebooks* were entitled, significantly, "At the Margins of History: History of Subaltern (Subordinate) Social Groups." They first discuss the brutal killing of David Lazzaretti, an Italian religious fanatic who in 1878 proclaimed the advent of "The Republic and the Kingdom of God." (The Italian authorities who ordered his murder were apparently less concerned about his claim to represent the kingdom of God than with his claim that said kingdom was a republic, Italy having been unified under the Piedmontese monarch.) Why has Lazzaretti been studied in Italy as a case of individual mental pathology instead of as an indication of the feelings of alienation he and his followers experienced toward the newly unified Italy? Because history has been written from the perspective of the powerful, notes Gramsci.
2284	MAR CUL OP	Gramsci calls for the publication of a series of monographs on revolts (by slaves, serfs, and so forth) of marginal groups throughout history. "Every trace of autonomous initiative by subaltern groups is of inestimable value for the integral historian," he concludes. The new politics of overcoming marginalization will be the fulfillment of these often pathetic attempts by the marginalized sectors of society to break out of the prison into which they have been consigned by the politics of prestige.
2286–87	MAR	The marginalized groups of history include not only the economically oppressed but also women, racial minorities, and many "criminals." In general, in this section Gramsci joins his peripheral perspective (of all those excluded from the center regardless of economic condition or conditions of servitude) with Marx's class perspective (all of those in the subordinate, or subaltern, classes). (See the end of chapter 2 for an elaboration of this point.)

2290–93	MAR PL	Utopias in the history of political thought—including Plato's *Republic* and More's *Utopia*—need to be studied to see whether they unconsciously reflect the most elementary and profound aspirations of the subaltern social groups, including those lowest down the social hierarchy, even if those aspirations are filtered through the brain of dominant intellectuals with other preoccupations. In a deformed fashion, utopias reflect the conditions of instability and rebellion latent in the great masses of the period. They are essentially political manifestos by intellectuals who want to attain the best state.
2293–94	MAR CUL I	In a confused way, the sociology of the left in Italy contributes to the advent of a new culture oriented to the majority at the margins by demanding penal reform. However, there is also the danger that some among them will succumb to the fantasy that one can scientifically explain different types of criminality. Such "scientism" is a form of "low romanticism" that can only result in the continued oppression of marginal elements by even more sophisticated means than those used in the past.
2299	L F NP	It is neither possible nor desirable for a leader to be above and immune from the passions of the people. On the contrary, for the new politics the leader feels the passions of the people with them. He knows and understands those passions from a perspective of sympathy and does not conceive of himself as above the people manipulating them.
2301	M H CUL	*Marxism,* or critical communism, or the philosophy of praxis, if true to itself, cannot be expressed in apodictic and preachy terms. The new politics perceives the need to create a new stylistic taste (*un gusto stilistico nuovo*), even a new language, as the means of intellectual struggle.
2311–12	MAR H OS	Properly understood, folklore is a "conception of the world and of life implicit . . . in certain strata . . . in juxtaposition (*in contra-opposizione*) . . . to 'official' conceptions of the world." To propagate the new conception of the world essential to the new politics, one must understand folklore.

"The people" is the ensemble of subaltern and instrumental classes in every kind of society that has ever existed until now. As a collection of oppressed and marginal groups, "the people" at first lack unity. Folklore is as varied, fragmentary, and diverse as are the marginal groups that make up "the people."

2314   TR
      CUL
      H
      E
      NP

In the new politics the gulf between folklore and modern thought, or popular and modern culture, will gradually be bridged. Folklore should not be conceived of as something bizarre, strange, or picturesque, but as something very serious that ought to be taken seriously. Only in this way can educators assist in the birth of a new culture in the great masses of the people, and the separation between modern culture and popular culture or folklore be overcome. An activity of this kind, carried out in depth, would correspond in the intellectual sphere to what the Reformation had been in the Protestant countries.

2324–25   LOR
      F

"Lorianism," or the tendency to explain complicated events by reducing them to a single material factor, has been typical of numerous intellectuals in Germany and Italy and has done incalculable damage to both societies. Because of the prison censor, Gramsci could not come out and say that Italian fascism is a form of Lorianism. He did feel confident enough (in 1935) to single out Hitler by name. "Hitlerism is a monstrous form of Lorianism that has broken the official crust" of the higher German intellectual world and become "diffused as the scientific method and conception of a new 'officiality.'"

2326   LOR

That the figure of Achille Loria existed in Italian culture is scarcely strange, Gramsci notes. (Left to himself he would have been just another morbid symptom of the transitional age. What is strange is that he became accepted as a pillar of Italian culture, receiving countless prizes, membership in the Academy, and so forth.)

2326   F

"Only today (1935), after the unheard of brutality and ignominy of a German 'culture' dominated by Hitlerism, are some intellectuals noticing how fragile is modern civilization."

2343   OS   Gramsci's final entries in his *Prison Notebooks* are
        NP   grouped together under the heading "Notes for an
              Introduction to the Study of Grammar." As if to il-
              lustrate in an unmelodramatic way the inclusiveness
              of the new style of politics for which he gave his life,
              he laid down his pen after entering his reflections
              on so recondite and seemingly academic a subject.
              He did not do so before explicitly arguing that even
              the choice of grammar was a political act: "Histori-
              cal grammar can only be 'comparative': an expres-
              sion which, analyzed in depth, shows that . . . , like
              any other historical fact, the linguistic fact cannot be
              confined within national boundaries, but that his-
              tory is always 'world history,' and that particular
              histories live only within the framework of world
              history."

THE *LEITMOTIF* OF THE *QUADERNI*

From following the road map through the *Prison Notebooks,* we have discovered that the *leitmotif* holding the parts together is a vision of a new
politics oriented toward the *emarginati* rather than toward the prestigious and the powerful. Nothing in the *Notebooks* is irrelevant to this
vision, because "everything is political" (886 and 977). In order most
graphically to convey the omnipresence of the political, Gramsci had
frequent recourse to architectural metaphors. Architecture, the most
collective of the arts (1656), was concerned with the arrangement of
space to accommodate the social body. Unlike the biological body, the
social body is malleable and lends itself to experimentation directed at
knocking down the barriers that have hitherto divided its inhabitants
into the privileged and powerful at the center and the impoverished and
powerless at the periphery.

Gramsci compared himself to an architect who can be judged by his
designs even if he could not build anything materially (or if what he had
built—the party—had been reduced to ruins by fascism). The comparison is not to be taken literally. The political architect deals with the
impalpable relationships that lie hidden in material things. His space is
more elusive and does not respond to fixed designs.

Still, the shadowy outlines of a new political architecture can be
made out in the thousands of pages of notes drafted in the darkness of a

Fascist prison. They indicate a new kind of social space in which the distinction between leaders and led has been "attenuated . . . to the point of disappearance" (1752).

Antonio Gramsci must have known that the mere existence of an outline of a new politics by a great political architect creates new space for the liberation of those on society's margins—and those who have trapped themselves in the center as well. His last great political act was to write the *Quaderni*.

Gramsci appears to give us the key to interpreting his own thought when, commenting on Marx, he wrote that if one wants to understand a writer who never systematically expounded his teaching, one must first reconstruct the process of the thinker's intellectual development and pay particular attention to his biography, both as to his practical activity and his intellectual production. One should aim to discover the author's *leitmotif,* or the rhythm of his thought, as it develops (1840–1841).

Having already attempted in this book to reconstruct Gramsci's "process of intellectual development" through paying attention both to his practical and intellectual activity, let us now go in search of the *leitmotif* of the *Prison Notebooks*. Knowing what we do about him, we do not have far to search, for the central theme, the connecting thread, of the *Quaderni* is none other than his quest for a new politics of inclusion.

How, one might ask, can such subjects as Canto X of Dante's *Inferno,* Pirandello's plays, the linguistic theories of Bartoli, and the literary criticism of De Sanctis be subsumed under the heading of politics, whether old or new? To such a question we must respond with the words of Gramsci himself, who wrote in the *Quaderni* that "tutto è politica" and "tutta la vita è politica" ("that everything is political" and "all of life is political") (886, 977). We already know (from chapter 2) that Bartoli's linguistic theory was important to Gramsci because it went beyond philology and grammar to emphasize the role of prestige in shaping a language; De Sanctis was praised in the *Quaderni* because as a literary critic he was not "frigidly aesthetic" but took the side of the people in their struggles for a new culture (426). Pirandello was praised for introducing the Sicilian dialect into his plays and for his view of reality as something to be created rather than as something objectively given (703). Dante, the supremely political poet, interested Gramsci greatly, and although he displayed his unusual interpretive skills in analyzing Canto X of the *Inferno* (516–530), even in this "pure" analysis he finds relevance to contemporary Italian politics (1682).

The outlines of the arguments Gramsci advanced in the *Prison Notebooks* are clearly visible in the journalism of his Turin period. The rejection of deterministic Marxism (871–73), ridicule of intellectual reductionism, or "Lorianism" (883–84, 1145, 1287), advocacy of nonauthoritarian leadership styles (73, 236, 771–72, 1639), condemnation of state-worship (*statolatria*) (1020–21), contempt for Fascist "gladiatorial politics" (771–72), insistence on the educative role of the party (1329, 1383, 1543, 1561), commitment to internationalism (928, 1776, 2194), opposition to the working class's acceptance of philanthropy (821, 1320), insistence on linking party policy to effective social forces (1116, 1639), disgust with mandarin bureaucrats in the party and the unions (1191, 1383, 1752)— these and other themes prominent in the *Quaderni* were anticipated in his pre-prison writings.

Other than illustrating concretely through their very erudition, originality, and intellectual breadth and depth how to go about building a new culture and a new network for diffusing its influence in "civil society," the *Prison Notebooks'* greatest achievement is further to illumine the contours of the architecture of the new politics through sustained discussions of concepts such as "civil society," "hegemony," "the war of position," "the passive revolution," "the historical block," and "the regulated society."

It is necessary to reiterate that Gramsci held it to be fundamentally incorrect to use the terms *civil society, hegemony,* and so forth, as if they were "pure" ideas. Rather, they must be understood to have arisen from the practical sphere and, once clarified, to be usable as implements for building the new politics of inclusion, which is what Gramsci understood by the term *revolution.*

It would also be misleading to discuss these general terms in isolation from each other (for they are all interconnected), or as if they were written by a university scholar for publication in an academic review. It is impossible to draw neat, precise definitions of these terms from the *Quaderni.* This is not attributable to a defect in Gramsci's cognitive powers but was the result of his deliberate method, because Gramsci does not want abstract ideas imposed on concrete reality. The ideas have value only insofar as they emerge from and refer to practical social forces and contribute to the emergence of a new politics of inclusion.

Gramsci's general concepts are not *definitions* of a reality that is fixed but are *intimations* of a reality that can emerge only through organized human willing.

Thus, civil society and hegemony are indices of the constellation of social forces: "Civil society . . . is the political and cultural hegemony of a social group over the entire society. . . ." (703). The road to revolution in the West leads through the territory of consent. This consent, however, is not arrived at simply through counting the votes in an election taking place in the framework of the old politics of prestige and exclusion. What must be done is to bring the large majority of the people who have lived at society's periphery to a consciousness of their potential for living a life of full and meaningful participation. This change of sentiments about themselves can come about only through creating a new popular literature, new styles of art and taste, and even a new attitude toward sarcasm, usually employed in a reactionary way to put down the weak and powerless (2300). Above all, it must entail an alternative notion of common sense, for the prevailing understanding of this term is weighed against fundamental change and in favor of the idea that a fixed human nature ensures the perpetual defeat of efforts to create a qualitatively different political order (1483).

There are two modes of supremacy that a social group exercises over a society: dominion (force) and intellectual and moral direction (consent). A social group can become "directing" even before it dominates society; that is, even before conquering governmental power it may become the directing influence in civil society. After such a group acquires control of the machinery of coercive power, it must continue to be directing at the level of civil society if it truly possesses the staying power of hegemony (2010–11).

To acquire hegemony, mere one-to-one conversions will never suffice; rather, the support of whole groups of intellectuals, together with their less-educated followers, must be acquired. This support will not be achieved through grandiose preaching by a charismatic figure, but must come through the recognition that a "historical block" exists based both on common economic interests and a shared mental universe. The party—conceived of not as a bureaucratic entity but as a band of self-conscious, dedicated, and active supporters of the new hegemony—will help the people themselves build their historical block. Whereas the era of the lone founder—Machiavelli's Prince—is dying, that of the party—the "modern prince"—is dawning.

A true revolution actively involves the "people-nation" and not just restricted circles of elites. It does not occur passively over the people's heads, as was the case with the Italian *Risorgimento*. An active rather than a passive revolution in western Europe will be won not through *una guerra manovrata o frontale* (a frontal or maneuvered war) but through *una guerra di posizione* (a war of position) (865). A war of position is comparable to trench warfare. Unlike the frontal attack, in which one invests all one's forces in hopes of achieving victory with one decisive blow, the war of position involves a slow, step-by-step conquest of one vantage point after the other. Because capitalist hegemony in the West is so firmly established in the various areas of civil society, the war of position is the only path to revolution in the West. (Lenin could lead the Bolsheviks to victory in a "war of maneuver" in October, 1917, only because civil society in Russia was "gelatinous.")

A key symbol for understanding Gramsci's architecture of a new politics is the *società regolata* (882). (The term literally translates as "regulated society," but its meaning is a society that regulates itself from below rather than one that is regulated from above.)

One might describe Gramsci's image of the regulated society as a more realistic version of Marx and Engels' "withering away of the state" (*Absterbung des Staates*). Gramsci is more realistic in that he refrains from setting any scientifically predictable date for the transition, saying cautiously that *"one can imagine . . .* state coercion exhausting itself" (763) and that the transition will *"probably"* take centuries.

In a discussion of state-worship (*statolatria*), Gramsci gave a further indication of what he meant by the regulated society. In what is almost certainly a criticism of Stalin's policies in the USSR, and while granting that there may be periods in the creation of a new order when power must be concentrated in the state's coercive apparatus (to eliminate remnants of feudalism, and so forth), Gramsci insists that such concentration of power must be continually criticized and in no sense should be accepted as perpetual in the regime's ideology. Gramsci's paradigm for Communist development after the revolutionary seizure of power was the

> construction within the shell of political society of a complex and well-articulated civil society, in which the single individual is self-governing, without this self-government coming into conflict with political society but, on the contrary, becoming its normal continuation and organic completion. (1020)

Under no circumstances should Gramsci be viewed as a utopian thinker. As he wrote specifically in the *Quaderni,* utopianism must be rejected because it is grounded on the belief that a governing group can introduce economic equality through arbitrary laws or by an act of will. Political equality can exist only when there is economic equality. So long as there are classes—that is, so long as there is a division between those at the center and those on the periphery—the regulated society will not have been constructed (693).

Antonio Gramsci knew that "to destroy is very difficult—just as difficult as to create." This is because one is dealing not with material things but with invisible, impalpable relationships even if the latter are concealed in material things (708). He made no secret of his desire to contribute to the emergence of a new conformism from below that would at the same time "create liberty for the individual."

At first glance, Gramsci's statements appear vulnerable to the same kinds of objections one can raise about the paradoxes of Rousseau (one can be "forced to be free"). If we are fully to understand Gramsci, however, we cannot divorce these statements from their experiential context and treat them as mistakes in logic.

Antonio Gramsci had been in prison for five years when he wrote these remarks about the meaning of freedom. In the ensuing year (1932), he wrote that "prison is a file so sharp that it completely destroys thought" (1126). What is impressive, however, is that not even prison could destroy his empathy for the poor, the marginalized, and the powerless like the young man in a nearby cell who cried out in his sleep, "I want to die!"

Gramsci held that it was all very well if you have education, power, prestige, and property to talk of freedom of the individual and to oppose conformity. But one should not delude oneself into thinking that he has such freedom, for man is not an individual but an ensemble of social relationships. The choice is not *whether* to conform but *to what* one conforms.

I wish to conclude this final chapter with a consideration of the question whether in the *Quaderni* Antonio Gramsci presented a totalitarian vision of politics. The earliest use of the term *totalitarian* in the *Quaderni* is on pages 800–801, where reference is made to *una politica totalitaria* (a totalitarian politics), wherein the members of a party find in the party itself all the satisfactions that they found before in a multiplicity of organizations. Gramsci then distinguishes between two types of totalitarian parties: progressive and reactionary. Progressive totalitarian parties are the bearers of a new culture. Reactionary totalitarian parties pretend to initiate a new culture but actually reconstitute the old order in a pseudorevolutionary disguise.

Beginning with *Quaderno* 12, Gramsci's use of the adjective *totalitarian* becomes more frequent. Thus, those parties that are vitally and radically innovative are said to be "elaborators of new integral and totalitarian forms of intellectuality; that is, they are the crucible for the unification of theory and practice, understood as a real historical process" (1387). In *Quaderno* 13 Gramsci refers to regimes that are classified as totalitarian, where the party claims to function as an impartial force, substituting for the traditional function of the monarchy. This passage reads like an attack on Mussolini's fascism (1601–1602).

Thus, for Gramsci there are genuine and spurious, progressive and reactionary, forms of totalitarianism. In *Quaderno* 15 he returns to the progressive form of totalitarianism by observing that when a movement achieves wholeness, independence, and maturity—something that happens only gradually—it becomes an active force for modifying the environment and may be said to possess genuine *totalitarietà* (1760–61).

In *Quadaerno* 17 (written between 1933 and 1935) Gramsci attacks Italian fascism and German national socialism as systems in which the single party functions exclusively as a police and censorship apparatus. As a result the party no longer has specifically political functions, but forces the *de facto* parties to fight behind the scenes (1939). This passage could also be a criticism of the Stalinist deformation of Marxism.

In *Quaderno* 20 (2086–87) Gramsci calls Italian Catholicism during the centuries of its unquestioned hegemony totalitarian in a double sense, warning that it represented a total conception of the world held by a society in its totality. At the time he was writing (in the mid-thirties), Catholicism had become "partial" in Italy, because it had formed its own party in the Catholic Action organization. (The *popolari* existed also in uneasy relationship with the Church as a Catholic party.)

Finally, in *Quaderno* 25, written in 1934, Gramsci attacks the contemporary dictatorships (presumably chiefly Italian fascism, German national socialism, and Stalinism) for having abolished the forms of autonomy that had sprung up in the civil society of the modern state, forcing them to be incorporated into the state. In such a situation, he asserts, the dominant group becomes totalitarian in a reactionary sense because by law it concentrates all of the national life in the state (2287).

Antonio Gramsci's political theory ought not be subsumed under any of the usual categories of political analysis. As not only the above references but all the actions of his life demonstrate, he does not deserve to be classified a totalitarian thinker in the police-state sense, but rather ought to be hailed as an opponent of the same. On the other hand, he is scarcely a liberal constitutionalist, either.

Gramsci was a proponent of a *new* politics that has for its point of reference the inclusion of the hitherto marginalized sectors of society. Such a new politics cannot come about by philanthropy or partial concessions from those in power; for every government, no matter how reactionary, does some things to aid its inhabitants in greatest need. Such actions do not add up to a new politics any more than an oasis signifies the abolition of a desert (821).

In an important passage of which there are two slightly different versions, Gramsci makes clear that the new politics can come about only through an intellectual and moral *metanoia,* or transformation, of consciousness. The initiative for such a transformation must come from the depressed strata themselves. The role of the party—or "modern prince"—is twofold: to assist in the formation of a national-popular collective will and to be the town-crier (*banditore*) and organizer of an intellectual and moral reformation. The intellectual and moral reformation is indissolubly tied to a program of economic reformation, which is the concrete mode in which one presents any intellectual moral reformation (752–53, 1560–61).

Gramsci ends his treatment of the need for an integral, or total, intellectual, moral, and economic reformation of society in order to achieve the new politics with one of his most controversial passages:

> As it develops, the modern prince uproots the entire [prevailing] system of intellectual and moral relationships insofar as its development signifies precisely that every action comes to be conceived of as useful or harmful, virtuous or vicious, solely insofar as it has the modern prince itself as its point of reference and serves to increase or oppose its power. The prince takes the place in the consciences [of its members] of the divinity or the categorical imperative and becomes the basis for a modern secularism (*laicismo*) and a complete secularization of all of life and of all customary relationships. (1561)

The above passage has often been interpreted as having sinister implications of a totalitarian police-state character. To interpret it correctly, however, one should note that on the immediately preceding page (1560) Gramsci has specifically disassociated himself from any "Jacobin" implications. The passage needs to be read in the light of Gramsci's entire thought and action regarding the party, recalling his rejection of any soldierlike conception of the same in the Vienna letters and repeatedly in the *Notebooks* (771–72, 926, 1639, 1643, 2267–68).

Gramsci's assertion that the party takes the place both of God and of Kant's categorical imperative in the minds of its members does not mean that he is deifying the party. The whole point of a complete secularization of life is to show that the earth is the earth, and, just as there is no heaven beyond the world, there can be none within the world either. Just as Gramsci the atheist meant to exclude an appeal to faith in a transcendent God as the arbiter of men's consciences, he also meant to exclude liberal (Kantian) individualism as well. He held Kant's imperative to be an abstraction unhelpful in making disinterested ethical decisions because everyone tends to be indulgent with himself and rationalize his actions as the basis for a universal law (1484).

In saying that the modern prince—the revolutionary party devoted to stimulating the formation of a national-collective will and promoting intellectual and spiritual reformation—should become the touchstone of men's consciences, Gramsci is calling on those who support the new politics of inclusion to discipline their selfish individual interests in the name of advancing the cause of the marginalized majority (1706). The immediate practical objective, of course, was to defeat fascism, and toward that end, as "captain of the ship," he had personally sacrificed everything (1762). Fascism could never be defeated if Bordiga's brand of deterministic Marxism prevailed in the party, because it only encouraged passivity (1133, 1639, 1682).

THE NEW POLITICS AND THE OPEN SOCIETY

It is altogether remarkable that, given the materials with which he had to work, both in the *Prison Notebooks* and throughout his life, Antonio Gramsci produced a profound version of the theory of the open society—of humankind as a universal intellectual and spiritual community. Gramsci could work with only the books and periodicals his jailers would allow him to read. By "materials," however, I refer also to the intellectual and spiritual resources available to him from the age in which he lived. Gramsci had to struggle in his youth against both the deformed and petrified religiousness of Sardinian village Catholicism and reductionist materialist positivism. With only the aid of Benedetto Croce's philosophical idealism—an orientation he attacked for contributing to the defense of the old politics (1231, 1233–34, 1293, 1303, 1328, 2188–90)—Gramsci single-handedly created a critical, antieconomistic version of Marxism in Italy. To do so, he had to fight the positivistic and reductionist interpretation of Marx prevalent in Italy since the founding of the PSI in the 1890s.

With only his remarkable intellectual and preintellectual gifts, enlivened by his experience of exclusion as a hunchback and a Sardinian, to aid him, Antonio Gramsci reached out to empathize with the sufferings and aspirations of all marginalized human beings wherever and whenever they existed. He wrote appreciatively of Chinese culture (562), Japan (585), and Islam (622). "The greatest and most common error is not to know how to break out of one's own cultural shell," he wrote in calling for a new journalism (928). He hailed the universal significance of great art and music (2194).

Gramsci defined "the people" as "the ensemble of subordinate and instrumental classes in every kind of society that has ever existed until now" (2312). In so doing he showed his profound respect for the past, a respect altogether remarkable in a revolutionary. In one of his last entries in the *Quaderni*, presumably written in 1935 just before a further deterioration in his health prevented further sustained intellectual work, Antonio Gramsci wrote that "history is always 'world history'" and "particular histories live only within the framework of world history" (2343).

✒ Conclusion

In the *Prison Notebooks,* Antonio Gramsci wrote that "an architect can be judged a great artist by his plans, even if he has never built anything materially" (406). These words may be applied with justice to their author's own work as a political theorist and leader. The vast Gramscian corpus, extending from his massive journalistic writings in Turin to the last page of his meditations in prison, may be regarded as a series of designs for a new politics. These sketches or designs indeed reveal Antonio Gramsci to have been a "great artist."

One could say that Gramsci accomplished a Copernican revolution in politics by giving the world of political and social relationships a new sun. What had previously been described as "marginal" territory—the everyday lives of the impoverished and illiterate majority of humankind—becomes for Gramsci the center around which the political world evolves. The whole human world of language, art, literature, philosophy, and—yes—architecture is enlisted by Gramsci in the task of overcoming the oppressive state apparatus, together with its supporting societal caste, whose *raison d'être* has been to perpetuate the distinction between the powerful and prestigious few at the expense of the powerless and despised many. For Antonio Gramsci, it is far more important for a political theorist to know how the ordinary members of society think, feel, and endure life than it is to linger in the palaces of the powerful, eager to catch whatever morsels drop from their hands.

One could say, furthermore, that with Gramsci the world of everyday transactions, alliances, and aversions comes alive for a theory of politics. As we have seen, there is an incredibly tactile quality to his mind. Gramsci wrote thousands of newspaper articles and reviews, the majority of them in retrospect on subjects of seemingly transient or even trivial importance. Appearances can be deceiving. Most of these fragments fit into their author's grand design to find the sun where previously society had found only shadows, rot, and stench. The smell of billy goats in Sardinian yogurt was where life flourished rather than in the cold abstractions of pompous party programs and merely intellectual philosophies.

In the Foreword to his well-known biography of Antonio Gramsci, Giuseppe Fiori writes: "The only ambition of this book is to complete the portrait of Gramsci . . . : to add 'body and legs' to the 'head' we already know—Gramsci the great intellectual and political leader." As I have repeatedly shown, I admire Fiori's study and welcome it as a necessary corrective to the prevailing tendency in Gramsci studies to paint a portrait of the "head" without the "body."

What I have tried to do, however, is to provide an *integral* approach to Gramsci, combining both political theory (Gramsci's "head") and biography (his "body") instead of separating them, as Fiori chose to do.

My decision to link Gramsci's theory to his biography is based on my reading of Gramsci himself. As he wrote in the *Quaderni,* an interpreter must concern himself with the entire personality of a thinker who expounds a new conception of the world. We have a duty to reconstruct the process of the thinker's intellectual development and indicate the elements that become stable and permanent. We must search for the *leitmotif,* for the rhythm of the thought and development of such a thinker (1844).

In concerning myself with Gramsci's entire personality, I have stressed the importance of the impact of his deformity on his sensibility. I have then attempted to reconstruct his intellectual development and to illumine the *leitmotif* and rhythm of his thought.

Let me emphasize that my book is not an attempt at psychobiography or psychohistory. Gramsci himself was too conscious of the fallacies of reductionism (he called it Lorianism) to allow his thinking to be interpreted as the reflex of some unconscious or extraconscious force. What needs to be recognized from the evidence presented in this book is that Gramsci was acutely aware that both his physical handicap and his Sardinian roots conditioned his mature political thinking by equipping him with the perspective of a person at society's periphery.

Gramsci's legacy is that of a man who lived according to a new and distinctive style of political existence. Because of that, he deserves serious study by everyone.

Gramsci was a philosopher who rejected philosophy (as academically conceived), a man of culture who fought the idea that culture is the preserve of a small minority, a party leader who despised the spirit of intrigue and the pompous trappings of office, and a militant who spurned activism (as vulgarly understood).

To read Gramsci is never boring because his thought is always related to his life in such a way that one illumines the other. Gramsci's genius, his originality, consists not in his having elaborated a new doctrine, but in his having offered the world a new style of life that integrates high and low, active and contemplative, the center and the periphery.

His architectural "designs" are not to be taken as etched in stone, for with Heraclitus he was aware that one never steps twice into the same river. Rather, Gramsci's designs were etched in his bones, the bones of an outsider and a rejected person. For a new society and a new world to be built, a new coalition of human beings capable of empathizing with those at society's margins must be formed, a coalition solid enough to constitute a new economic, intellectual, and aesthetic hegemony.

Realists and pragmatists will dismiss Gramsci as an idealist. "Pessimism of the intellect and optimism of the will" was his motto, however, and his understanding of politics as the theory and practice of overcoming emargination—and re-emargination—is more complete, more subtle, and more just than are most other images of politics current today.

Antonio Gramsci's design of a new centerless politics may never be implemented in the everyday world. One thing is certain, however: Gramsci proved himself to be a great architect by capturing the attention of many at the center and compelling them, at least for a time, to pay more than passing notice to a Sardinian hunchback from history's margins.

Index

American Federation of Labor, 144
Armenian Massacre, 43–44
Ascoli, Graziado, 26–28
Avanti! 36, 54, 89–93, 101, 105
Aventine Secession, 174–75, 179, 189

Bartoli, Matteo, 26–30, 194, 254
Bolsheviks, 62, 73–74, 87, 93, 154–55,
 169–70
Bordiga, Amadeo: compared with Gramsci, 38, 54–55, 109–10, 121,
 125–26, 134, 142–45, 150–53,
 157–64, 168, 169, 186, 241, 261; in
 PCd'I, 114–15, 184; in Cominterm,
 130, 136–37; Rome theses of,
 131–33, 233, 242; in prison, 190–91
Brandler-Thalheimer group, 155–56
Bukharin, Nikolai, 146, 154, 183,
 206, 225

Capitalism, 75–77
Carena, Pia, 32–33, 54, 95, 134
Center-periphery model, 14, 45, 50–53,
 91, 158–59, 170, 249–50, 253–55
Christianity, 41–42, 49, 215; compared
 with Communist revolution, 116–18
Club for the Moral Life, 33–34, 50, 160

Cominterm: and relationship with Italian
 Socialism, 103–104, 136–37,
 141–42, 150–51; Gramsci in,
 130–34; Gramsci on, 146–47,
 169–70, 184, 207
Corradini, Enrico, 59–60, 225
Cosmo, Umberto, 68–69
Croce, Benedetto: compared with Gramsci, 18, 214–16; influence of, on
 Gramsci, 38, 262; Gramsci on, 47–48,
 201, 214–17, 223, 228–30, 233–37,
 240; mentioned, 2, 7, 46, 248

D'Annunzio, Gabriele, 88–89
Dante Alighieri, 200, 221–22, 242, 254
de Ruggerio, Guido, 18, 215
de Sanctis, Frederico, 248, 254
Determinism, 22, 28–29, 55, 61, 74,
 115, 132, 161, 235–36, 261

Elections: of 1913, pp. 20, 35; of 1923,
 p. 127
Engels, Friedrich, 61, 89, 93, 220, 257

Fascism(ists): development of, 88–89,
 102–103, 127, 132, 135–36; Gramsci
 on, 89–90, 128–29, 145, 152,